Career and Life Planning With Gay, Lesbian, and Bisexual Persons

Susan Gelberg, PhD
Joseph T. Chojnacki, PhD

CAREER AND LIFE PLANNING WITH GAY, LESBIAN, AND BISEXUAL PERSONS

10 9 8 7 6 5 4 3 2

American Counseling Association
5999 Stevenson Avenue
Alexandria, VA 22304

Acquisitions and Development Editor
Carolyn Baker

Managing Editor
Michael Comlish

Copyeditor
Lucy Blanton

Cover design by Brian Gallagher

Library of Congress Cataloging-in-Publication Data
Gelberg, Susan.
    Career and life planning with gay, lesbian, and bisexual persons /
Susan Gelberg, Joseph T. Chojnacki.
        p.   cm.
    Includes bibliographical references (p.   ) and index.
    ISBN 1-55620-153-2 (alk. paper)
    1. Vocational guidance for gays.   2. Gays—Counseling of.
3. Homophobia.   I. Chojnacki, Joseph T.
HF5382.68.G45   1996

Table of Contents

Dedication and Acknowledgements

To family and friends, clients and colleagues

This book could not have been written without the encouragement of those clients, colleagues, friends, and family members who have trusted us enough to discuss their concerns, thoughts, and feelings about being gay, lesbian, or bisexual men and women. Their enthusiasm for our work has helped us continue to develop both personally and professionally as we seek to continue to develop resources and programs for the gay, lesbian, and bisexual communities. In addition, the self-disclosures of allies have helped us better understand the process that they continue to go through as they strive to become more effective allies.

Our families, friends, and colleagues have supported us throughout both the happier and the more difficult times. Our special thanks go to those individuals who consistently encouraged us whenever we became discouraged over the monumental nature of our task. Their humor, loving encouragement, and important insights helped sustain our efforts during the more stressful times. We also thank the staff of the American Counseling Association and the anonymous reviewers for their enthusiasm, thoughtful feedback, and support of our work.

The help, expertise, and encouragement of these individuals has made this book possible and enabled exciting, interesting, and meaningful professional and personal journeys for us. It is our hope that readers find these materials equally supportive to the personal and career-planning needs of their career clients.

Susan Gelberg   Joseph T. Chojnacki

About the Authors

Susan Gelberg, PhD, is a licensed clinical psychologist and career counselor at BroMenn Counseling Services, BroMenn Healthcare, Bloomington, Illinois. She received a BA in psychology from Cornell University, an MS in speech pathology and audiology from Ithaca College, and a PhD in counseling psychology from the University of Illinois at Urbana-Champaign. Her doctoral program included a specialization in career development and multiple role planning. She has published in the area of career counseling with gay, lesbian, and bisexual persons and has presented at national conferences on lesbian, gay, and bisexual issues. She served as an elected member of the Standing Committee for Lesbian, Gay, and Bisexual Awareness of the American College Personnel Association (ACPA), and she is a member of Commission VI (Career Development) of the American College Personnel Association. She is also a member of the American Psychological Association and the American Counseling Association's National Career Development Association, American College Counseling Association, and Association for Multicultural Counseling and Development. Her work experience includes providing career and psychological counseling to lesbians, bisexual persons, and gay men in both individual and group formats; developing career services and programs for university career centers; doing organizational educational programming; consulting in the area of diversity; and training/supervising psychology interns and other mental health professionals in gay, lesbian, and bisexual issues. She has also taught career choice classes for undergraduate students at the University of Illinois and Illinois State University. She is currently working on an MBA at Illinois State University.

Joseph T. Chojnacki, PhD, is a licensed clinical psychologist and career counselor at Counseling and Career Services at Illinois State University. He received his BA in philosophy and psychology from Cornell College, and his MA and PhD in counseling psychology from Ohio State University.

He has published many articles on career issues with gay, lesbian, and bi-sexual persons, and made numerous presentations at national conferences. He has also published in the area of psychological assessment. He has served as a consultant/trainer to organizations on gay, lesbian, and bisexual issues. His work experience includes cofacilitating lesbian/gay/bisexual support-therapy groups, coordinating a large career paraprofessional program, su-pervising predoctoral and master's level therapists, and consulting with lesbian, gay, and bisexual staff and student groups. He is a member of the American Counseling Association, the American Psychological Association (including Division 17, Counseling Psychology), the American College Per-sonnel Association, and Psychologists for Social Responsibility. He is listed in the National Register of Health Service Providers in Psychology.

Preface

In our work as career counselors, educators, and psychologists, we have sought to develop programs and resources for individuals who have special career and life planning needs. We have assisted people from different racial, cultural, and ethnic backgrounds; people who had special physical or medical needs; and older people who wished to return to work or change jobs. We have helped women address a number of gender-related special needs. We have also counseled gay, lesbian, and bisexual (g/l/b) persons who sought assistance because of career concerns linked to sexual orientation. In our work as career counselors, we have helped our career clients address a number of "isms" that influence career and life planning: racism, ethnocentrism, ableism, ageism, sexism, and heterosexism.

In our efforts to address these isms, we were dismayed to find very few resources for g/l/b career clients. Because of this, we began to study the career literature as it focused on the career development of g/l/b persons. We also looked at the psychological literature as it explored the identity development of g/l/b persons. In addition to surveying the career and psychological literature, we began attending conferences that we hoped would address these issues and help fill the gaps in our information and resources for these populations.

We were looking for the answers to questions posed by our clients such as:

- "How 'out' as a g/l/b person should I be during a job interview?"
- "I want to show that I have leadership potential, and I was the president of our g/l/b student organization. How should I word my résumé to demonstrate this potential? Should I give the name of the student organization? What if I then encounter homophobia from whomever reads the résumé?"

- "How can I network with other g/l/b persons in my field of interest and protect myself from homophobia at the same time?"
- "When I am interviewing, what is the best way for me to find out about potential job benefits for my partner?"
- "I was told by my adviser that I can never be out if I enter certain careers because of homophobia. Should I change my career goals?"
- "I believe that I am being sexually harassed at my job because of my orientation. How should I handle this?"
- "It is important for me to be out professionally. How can I predict and cope with homophobia in the work environment?"
- "How easily will I meet other g/l/b people if I take a particular job or move to a specific geographical area?"
- "How should I respond if an interviewer asks me questions about my sexual orientation during a job interview?"

As we studied the literature, we came to several conclusions. First, we felt that the career literature inadequately addressed the impact of sexual orientation on career and life planning. There just wasn't enough written on g/l/b career development issues to meet our professional needs as counselors. Second, we felt that the psychological and counseling literature on the identity development of g/l/b persons did not address career and life planning needs in suffcient detail. The two fields—career counseling and g/l/b studies—were, for the most part, distinct and separate from each other. Those who wrote in the field of career counseling did not address sexual orientation, and those counselors who were well versed in sexual orientation issues often did not consider the full range of career issues.

As we began to better integrate the two fields of career counseling and g/l/b studies, we found ourselves developing a more comprehensive career counseling framework for our g/l/b clients, and our services for g/l/b individuals expanded. In our attempts to continue to learn, as well as to encourage other career counselors as they seek to enhance services for g/l/b clients, we began to write professionally about these topics. We also began to present programs at national conferences that addressed these issues.

As we helped other professionals focus on career counseling with g/l/b clients, two types of questions were posed by those who provided various forms of career counseling. One group of questions focused on the career needs of g/l/b persons:

- "How can I learn more about g/l/b identity development—and how it affects career planning?"
- "Can you give us a useful, overall framework for providing career counseling with g/l/b persons?"

- "What specific career resources can you recommend for g/l/b career clients?"

The second group of questions dealt with professional effectiveness in working with g/l/b clients:

- "How does our own sexual orientation affect our credibility or effectiveness in working with g/l/b clients?"
- "How can we cope with the homophobia we experience from others if we work to develop better resources and programs for g/l/b persons?"
- "How can we understand and deal with the stereotypes and myths that we may hold about g/l/b persons?"
- "How do I train my staff about g/l/b issues?"

As we addressed these questions, diverse groups of professionals began to see the issues as being interconnected. That is, counselors saw how career and life planning is affected by g/l/b issues and how the personal development of g/l/b persons is affected by career and life planning. Student affairs professionals began to see the need to move their divisions toward greater affirmation of sexual orientation. Instructors began to include affirmation of sexual orientation into their teaching programs as they addressed other types of diversity. Academic advisers began to see the impact of sexual orientation on students' educational planning.

The discussions that were generated from these types of questions helped us clarify our professional goals in working with g/l/b persons, and led to our own personal and professional growth. Questions led to more questions, and discussions to more discussions. We started to feel a strong need to help others who had begun the challenging task of developing g/l/b-affirmative services. We continued to study, discuss, propose, write, learn, suggest, and ask. With each question came a new answer—and new questions.

Our efforts to fill the information and resource voids for g/l/b career clients have been both challenging and rewarding. We have appreciated the enthusiastic responses to our efforts from professionals in human services fields. We have been pleased to find our own counseling techniques, materials, and conceptualizations of career counseling with g/l/b persons growing in depth and breadth. We felt that with each new professional paper we wrote, conference presentation we led, or training seminar we conducted, our thinking grew clearer and more focused, and resulted in continued improvements in the quality of career counseling services that we were able to offer g/l/b clients.

To our knowledge, there is no book that addresses the important issue of the career development of g/l/b persons. *Career and Life Planning With Gay, Lesbian, and Bisexual Persons* seeks to fill this information void. We hope that this book assists helping professionals to better nurture the career and life planning needs of all g/l/b individuals with whom they work. We also hope that this book helps g/l/b persons find the information, resources, and support they need to attain meaningful career and life planning goals. Career counseling with g/l/b clients is a new field of study. With that newness come personal and professional challenges as well as great satisfaction and unique opportunities for professional growth.

1

Introduction:
The Importance of Career
and Life Planning Skills

It is important for all individuals, whatever their sexual orientation, to become skilled at career and life planning. (We use the term *sexual orientation* in the broadest sense to refer not only to sexual behaviors but also to sexual attractions, emotional preferences, social preferences, sexual fantasies, lifestyle choices, and sense of identity—Klein, Sepekoff, & Wolf, 1985.)

One reason that career and life planning is important is that frequent job changes are the norm rather than the exception, with people changing jobs numerous times during their lifetimes (Hopson & Hough, 1973). Career planning is often described as a continuum of decision making that begins in early childhood and extends into retirement: "It is a process . . .that for many people never stops" (Harris-Bowlsbey, Spivack, & Lisansky, 1991, p. 3). Promotions, job loss, financial pressures, and changes in career needs, values, or abilities force people to think about career changes. For g/l/b persons, both personal factors (such as dual career issues) and environmental factors (such as homophobia in the workplace) may further affect the number of lifetime job changes.

Another reason that systematic career and life planning is important is that people today may work longer and retire later than they may have originally expected. By the year 2000, about 13 percent of the population will be age 65 or older (Tinsley & Schwendener-Holt, 1992). Average life expectancy in the United States will be about 79.5 years for women and 72.1 years for men. This contrasts with the 1950s and 1960s when the average life expectancy was about 73 years for women and 66 years for men (Harris-Bowlsbey et al., 1991).

Economic factors further emphasize the critical need for and importance of systematic career and life planning. For example, most couples today are not able to live on only one income—which may be especially

1

salient for g/l/b couples because benefits, such as health insurance, are often not extended to the partners of g/l/b workers. For another example, the development of economic global interdependence means that workers are increasingly affected and may face demotions and layoffs as governments dissolve, reorganize, or are created, and as businesses dissolve, reorganize, merge, downsize, and relocate (Bridges, 1994; Dent, 1995; Hakim, 1993). Changes in national and local political issues surrounding g/l/b matters also have an impact on workers.

Research indicates that poor work performance, difficulty in managing work stress, and reduced work satisfaction are due, in part, to making career or lifestyle decisions that do not maximize the individual's unique personality, including career interests, values, experiences, and skills (Rounds & Tracey, 1990). Capitalizing on personal characteristics tends to enhance career and life satisfaction. People who make career and life planning decisions consistent with their interests, values, and skills generally have careers that are more satisfying and productive. When people select careers that suit their personalities, their self-esteem is often enhanced. In contrast, when people choose jobs inconsistent with their interests, values, experiences, and skills, they may enjoy their work less, be less motivated, have lower self-esteem, and experience anxiety, confusion, and depression.

Important questions for career counselors and other professional helpers to address thus include

- How do most people typically go about making decisions about their work and their personal lives?
- How good are the approaches they use in making these decisions?
- What is the best way to help g/l/b persons maximize their chances of making career and life decisions that will lead to happy, productive, and successful lives?

Most researchers have focused on answering the first two questions. That is, they have focused on career and life planning as it affects the majority population rather than as it affects g/l/b persons. Much has been written about the importance of a career client's psychological characteristics, work-related interests, values, experiences, and skills (e.g., Holland, 1992), life developmental history (e.g., Chickering, 1969; Chickering & Reisser, 1993; Gilligan, 1982; Gottfredson, 1981; Jepsen, 1984; Super, 1980, 1983), and the role of cultural factors in shaping career decisions (e.g., Salomone, 1991).

Career counseling approaches developed to help individuals make good career decisions include developmental career counseling (e.g., Jepsen, 1984, 1990; Super, 1980, 1983; Vondracek, Lerner, & Schulenberg, 1986), person-centered career counseling (e.g., Bozarth & Fisher, 1990; Spokane, 1987), psychodynamic career counseling (e.g., Watkins & Savickas, 1990), trait-and-factor or person-environment fit career counseling (e.g., Moos, 1987; Osipow, 1987a; Rounds & Tracey, 1990; Walsh, 1987), social learning career counseling (e.g., Krumboltz & Nichols, 1990), social psychological career counseling (e.g., Dorn, 1990), and computer-assisted guidance (e.g., Rayman, 1990). Although sexual orientation is not a primary focus of any of these approaches, each has a number of general principles relevant to career and life planning for g/l/b persons. Many of these principles are incorporated throughout this book.

Few researchers have addressed the third question concerning the best way to help g/l/b persons make career and life decisions. However, issues linked to the impact of sexual orientation on the job search process and on securing benefits as well as issues linked to the impact of dual careers have been addressed by Fassinger (1994); Hetherington (1991); Hetherington, Hillerbrand, and Etringer (1989); Hetherington and Orzek (1989); Orzek (1992); and Schmitz (1988).

The Need for Special Resources for Gay, Lesbian, and Bisexual Career Clients

Many materials are currently available that help people explore their work-related interests, values, experiences, and skills (e.g., Bolles, 1995; Carney & Wells, 1987; Figler, 1988; Harris-Bowlsbey et al., 1991; Lock, 1988; Osipow, 1983; Walsh & Osipow, 1990). Other currently available materials deal with the impact of gender, age, race, ethnicity, physical health, and religious beliefs on the career and life planning decisions people make (e.g., Betz & Fitzgerald, 1987; Leong, 1995). However, sexual orientation is rarely discussed in any of these.

This lack of career and life planning materials for gay, lesbian, and bisexual (g/l/b) persons is surprising given that an estimated 5 to 25 million g/l/b persons live in the United States (Henderson, 1984; Kinsey, Pomeroy, & Martin, 1948; Kinsey, Pomeroy, Martin, & Gebhard, 1953; Michael, Gagnon, Laumann, & Kolata, 1994). Estimates in studies vary depending on the methodologies and definitions employed (Henderson, 1984; Kinsey et al., 1948; Kinsey et al., 1953; Michael et al., 1994). If we avoid polarization in thinking about sexual orientation (i.e., if we avoid classifying people only as *g/l/b* or *heterosexual*), the 5 to 25 million figure may be an underestimation. If we view each aspect of sexual orientation as being a distinct factor, we create an almost limitless number of possible combinations of attractions, preferences, fantasies, lifestyles, and identities, and we find that distinctions between sexual orientations blur.

Coming out as a g/l/b person is a complex process that can take a number of years (Task Force on the Status of Lesbian and Gay Male Psychologists [Task Force], 1977) and can greatly impact career and life planning. Coming out as a g/l/b person can be an exhilarating process as people gain an appreciation of their individuality and develop close social, emotional, and physical relationships with others. Because of societal homophobia and heterosexism, however, the process of coming out can also have a negative influence on g/l/b persons' feelings about themselves and their relationships with their peers, family, friends, and romantic partners. (*Heterosexism* refers to the tendency to assume that all individuals are heterosexual in their values, interests, needs, and behaviors, and *homophobia* refers to both the negative stereotypes and myths about g/l/b persons as well as the irrational fear, hatred, and intolerance of g/l/b persons—Pharr, 1988.)

Often in our counseling with individuals who are just beginning to come out, two basic fears emerge: One is "As a g/l/b person, will I be accepted by others?" The other is "Will I as a g/l/b person be able to engage in meaningful and fulfilling activities in my life (e.g., a career)?" If, indeed, the two main tasks of adulthood are work and love (as Freud has been credited with saying), then we might expect to address these two main tasks in our work with individuals who are coming to know and understand their sexual orientation.

Legislation has protected a number of oppressed groups in this country from overt discrimination in the workplace (e.g., the Civil Rights Acts, the Age Discrimination in Employment Act, the Equal Pay Act, the Immigration Reform and Control Act, the National Labor Relations Act, and the Americans With Disabilities Act—Yates, 1994). No national protection exists for g/l/b persons. Concerns about pursuing meaningful career paths are grounded in the political and societal reality of the day.

Because of a lack of legal protection and because of societal heterosexism and homophobia, g/l/b people

- may be fired for their sexual orientation,
- may be denied employment or promotion because of their sexual orientation,
- are denied the right to file joint income tax returns,
- may be physically or verbally harassed both on and off the job,
- may be denied health insurance for their partner,
- may find that social activities at work assume that employees are heterosexual, and
- may conduct differing types of job searches, depending on how out they are in the workplace.

Heterosexism and homophobia negatively influence both educational settings and work environments. Because of heterosexism and homophobia, career and life planning resources should acknowledge not only the positive aspects of coming out as gay, lesbian, or bisexual but also the struggles of coping with homophobia and heterosexism in the work environment.

Sexual orientation is inextricably connected to the career and life planning process. It affects career choices; the ways in which the job search is conducted; the development of work-related interests, values, experiences, and skills; the nature of personal and professional relationships; and the degree of stress experienced at work and at home.

Professional Perspectives

This book seeks to achieve a balance between theory and application. We present theory in order to provide a useful overall framework in which to provide career counseling. We also seek to translate theory to application by suggesting interventions, action steps, and resources for implementing this framework and developing better services for g/l/b persons.

Throughout the book, we provide case examples in order to illustrate the application of specific theories, approaches, or points. These examples are anonymous composites. All identifying details have been changed in order to protect the confidentiality of the individuals with whom we have worked.

This book is designed to be used by helping professionals with an interest in career and life planning with g/l/b persons. Professionals who may find the information in this book useful include student advisers, guidance counselors, psychologists, therapists, career counselors, social workers, job coaches, and educational administrators. For professionals in training, this book could be useful because it helps fill the immense need for greater training on g/l/b issues (Buhrke, 1989; Buhrke & Douce, 1991; Eldridge & Barnett, 1991; House & Holloway, 1992; Iasenza, 1989).

Others who may find the book a useful resource include g/l/b persons seeking assistance in career and life planning, their friends and family members seeking to become more aware and understanding of the complexities involved in career and life planning for g/l/b persons, and employers, recruiters, and managers seeking to sensitize themselves to the issues faced by their employees.

Although we group gay, lesbian, and bisexual topics together throughout much of the book, we do not believe the career and life planning needs are exactly the same for each of these orientations. Differences exist among groups, and from time to time, we highlight these differences.

When we consulted with other professionals about the best way to refer to these three sexual orientations, we found no consensus. All suggestions had both strengths and limitations. Our imperfect solution is to use the acronym *g/l/b* to refer to the three sexual orientations. This acronym is used only for fluidity. It is in no way intended to imply that one group has greater importance or priority relative to another group.

In writing this book, we draw from our professional work as clinical psychologists and career counselors. We also draw from the experiences of g/l/b friends, family members, and allies. (We use the term *ally* to refer to heterosexuals who are professionally and personally affirmative to g/l/b persons.) In our professional capacities, we provide individual career counseling to g/l/b clients, and we plan programs designed to address these needs in a group format. We have developed and co-led g/l/b support-therapy groups in two counseling agency settings (Chojnacki & Gelberg, 1995). We have also provided individual training and supervision for g/l/b counselors and allies. Additionally, we have helped a number of professional agencies address personal or institutional homophobia and heterosexism (Gelberg & Chojnacki, 1995; Gelberg, Foldesi, Prieto, Rademacher, & Spearman, 1993).

In helping g/l/b persons make career and life planning decisions, we take a developmental psychological perspective (e.g., Jepsen, 1990). Using a developmental career counseling perspective, we encourage g/l/b persons to look at their past, current, and future career needs and to also consider their psychological needs, including their present development as g/l/b persons.

We view career and life planning as an interactive, developmental process between people (P) and environments (E) (e.g., Rounds & Tracey, 1990). In previous writing (Chojnacki & Gelberg, 1994), we have applied some person-environment (PE) career counseling concepts to the specific career needs of g/l/b persons. We further develop this career counseling approach in this book.

Overview of Book

Chapter 2, Adapting Career Counseling Approaches, surveys the most common general counseling approaches used by career counselors and shows how parts of each approach can be applied to the career needs of g/l/b persons. We elaborate on the use of person-environment and developmental career counseling approaches to career and life planning with g/l/b clients.

Chapter 3, Assessing the Person: Interests, Values, Experiences, and Skills, describes instruments for evaluating the worker characteristics of the person portion of the person-environment approach. This chapter also notes problems related to existing career inventories and assessment procedures for g/l/b persons.

Chapter 4, Assessing the Person: The Role of Adult Development in Career and Life Planning, considers how other person factors such as sexual identity development and adult life-span development affect career and life planning. This chapter highlights the impact of gender, age, physical health, cultural background, and ethnicity on career and life planning.

Chapter 5, Assessing the Work Environment, explores the environment part of the person-environment approach. This chapter details how an individual can assess work environments for the level of g/l/b affirmation or discrimination. Techniques and resources for the assessment of work environments are described.

Chapter 6, Career Decision Making and Goal Setting, focuses on ways to assist g/l/b persons in being more effective at setting and implementing career goals through the enhancement of decision-making skills and goal-implementation skills. This chapter provides a six-step career decision-making model to help g/l/b persons make specific career and life planning decisions.

Chapter 7, The Job Search, emphasizes the development of employability skills such as writing resúmés, conducting electronic job searches, and sharpening interview techniques. This chapter includes an examination of personal characteristics that may affect conducting an effective job search.

Chapter 8, A Comprehensive Model of Career and Life Planning for Gay, Lesbian, and Bisexual Persons, integrates concepts from preceding chapters into a more detailed comprehensive framework of career and life counseling with g/l/b persons.

The appendixes provide additional resources for career counselors. Appendixes 1 and 2 present practical sample forms for use by the professional helper and career client. Appendix 3 suggests additional career resource materials. Appendix 4 addresses both personal and professional issues of ally development and the use of mentoring to facilitate this professional development.

The career decision-making process is too important to leave to chance. With some forethought, we can help g/l/b career clients maximize their chances of developing job goals that lead to more successful and productive work lives. We hope that this book helps counselors better appreciate both the joys and the struggles that g/l/b career clients experience as they strive to integrate their identities more fully as g/l/b persons into career and life planning decisions.

The cards may be stacked against g/l/b persons in the world of work, and the playing field is not always level. Our hope is that this book helps g/l/b persons, and those who assist them, begin to level the field and create optimal life circumstances and opportunities for g/l/b persons.

2

Adapting Career Counseling Approaches

In developing frameworks for approaching career counseling with g/l/b persons, career counselors and other professional helpers do not have to "throw the baby out with the bath water." Many of the traditional approaches, particularly the person-environment fit and developmental approaches, are useful in helping g/l/b persons make career and life planning decisions. Person-environment fit career counseling focuses on the qualities of the person (e.g., the person's interests, values, experience, and skills), the type of work environment the person has entered (e.g., eligibility requirements for a particular job, work opportunities, and the interpersonal climate of a workplace), and the interactions between people and their environments. Developmental career counseling views career planning as a lifelong process. When used with g/l/b persons, however, these and other traditional approaches require modifications and, in some cases, the addition of important new dimensions. This chapter details the modifications and elaborates on those additional dimensions.

In considering what helping and counseling skills to use with g/l/b persons, career counselors and other professional helpers also do not have to throw out the basics or start anew. Similarly, because the issues that g/l/b persons bring to counseling may require greater counselor knowledge and awareness, modifications and special considerations are often required. This chapter explores these modifications and considerations.

The first two sections in this chapter review the person-environment fit and developmental approaches, which together form the basis for many of the recommendations contained in this book. The third section reviews contributions from other major perspectives, including client-centered counseling, psychodynamic counseling, social learning counseling, social psychological perspectives, career decision-making perspectives, and computer-assisted guidance systems. The final section discusses general counseling issues and considerations—including stereotyping, homophobia and heterosexism, language, symbols of affirmation, and the need for lifelong education.

Person-Environment Fit Career Counseling

Person-environment (PE) counseling, referred to in the past as *trait-factor*, *matching*, or *congruence*, is at the core of career counseling. As Osipow (1987a) wrote, "Person-environment is what vocational psychology is all about. Starting from the days of Frank Parsons (1909)...the idea of a good match between people and their work remains at the core of career psychology" (p. 333). Traditional dimensions relevant to this matching process include interests, values, and abilities (Rounds & Tracey, 1990; Walsh & Betz, 1990).

Person-environment fit counseling has as its three foci the evaluation of individuals, the assessment of work environments, and the consideration of the interaction between individuals and their work environments (Moos, 1987; Osipow, 1987a; Rounds & Tracey, 1990; Walsh, 1987). This approach looks at the impacts that individuals have on their work environments and the impacts that work environments have on individuals.

The Person (P)

The PE approach stresses the importance of assessing a number of person characteristics. Traditional person variables include vocational interests (Benyamini & Gati, 1987; Gati, 1979; Holland, 1992); values, needs, and preferences (Dawis & Lofquist, 1984; Super & Nevill, 1986); and abilities and aptitudes (Jackson, 1984). In our own work, we also include consideration of such areas as career maturity (Savickas, 1984), gender (Betz, 1992), sexual orientation and level of identity development (Chojnacki & Gelberg, 1994; Hetherington, 1991), race and ethnic background (Hoyt, 1989), age (Levinson, 1986), health, and physical characteristics. We believe that all of these attributes help shape the career and life planning decisions that people make. In addition, career clients' life histories, their work experiences, and the vocational interests of their family, friends, and teachers, influence the career decisions that people make. (For discussion of person factors, see chapters 3 and 4.)

The Environment (E)

The PE approach looks at environment factors such as the type of interests that are desirable in a particular work environment, the opportunities that are offered in those work environments, and the skills that people should have in order to succeed at particular jobs.

As g/l/b persons reflect on their past histories as workers, some consider how their jobs may have been affected by other environmental factors such as the degree to which the work environment is affirmative to g/l/b persons. For example, some work environments have official policies that are openly discriminatory. Others have official nondiscrimination policies, but the work environments may be covertly discriminatory. Still other work environments are g/l/b affirmative (Chojnacki & Gelberg, 1994). (For discussion of environment factors, see chapter 5.)

The Person-Environment Interaction

PE theory predicts that if there is a strong match, or high degree of congruence, between a person and a work environment, (i.e., if there is a good PE fit), worker satisfaction and productivity will be high. Also, with a good PE match, turnover decreases and people deal more effectively with the stressors associated with the job (Moos, 1987; Osipow, 1987a; Rounds & Tracey, 1990; Walsh, 1987).

The interaction between workers and their work environments considers how the incongruence between a worker's personality and a particular work environment is addressed. Thus heterosexism and homophobia in the work environment can be viewed by the PE approach as an incongruence between two parties: the worker (person) and the work environment (environment). According to PE theories, the interaction between these two parties, as they respond to potential sources of difference, can affect both workers and their work environments.

By considering the fit and quality of interactions between the worker and the work environment, the person-environment approach suggests that people should select environments that offer the possibility of actualizing their needs, interests, values, and skills. If work environments fail to do this, workers may experience dissatisfaction, confusion, low self-esteem, anger, frustration, anxiety, or depression. By modifying the PE approach and increasing the number of variables considered, including sexual orientation, the PE approach helps us attend to the unique career planning needs of g/l/b persons.

Developmental Career Counseling

Traditional developmental theories do not directly address issues related to sexual orientation. However, by modifying traditional theory and increasing knowledge of new identity developmental models for g/l/b persons (e.g., Cass, 1979, 1984a, 1984b), developmental approaches can be extremely effective in career counseling with g/l/b persons.

Development Across the Life Span

Career and life planning is a process that begins in childhood and continues throughout the life span. Career interests develop when we pursue our hobbies as children, select courses in school, hold summer jobs, participate in extracurricular activities, or hold part-time jobs as students. We make career and lifestyle decisions in the choice of our first jobs and in the goals we set for job promotions or subsequent job changes. Even retirement planning requires career and lifestyle decision-making skills (Tinsley & Schwendener-Holt, 1992).

General development theories (e.g., Chickering, 1969; Chickering & Reisser, 1993; Gilligan, 1982) and developmental career counseling approaches (e.g., Gottfredson, 1981; Jepsen, 1984, 1990; Super, 1980, 1983) help career counselors focus on how adult development over the life span affects career and life planning. Thus developmental career counseling takes into account the fact that the career decisions individuals made in adolescence may differ from the decisions they make in early, middle, or late adulthood. For example, the decisions career clients make when entering the job market as young adults are likely to differ qualitatively from the decisions they make when considering a change in job status, job promotions, career redirection, or retirement. These differences occur in part because of a shift in priorities or changes in workers' values, needs, experiences, or interests.

Developmental career counseling approaches move beyond the sole consideration of such factors as work-related values, abilities, skills, experiences, and needs, and also consider the person's cognitive maturity level, life experiences, and developmental tasks. The whole person is considered in these theories.

Critical to considering the whole g/l/b person is considering the person's level of sexual identity development (e.g., Cass, 1979, 1984a, 1984b). Because peoples' thinking may be quite different across developmental stages of coming out, g/l/b identity development may affect willingness to enter homophobic work environments, ability to assess effectively the level of homophobia in a particular job environment, skills in confronting homophobia, ways in which sexual orientation is incorporated into career planning, and level of self-esteem as g/l/b employees. (For discussion of adult, career, and g/l/b identity development theories, see chapter 4.)

Developmental Transitions

The developmental approach also helps g/l/b persons better understand the role of transitions in career development. These transitions are referred to as *turning points*, *developmental bridges*, or *life passages* (Levinson, 1986; Levinson, Darrow, Klein, Levinson, & McLee, 1978). When people are in a transitional state or are at a developmental bridge, they are in between two stages of development: the previous outdated way of thinking, and the newer, more advanced cognitive stage. During this time, they may experience feelings of confusion, fear, anxiety, anger, or depression. They experience these feelings partly because the old ways in which they view their work or life situations do not seem to work for them, yet they do not have a new way to view the situation. In other words, when they are in a state of transition, the old patterns of thinking do not seem to be helpful anymore, but new perspectives are not yet clear to them. During these times, people usually feel a sense of disequilibrium because their usual responses to life seem insufficient and ineffective. They may also feel a sense of loss because their previous beliefs or approaches, which seemed to be helpful in the past, no longer work for them. They have lost their old, comfortable ways of thinking. This is often a time when people seek out helping professionals to assist with new changes.

When g/l/b persons first sense that their own sexual orientation differs from a heterosexual orientation, they may enter a transitional period characterized by heightened emotions of anxiety, fear, confusion, anger, or depression. As they move through the process of coming out as g/l/b persons and begin to leave the transitional period, these feelings of anger, fear, depression, or confusion are often replaced by such positive feelings as pride, a clarity of purpose and identity, and a sense of being "grounded" as g/l/b persons (Cass, 1979, 1984a, 1984b). Information on g/l/b identity development (Cass, 1979, 1984a, 1984b; Coleman, 1985; Henderson, 1984; Levine & Evans, 1991; Troiden, 1989) should be incorporated into developmental career counseling approaches, so that the transitional stages in coming out as g/l/b persons can thus be more effectively facilitated during career and life planning (Chojnacki & Gelberg, 1994).

Other kinds of developmental bridges or transitions that g/l/b persons may experience occur when these individuals first enter a romantic relationship, begin their first jobs, leave home for the first time, or receive job promotions. Although these are usually viewed as positive marker events, clients may feel that they have made a poor decision because of the strong transitional feelings. Professionals should help clients understand the developmental tasks associated with these strong transitional feelings, so that clients may then work toward meeting those developmental goals.

Other Career Counseling Approaches

Although we emphasize developmental and PE approaches to career counseling with g/l/b persons, other approaches can provide useful contributions. These are briefly summarized in this section.

Person-Centered Counseling

The application of this approach, first developed by Carl Rogers (1959) as a theory of psychotherapy rather than as a career counseling approach, has led to what is termed *client-centered vocational counseling* (Bozarth & Fisher, 1990). Client-centered counseling focuses on the person's career concerns as determined by the person rather than the counselor or professional helper. By encouraging greater autonomy, this approach can enhance self-esteem and self-confidence as g/l/b persons begin to determine the types of career and life planning concerns they will address in career counseling. Thus this approach can enhance such person factors as self-esteem and autonomy.

Psychodynamic Career Counseling

In this approach, the theories of Freud and of neo-Freudian theorists (e.g., Erikson, 1968, whose principles are discussed in chapter 4) are used to understand the client's drives, purposes, and motives (e.g., Watkins & Savickas, 1990). Adler (1964), another neo-Freudian, explored the impact of four variables on career and life planning decisions: the client's lifestyle, life tasks, family atmosphere and family relationships, and early recollections. Adlerian approaches seek to help clients find careers that will help them develop their life themes. A special issue of *Individual Psychology: The Journal of Adlerian Theory, Research, and Practice* (Carlson, 1995) has been devoted to revising Adlerian theory in order to provide affirmative counseling to g/l/b persons.

The application of Freudian principles to g/l/b identity development has been criticized because of Freud's view that g/l/b development resulted from disrupted development and was thus pathological (Carl, 1990). This criticism is supported by guidelines provided by the American Psychological Association Committee on Lesbian and Gay Concerns (CLGC) stating that approaches based on the belief that "homosexuality per se is a form of psychopathology" are "biased, inadequate, or inappropriate" (Garnets, Hancock, Cochran, Goodchilds, & Peplau, 1991, p. 21). The application of Freudian principles to the psychosocial development of women has also been criticized because it "takes male experience as the universal norm" (Kaschak, 1992, p. 15). Thus some Freudian principles may be particularly problematic when working with g/l/b clients.

Some writers have been able to utilize certain aspects of Freud's theories to describe g/l/b developmental dynamics. Starzecpyzel, for example, developed a theory drawn from the work of Freud, Chodorow, Slipp, and Kohut to describe the dynamics for lesbian survivors of father-daughter incest (Starzecpyzel, 1987). Klein (1993) revised classical Freudian principles surrounding the Oedipus complex because he felt that the classical view did not explain healthy g/l/b development. Thus some revised Freudian principles have been applied to g/l/b developmental theories in ways that do not pathologize g/l/b persons.

Social Learning Career Counseling

This approach highlights the role of learning experiences in shaping peoples' preferences for various activities (Krumboltz & Nichols, 1990). Although social learning theories have not been directly related to g/l/b career development, many social learning theory principles do have relevance. For example, these theories predict that certain occupations are more valued by a person if that person has succeeded, or believes she or he can succeed, at the tasks performed by people in that particular occupation. Thus career stereotyping based on sexual orientation could be predicted to affect an individual's valuing of certain occupations and belief that she or he can succeed in a particular job or profession.

The social learning approach to the career needs of g/l/b persons also highlights the importance of having positive role models at work (Krumboltz & Nichols, 1990). Because the degree to which a g/l/b person is out at work may depend on the level of homophobia or heterosexism of a particular work environment, g/l/b role models may be less visible in certain occupations or work environments. According to social learning theory, an absence of g/l/b role models in certain occupations could have an important impact on the level of desirability of those occupations in the eyes of g/l/b persons. Without positive g/l/b role models or mentors in certain work environments, g/l/b workers could feel a greater sense of isolation and may feel more negative about those particular work environments.

Social Psychological Perspectives

These approaches examine the role of social influence on the formulation of people's work attitudes (Dorn, 1990) and focus on the negative impacts of career myths (e.g., that certain careers are best for only one gender). In applying social psychological approaches to the career needs of g/l/b persons, career counselors and other professional helpers should be aware of the stereotypes that surround g/l/b career behaviors (Botkin & Daly, 1987) and should be knowledgeable about the homophobic or heterosexist stereotypes that surround g/l/b persons in general (Obear, 1991).

Social psychological approaches stress the need for career counselors and other professional helpers to be perceived as being expert, trustworthy, and having a positive regard for clients (Dorn, 1990). Counselors and other professional helpers may enhance these qualities by being educated about g/l/b identity development, being skilled in addressing career issues, and, finally, addressing their own internalized homophobia and heterosexism.

Career Decision-Making Perspectives

Phillips (1992) and Rounds and Tracey (1990) have discussed these approaches. Rounds and Tracey summarized common characteristics of several decision-making models as including "the definition and diagnosis of the problem, provision of information, alternative search and selection, and finally action" (1990, pp. 24-25). (See chapter 6 for a six-step decision-making process that includes these factors.)

Computer-Assisted Guidance Systems

Career needs are assessed in these approaches through the administration of a number of career assessment batteries. Based on the results, career clients may then receive information about occupational alternatives. Clients may also receive information about educational opportunities. The most common computer-assisted guidance systems are DISCOVER, developed by the American College Testing (ACT) Program, and SIGI-PLUS, developed by the Educational Testing Service (ETS).

Computer-assisted guidance systems were developed using such career counseling theories as Super's (1957) developmental theories, the decision theories of Tiedeman and O'Hara (1963), and Holland's (1973) hexagonal occupational and personality classification system.

Because the computer does not have information about such personal characteristics as the user's race, gender, or sexual orientation, the use of computers for career counseling may help prevent some types of bias. In addition, computers are commonly perceived to be nonthreatening (Rayman, 1990), and clients may be less hesitant to interact with computers than with career counselors and other professional helpers (Rayman, Bryson, & Bowlsbey, 1978). Thus g/l/b users who have concerns about homophobic or heterosexist counselors and other professional helpers may feel less hesitant to interact with computers. The potential for biased computer information still remains, however, because the career counseling theories used in developing the computer programs have not focused on sexual orientation as it affects career and life planning.

Computers have recently been used more extensively in the job search process. For example, electronic job searches are now possible with the arrival of the information superhighway, CD-ROM, teleconferencing, and the Internet. Users can tap into the Internet to check for job postings. Databases of résumés and positions are also available on the Internet. One benefit of an electronic job search is the fact that databases are updated more frequently and tend to have jobs not listed elsewhere. Databases for job seekers include Classifacts, Federal Job Opportunities, Career Link Worldwide, and Computer-World Careers Online (Waldrep, 1994). (For further discussion, see chapter 7.)

A potential use of computer information systems is the networking of g/l/b workers. Because it may be difficult for g/l/b persons to find g/l/b mentors at work, the development of national network databases could help offset the lack of g/l/b mentors in the local work environment.

General Counseling Issues and Considerations

Just as we do not advocate starting from scratch using career approaches with g/l/b persons, we also do not suggest changing fundamental counseling skills and techniques. Such basic counseling skills as the communication of care, empathy, and positive regard, as well as the ability to provide accurate reflection, are necessary conditions for any type of counseling.

There are, however, unique issues that g/l/b persons bring into counseling, and helping professionals must be knowledgeable about these issues in order to provide effective counseling with these individuals. Training of counselors in the area of g/l/b issues has been lacking (Buhrke, 1989; Buhrke & Douce, 1991; Eldridge & Barnett, 1991; House & Holloway, 1992; Iasenza, 1989). Training counselors, whatever their sexual orientation, in the area of g/l/b issues is critical because all people inherit societal values that are homophobic and heterosexist (Eldridge & Barnett, 1991).

G/l/b persons may approach counseling with some degree of trepidation. The client may reason that society is homophobic, and because the counselor is a member of society, there is a reasonable chance that the counselor may also be homophobic. Further, until recently, mental health providers have viewed g/l/b persons as having an illness that the mental health care providers needed to "cure." Cures included the use of electrodes in aversive conditioning techniques (Eldridge & Barnett, 1991). Only recently has the word *homosexuality* been eliminated from the official list of mental illnesses by the American Psychiatric Association (1987).

Schwartz and Hartstein (1986) described six interlocking assumptions that characterize g/l/b-affirmative counseling:

1. Being gay, lesbian, or bisexual is not a pathological condition.
2. The origins of sexual orientation are not completely known.
3. G/l/b persons lead fulfilling and satisfying lives.
4. There are a variety of g/l/b lifestyles.
5. G/l/b persons who attend counseling without a desire to change their sexual orientation should not be forced into change.
6. G/l/b-affirmative individual and group counseling should be available.

Eldridge and Barnett (1991) wrote that a critical factor in becoming a g/l/b-affirmative counselor is increased awareness. This should include awareness of the stereotyping issues facing g/l/b persons in this society, awareness of internalized homophobia and heterosexism, the need for affirmative symbols, and awareness of the ever-shifting political, legal, and societal changes regarding sexual orientation issues. The awareness needs to be maintained through lifelong, continuing education.

Stereotyping

In our conference presentations, we have asked people to share their stereotypes about which jobs they believe lesbians or gay men commonly hold. Invariably, audience members have associated such jobs as interior decorator or hair dresser with gay men. Jobs commonly associated with lesbians included firefighter, truck driver, and auto mechanic. Anecdotal evidence, combined with empirical data, indicate that some job stereotypes seem to split along gender lines (Botkin & Daly, 1987; Eldridge & Barnett, 1991; Herek, 1984). Society seems to associate gay men with traditionally female jobs and lesbians with traditionally male jobs. Professional helpers, as members of society, fall prey to these culturally inherited biases.

Gender Role Stereotypes

Career stereotyping of g/l/b persons is based, in part, on gender role stereotyping, and one reason that individuals may make career decisions that do not maximize their potential is that they may be negatively influenced by gender role stereotyping. Gender role stereotyping may influence the career goals that people set for themselves (that is, people may set goals that are too low, given their abilities). Gender role factors may further make individuals feel less confident in their ability to be successful at jobs to which they aspire, even if they do, in fact, have the abilities to succeed at those jobs.

The influence of gender factors was highlighted in a study of high school valedictorians. Arnold and Denny (1985) and Arnold (1987) found that gifted females tended to underestimate their potential, especially as they grew older. That is, intellectual self-esteem in 46 high school female valedictorians deteriorated over time. The self-esteem of the male valedictorians, in contrast, dropped less over time. Thus because gender seems to play a crucial role in how we view ourselves intellectually, it may subtly shape the career objectives we set for ourselves.

Linda Gottfredson (1981) has speculated in detail about the impact of gender role stereotyping factors (as well as other factors) on career aspirations. According to Gottfredson, as children grow older, four factors influence their career aspirations and choices. The first is that some jobs are discarded by children as viable career options because these particular jobs hold too little *prestige* for the child. Over time, a second factor, *sex role stereotyping*, becomes more important to children in making career decisions. A third factor, how difficult people feel the *level of effort or training* might be for a particular job, additionally affects career decision making, as does a fourth factor, how well a person believes a job suits her or his *work personality*.

Stereotypes associated with socioeconomic class, religion, national origin, race, or ethnicity also have strong impacts on the career goals people set for themselves. Further, physical disabilities, emotional disabilities, learning disabilities, physical fitness levels, and physical appearance may shape career goals in subtle ways. Thus we believe that factors such as sexual orientation, socioeconomic status, religious orientation, ethnicity/ nationality/race, physical health/fitness, and perceived physical attractiveness may also affect peoples' zone of acceptable alternatives in addition to the four factors discussed by Gottfredson.

The potential impact of gender role stereotypes on career decision making is illustrated by the experience of one of our career clients who spoke about her childhood dreams to be a pilot. She kept this goal until a young boy told her that "girls can't be pilots." Despite the fact that this advice giver was another small child (not the ideal career counselor), the young girl gave up her dream of being a pilot. She did not reconsider that field until she sought career counseling as an adult. During career counseling, a conscious effort was made to help her once again reconsider those careers that she may have given up because of such factors as low prestige or sex role stereotyping. The expectation was that when she again considered careers she had given up, she might make career decisions that emphasized more strongly the role of her work-related interests, values, experiences, and skills rather than make career decisions based solely on prestige factors or gender role stereotyping factors. After career counseling, this particular career client did decide to pursue her dream of becoming a pilot again because that career was so closely tied to her present interests, values, experiences, and skills.

Gottfredson (1981) believed that very young children tend to see a wide range of careers as being feasible for themselves before stereotyping has had a chance to influence their career planning. She noted that with time, however, they may discard a number of career alternatives because those jobs do not have enough prestige, or because the child perceives that some jobs are not held by individuals of his or her gender. Thus the range of career alternatives people view as feasible for themselves may become restricted in adulthood partly because of stereotyping.

Only after an individual considers such factors as the prestige of the job, the perceived sex type of the job, and how difficult that person feels the effort or training might be for a specific job, Gottfredson (1981) speculated, will the person consider the degree to which a particular job matches that person's work-related interests, values, experiences, and skills. Thus stereotypes seem to take priority over interests, values, experiences, and skills during career decision making.

Gottfredson (1981) also noted that a person's career-related interests, values, and needs may be the first things that individuals compromise when forced to make choices about which careers to pursue. Thus when making career choices, people are likely to first consider gender role stereotyping of a job before thinking about the degree to which that job matches their interests, talents, values, or needs.

Stereotyping has long-lasting effects. According to Gottfredson (1981), only with conscious effort do people once again reconsider jobs they may have failed to pursue—even when those decisions were based on faulty stereotypes. Thus those who help g/l/b persons make career decisions should encourage these individuals to reflect once again on those careers they may have stopped considering because of stereotypes held about that job's prestige, sex type, or level of effort required to enter that position. These individuals should then be better able to consider the match between the requirements of specific jobs and their own unique work-related interests, experiences, and talents. Counselors must, therefore, take an active role in exploring and challenging stereotypes.

Stereotypes Associated With Sexual Orientation

The career goals people set for themselves may also be affected by stereotypes linked to sexual orientation. An individual may avoid some careers because of a belief that those careers are not held by persons of a particular sexual orientation.

Research suggests that people are more tolerant of gay men who conform to societal stereotypes. That is, a gay male hairdresser will be tolerated more than a gay male construction worker (Herek, 1984). In a study of sexual orientation stereotyping by Botkin and Daly (1987), a group of college students were asked to name careers that the students felt would be most interesting to lesbians, gay men, and heterosexuals. The students speculated that the jobs most interesting to gay males would be photography, interior decorating, and nursing. The students thought that lesbians would be most interested in being auto mechanics, plumbers, and truck drivers. Thus, as already noted, empirical evidence seems to support the notion that both career stereotyping and stereotyping of sexual orientation fall along gender stereotyping lines, with gay men being stereotyped as holding traditionally female jobs and lesbians being stereotyped as holding traditionally male jobs. It is interesting to note that in Botkin and Daly's study the careers listed for heterosexual women require a college education, but the careers cited for lesbians do not. The jobs listed for heterosexual women were nursing, working as a dietitian, and interior decorating.

Heterosexuals may also make career decisions reflecting the impact of career stereotypes linked to sexual orientation. For example, heterosexuals may not enter certain careers to which they are well suited because of a belief that these careers are commonly held by gay, lesbian, or bisexual individuals. One heterosexual male client was highly conflicted about going into nursing for fear of being stereotyped as gay. This exemplifies how all persons are impacted by sexual orientation career stereotyping, regardless of their sexual orientation. All people can face constricted career options as a result of this type of stereotyping.

Like other types of stereotyping, stereotyping associated with sexual orientation seems to exert its impact in two ways. First, it may influence g/l/b persons' own perceptions of the types of jobs they consider appropriate for themselves. Second, stereotyping may influence the expectations others hold about the kinds of jobs that g/l/b persons should enter. Because most career clients may be deeply impressionable at some points of their lives, the expectations others hold about the kinds of careers people should enter, given a particular sexual orientation, can have profound, negative impacts on the career and life planning goals people set for themselves.

Counseling Implications

Stereotypes must be of concern to the professional helper. Counselors and other professional helpers are members of society, a society that communicates strong messages about "appropriate" career options for g/l/b persons. Counselors must be aware of, and fight, their own stereotypes as well as those that clients may bring to them.

Consideration of the null environment hypothesis (Betz, 1989) suggests that counselors should take an active role in challenging stereotypes. According to Betz, "a null educational environment (Freeman, 1975) that ignores individuals is inherently discriminatory against women because external societal environments are different for men and women with respect to the amount of encouragement they receive for nontraditional career aspirations and achievements" (Betz, 1989, p. 136). We have already explored how gender role stereotypes may be linked to g/l/b career stereotypes. Betz argued that if counselors are neutral in their stance toward various career options, they are doing their clients a disservice. In a neutral or null environment, societal pressures push toward stereotypic choice. Counselors should thus actively explore, discuss, and pursue nontraditional options as well as traditional options. As Betz wrote, "we can do our best to. . .restore some of the options that societal pressures have taken away" (1989, p. 142).

Homophobia and Heterosexism

Homophobia is an irrational fear, hatred, and intolerance of g/l/b persons. It is a belief system that supports negative stereotypes and maintains that discrimination based on sexual orientation is justified (Lapierre, 1990; Pharr, 1988). It is deeply ingrained in our society. It is the force behind g/l/b persons being rejected by their families, dismissed from their jobs, losing custody of children, and becoming targets of violence. Parenthetically, recent figures indicate that hate crimes against g/l/b persons are on the rise (Freiberg, 1995).

G/l/b persons growing up in this society inherit its culture, a culture that includes pervasive homophobia. Consequently, g/l/b persons often internalize these societal beliefs; they come to dislike themselves. This is referred to as *internalized homophobia*. Persons in early stages of awareness of their orientation sometimes feel self-loathing for having affectional thoughts or feelings for persons of the same gender. They may feel a good deal of anxiety about having these thoughts or feelings, knowing how poorly society treats g/l/b persons.

Internalized homophobia often takes a toll on the well-being of a g/l/b person. Higher rates of suicide and substance abuse have been reported in the g/l/b population than in the population at large (Eldridge & Barnett, 1991). Not only do g/l/b persons face the dangers of a homophobic society (e.g., hate crimes), but they must also cope with internal conflicts resulting from being a part of a homophobic society.

G/l/b persons need to come to terms with internalized homophobia, and it is important for counselors and other professional helpers to be aware of this developmental process. It is also important to be aware that g/l/b persons may enter counseling with some degree of anxiety, both about themselves and the helpers they will be encountering.

Homophobic prejudice, the manifestation of irrational fear, hatred, and intolerance of people who are gay, lesbian, or bisexual, is associated with heterosexism, a belief in the superiority of heterosexuality (Obear, 1991). Our society often presents heterosexism as the only viable lifestyle. G/l/b relationships are seldom depicted in the media, and when they are, they are often sensationalized. Educators in the earliest of grades use materials that suggest that the only type of loving adult relationship is between persons of the opposite gender.

As helping professionals, we must monitor our own heterosexist assumptions. For example, when people talk about their *significant other*, a term that is nondisclosing as far as gender is concerned, do we automatically assume that person to be of the opposite gender? Counselors must examine their own subconscious reactions to intimate same-gender relationships. That is, for counselors and other professional helpers, awareness of their own homophobic and heterosexist biases is critical. As Eldridge and Barnett (1991) wrote, "therapists working with g/l/b students must challenge their own assumptions about sexual/affectional orientations when trying to understand and empathize with these clients. This is true regardless of a helper's sexual/affectional orientation because we have all been raised in a culture biased toward heterosexuality" (p. 148). House has designed a questionnaire for counselors to use to assess their own levels of homophobia (House, 1991; House & Taylor, 1992).

Helping professionals must also be aware of *heterosexual privilege*. Heterosexual privilege allows heterosexuals to walk down the street, holding the hand of their partner, without fear of comment or attack by others. It allows heterosexuals inheritance rights, access to a partner in a hospital, the legal right to marry, and the ability to adopt children. These are rights and freedoms taken for granted by heterosexuals. Counselors must become knowledgeable about the absence of rights for g/l/b persons because these rights can have an impact on career and life planning as well as on work behaviors.

Heterosexual counselors must also be aware of the privileges they themselves enjoy because of their sexual orientation. (See Appendix 4, which looks at issues surrounding heterosexual counselors who are striving to become g/l/b affirmative.)

The Importance of Language

The language counselors and other professional helpers choose to use is important because heterosexism and homophobia can be communicated through words. Helping professionals should use words that do not assume that significant others are the opposite gender. Gender free nouns like *partner* and *significant other* are useful.

The American Psychological Association (1991) has published a set of guidelines for avoiding heterosexual bias in language. The article recommends appropriate terminology and is a valuable resource for counselors.

A key recommendation is to avoid using the term *homosexual*. This term has negative connotations because it was associated with a diagnostic category of mental illness in the past and also because of its emphasis on the sexual aspect of a loving relationship. The term *sexual orientation* is a more appropriate term than *sexual preference* because sexual preference connotes choice in sexual orientation. Current thinking and research suggests that sexual orientation may not be linked to choice but rather to biological factors.

The Need for Affirmative Symbols

Currently, society's dominant message is the superiority of heterosexuality. Thus a neutral or null environment means one in which heterosexuality is assumed to be the norm. If g/l/b persons enter such an environment, they may be fearful or anxious about discussing their sexual orientation. Without any other information available, a person seeking help often assumes an environment of heterosexism and homophobia. Therefore, helpers must actively dispel this assumption.

Helping professionals can come out as affirmative through the use of symbols. Because the pink triangle is a symbol associated with g/l/b issues, counselors sometimes display pink triangles in their offices. Some universities have "safe zones," a program in which affirmative faculty and staff display pink triangles to indicate affirmative environments. Having books and publications about g/l/b issues in offices and waiting areas can also serve as symbols of affirmation.

Counselors and other professional helpers should be aware that g/l/b persons may respond differently to those clues about the sexual orientation of the helper. For example, some g/l/b persons who have experienced homophobia from heterosexuals may find it difficult to initially trust a helping professional whom they believe to be heterosexual. Other g/l/b persons may find that the sexual orientation of the helping professional is not a concern, and they may be comfortable working with a heterosexual helper. We have found that comfort in working with heterosexual or g/l/b counselors and other professional helpers may vary with the level of g/l/b identity development (Chojnacki & Gelberg, 1995). Heterosexual professional helpers should thus display symbols of g/l/b affirmation so that g/l/b clients need not struggle to answer the question, "Is this helper homophobic?" In order to help g/l/b persons make informed decisions about seeking help, we recommend that counselors and other professional helpers not purposefully hide signs of heterosexuality, but instead communicate g/l/b affirmation through visible signs of an appreciation of g/l/b issues and the valuing of a g/l/b orientation.

Hradsky and Comey (1992) developed a diversity report card that defined a number of career center characteristics reflecting a career center's responsiveness to g/l/b students' needs. These organizational characteristics included the use of publicly visible affirmative materials, the provision of g/l/b services and resources, staff education, network lists, inclusive language, liaisons with g/l/b student organizations, the addressing of recruitment issues and discrimination, and the level of comfort of both the staff and students in discussing sensitive issues. Eldridge and Barnett (1991) also described agency actions that communicate affirmation.

A recent study of student affairs professionals (Croteau & Lark, 1995) identified 10 behaviors that demonstrate exemplary professional practice concerning g/l/b persons. These behaviors focused on the open expression of g/l/b affirmation; supportive, educative, and legal responses to homophobic harassment and violence; the inclusion of sexual orientation in language, programs, written materials, social events, policies, and activities; the ability to treat g/l/b persons with the same level of regard as other students; an understanding of g/l/b identity development; a respect for issues relating to being out at work; the provision of staff and student awareness training for issues linked to sexual orientation; the facilitation of special g/l/b campus programs; serving as an advocate for g/l/b students and g/l/b organizations; and being equitable and affirmative in employment issues and benefits.

Lifelong, Continuing Education

As Eldridge and Barnett (1991) wrote, "Awareness. . .is assumed to be the best method to combat potential bias" (p. 164). Additionally, acquiring knowledge and increasing the level of awareness is not a one-time event but a lifelong process (Gelberg & Chojnacki, 1995).

Helping professionals need to know about g/l/b culture. Washington and Evans (1991) noted that "the gay, lesbian, and bisexual world is one that has its own language and culture" (p. 203). Reading fiction and non-fiction books, attending rallies and conferences, and immersion in situations in which g/l/b persons are in the majority help to increase cultural knowledge. Further, cultural differences exist among g/l/b persons (Blumenfeld & Raymond, 1988; Pope & Reynolds, 1991), and these differences must be understood and appreciated.

Coursework, workshops, and professional readings help professionals stay knowledgeable about current issues relevant to g/l/b persons (Buhrke, 1989; Buhrke & Douce, 1991). The media are full of current events and other topics impacting the lives of g/l/b persons. It is important to be as aware of them as g/l/b persons often are because these events and topics have direct and indirect effects on career and life planning. Even as we have been writing this book, laws and policies concerning g/l/b persons have shifted at national, state, and local levels. Counselors and other professional helpers need to stay informed and up to date on the nature of these changes.

AIDS is an example of a current issue that helpers should be knowledgeable about in order to address the myths and misinformation about the condition and the g/l/b community (e.g., the myth that AIDS is a gay disease) and be supportive of the members of the community who are affected by AIDS (Hetherington, 1991; Washington & Evans, 1991).

The use of consultants on g/l/b issues is highly recommended to further knowledge. Further, it is important for counselors and other professional helpers to become familiar with local agencies and services that are g/l/b affirmative (e.g., legal services and medical services) so that appropriate referrals can be made. Finally, the need for helping professionals to be aware of their own strengths and limitations in this area should not be understated. If counselors and helping professionals feel overwhelmed or ineffective, referral to other affirmative helping professionals is recommended.

Resources we have found particularly helpful for counseling g/l/b persons include *Counseling Gay Men and Lesbians: Journey to the End of the Rainbow* (Dworkin & Gutiérrez, 1992); "Counseling Gay and Lesbian Students," a chapter by Eldridge and Barnett (1991) in the book *Beyond Tolerance: Gays, Lesbians, and Bisexuals on Campus* (Evans & Wall, 1991); and *A Guide to Psychotherapy With Gay and Lesbian Clients* (Gonsiorek, 1985).

3

Assessing the Person: Interests, Values, Experiences, and Skills

The assessment of vocational interests, values, experiences, and skills is crucial to the person-environment matching process (Rounds & Tracey, 1990; Walsh & Betz, 1990). Although concerns of heterosexism must be addressed when using those basic career counseling paradigms that focus on the assessment of interests, values, experiences, and skills, these paradigms are still relevant when working with g/l/b persons. Thus counselors and other professional helpers should be knowledgeable about those basic career counseling approaches and theories that focus on the assessment of such work personality characteristics as interests, values, experiences, and skills. Because of heterosexism and homophobia, however, familiarity with these basic career assessment concepts is not by itself adequate. That is, these basic career assessment approaches must be modified to take sexual orientation factors into account.

In initially assessing the g/l/b person's work personality, it is recommended that the helping professional first use a semistructured interview approach in order to determine the client's own awareness of her or his career interests, values, experiences, and skills. Semistructured interviews may include such questions as

- What do you feel your current work strengths are? What classes or activities did you enjoy in school? What are your hobbies? What are the things you are not good at? (*measures interests*)
- Tell me about your past jobs and achievements in school. (*measures experiences*)
- What is important to you in your career? What have been the highlights of your life, work, or school experiences, and why were these highlights for you? (*measures experiences, skills, and values*)

- What are you good at in your job? What have people told you your strengths are? (*measures skills*)
- If you could have any job without having to worry about getting the training, what would be your ideal job? What about this job would be the most appealing to you? (*measures interests and values*)

Additional questions should be asked in order to understand fully the client's career history, educational history, awareness of the career decision-making process, knowledge of the world of work, occupational fantasies, level of interest in securing additional training, and personal/societal barriers to the implementation of career goals. In addition, useful information may be obtained through inquiring about the type of career advice that others have given the client. (See Appendix 1 for suggestions for areas of discussion during the initial interview.) After the helping professional has a general sense of the client's vocational personality from talking with the individual, a number of additional instruments may be of use.

Often in conjunction with a semistructural interview, career inventories are administered. A useful resource is *A Counselor's Guide to Career Assessment Instruments* (Kapes, Mastie, & Whitfield, 1994), which describes 52 career assessment instruments. For each instrument, the guide considers its use in counseling, discusses technical considerations, and presents information on computer-based versions. The guide also critiques 49 of the 52 assessment instruments and provides references.

This chapter focuses on the initial assessment of the g/l/b client's work personality. It first describes assessment instruments for classifying and inventorying the client's work personality (career interests, values/needs, experiences, and skills/abilities). Additional assessment instruments are suggested for inventorying the client's work personality and career beliefs. Resources that can help g/l/b clients understand the world of work are also enumerated. Finally, critical issues in using existing career inventories and assessment procedures for g/l/b persons are discussed, and the necessity for counselors and other helping professionals to consider the unique factors of sexual orientation in adapting career counseling assessments and approaches is emphasized.

Assessment Instruments

Assessing Career Interests

The Holland classification system (Holland, 1985a, 1985b, 1985c) is probably the most commonly used system to classify and assess career interests. Career interest inventories must be used with caution, given the lack of research development of these instruments with the g/l/b population. Three interest inventories are recommended for use with g/l/b persons:

- **Self-Directed Search (SDS).** Holland's classification system (Holland, 1985b) helps clients organize and clarify their work-related interests and preferences along the dimensions of six personality types. Once clients have a clearer sense of their realistic, investigative, artistic, social, enterprising, and conventional interests, they are better able to find a set of career options that matches those interests. Both occupations and educational majors are suggested from the SDS assessment.

- **The Strong Interest Inventory (SII).** The revised Strong Interest Inventory (Hammer, Borgen, Hansen, & Harmon, 1994) contains six general occupational theme scales: realistic, investigative, artistic, social, enterprising, and conventional. The SII also provides scores for 25 basic interest scales, 211 occupational scales, personal style scales, and administrative indexes. In using the occupational scales, the user's scores are compared with occupational samples that reflect individuals who are satisfied in their work, have at least 3-years' experience on a particular job, and perform the duties typical of members of a particular job. The *Strong Interest Inventory Applications and Technical Guide* (Harmon, Hansen, Borgen, & Hammer, 1994) includes sections on cross-cultural uses of the SII. In addition, guidelines are offered for using this inventory with people who have disabilities, and the importance of considering gender issues in interpreting the inventory is discussed.

- **Campbell Interest and Skills Survey (CISS).** The CISS (Campbell, 1994) measures self-reported interests and skills. Scores are reported for orientation scales, which cover seven themes of occupational interests and skills; basic interest and skill scales, subscales of the orientation scales; and occupational scales, which compare interests and skills with workers in a range of occupations.

Career interests and aspirations may differ for g/l/b persons, compared with heterosexual men or women. For example, Chung and Harmon (1994) found that gay men scored higher on artistic and social scales of an interest inventory than do heterosexual men. This may be due to some occupations evidencing less homophobia than others rather than to individual or personal factors (Murray, 1991). This may also be the result of conforming to societal expectations (Herek, 1984). Because there is controversy about whether these differences reflect outside forces rather than intrinsic characteristics, these findings should not be used to "perpetuate

stereotypes and instill limiting and potentially harmful ideas in career counselors about appropriate careers" for g/l/b persons (Hetherington, 1991, p.
133).

Because lesbians may value androgyny, they may seek nontraditional
employment more often than do heterosexual women (Elliott, 1993). Lesbians may rely less on traditional gender role stereotypes than heterosexual
women (Hetherington & Orzek, 1989), and this may also affect career
interests. As already noted, anecdotal and empirical evidence suggests that
job stereotypes seem to split along gender stereotyping lines, with gay men
often in traditionally female jobs and lesbians often in traditionally male
jobs (Botkin & Daly, 1987; Eldridge & Barnett, 1991; Herek, 1984).
Whether these interest inventories are measuring natural differences between genders or are reinforcing gender-based pressures toward certain interests is not clear. Anderson, Tracey, and Rounds (1995) reported that
their research did not indicate gender differences in the overall fit of Holland's model. That is, their research suggested that the meanings and interpretations associated with particular scores on one inventory, the Strong
Interest Inventory, were equally valid for males and females. Caution should
still be exercised in interpreting interest inventories (Hansen & Campbell,
1985).

Assessing Values/Needs

Standardized inventories of vocational values and needs include the
Minnesota Importance Questionnaire (MIQ) (Rounds, Henley, Dawis,
Lofquist, & Weiss, 1981), the Work Values Inventory (Super, 1973) and
the Values Scale (Super & Nevill, 1986). However, although these inventories help clients clarify their work-related needs and values, values and
needs linked to sexual orientation are not considered.

- **Minnesota Importance Questionnaire (MIQ).** The MIQ
  (Rounds et al., 1981) measures such vocational needs as com-
  pensation and co-workers (Betz, 1992). Vocational needs are
  described as "preferences for reinforcers expressed in terms of
  the relative importance of each reinforcer to the individual"
  (Rounds et al., 1981, p. 8).
- **Super's Work Values Inventory (WVI).** The WVI (Super,
  1973) measures such vocational values as altruism, aesthetics,
  intellectual stimulation, and economic returns.
- **Values Scale.** This scale (Super & Neville, 1986) identifies
  extrinsic and intrinsic core work values, such as ability, utilization, achievement, advancement, aesthetics, and altruism.

Maslow (1970) has proposed a hierarchy of psychological needs, and
other lists of needs have been developed by Dawis, Lofquist, and Weiss

(1968); Murray (1938); and Vroom (1964). Items from these lists can be used informally during a semistructured intake assessment interview.

Assessing Experiences

Such semistructured reflective activities as the New Quick Job Hunting Map (Bolles, 1990) can provide information about skills that have been developed from a particular set of career experiences. The New Quick Job Hunting Map asks clients to draw their experiences from satisfying accomplishments that occurred either during leisure or work, from previous jobs, or from experiences linked to life roles such as student or volunteer worker. Thus the assessment of experiences need not be based solely on work experiences. The key is to find those experiences during which the individual felt a strong sense of pride, accomplishment, or meaning.

Assessing Skills/Abilities

There are a number of concerns about the use of specific aptitude measures with minorities. These include concerns about gender, race, cultural, and social class test bias (Walsh & Betz, 1990). G/l/b persons have been described as a type of minority (Hetherington, 1991). Thus the use of aptitude measures should be placed within the context of race, gender, culture, and socioeconomic background (Betz, 1992) as well as sexual orientation. Typical measures of abilities include the following:

- **American College Testing (ACT) Assessment.** This academic aptitude test yields a total of 12 subscores and includes subtests in English, math, reading, and science reading.
- **Differential Aptitude Tests (DAT).** The DAT (Bennett, Seashore, & Wesman, 1990) measures a number of aptitudes for adolescents and adults, including verbal reasoning, numerical reasoning, abstract reasoning, and perceptual speed and accuracy. The DAT also provides the Career Interest Inventory (CII) as a career exploration option.

Academic aptitude tests such as the SAT, ACT, or GRE can provide some information about skill areas. In addition, information gathered about previous jobs and academic performance is also useful in assessing skills and abilities.

Comprehensive Assessments

Comprehensive computer programs can supplement career and life planning counseling through use of interactive dialogues between users and computer programs. These comprehensive programs, which include assessments of a person's interests, values, experiences, and skills, aid in test administration, instruct users about the world of work, store large data banks of occupational and educational information, assist in generating lists of occupations/educational majors based on assessment results, facilitate career decision making, and assist in job search networking with employers. Two commonly used computer-assisted comprehensive assessment and guidance approaches are DISCOVER and SIGI-PLUS.

- **DISCOVER** (developed by ACT). DISCOVER uses nine modules to orient the user to career planning. DISCOVER also provides instruction on the world of work, assists in self-assessment, helps the user locate occupations based on the assessment, provides educational and occupational information, facilitates educational decision making, assists in the development of a plan for educational preparation, facilitates additional career planning, and provides suggestions for transitioning milestones. Module 3 (Learning About Yourself) of this computerized guidance system helps in the self-assessment of interests, abilities, experiences, and values. Modules 4 (Finding Occupations) and 5 (Learning About Occupations) provide information about a large number of occupations based on the results of the assessment inventories in Module 3.

- **SIGI-PLUS** (developed by ETS). SIGI-PLUS takes clients through a number of steps including self-assessment, information gathering, preparation and coping, decision making, and making action plans. Section 2 (Self-Assessment) helps the user of this computerized guidance system look at values, interest fields, and skills.

As noted earlier, there are a number of positive aspects about the use of computers for career assessment. However, the career counseling theories used in developing the computer assessment programs have not focused on sexual orientation as it affects career and life planning. Thus comprehensive computerized assessment programs have the same potential for heterosexual bias as do other career counseling assessment models.

Other Assessment Instruments

- **Myers-Briggs Type Inventory (MBTI) Career Report.** The Myers-Briggs Career Report (Myers & Myers, 1992) uses four personality scales (extrovert/introvert, sensing/intuition, thinking/feeling, and judgment/perception) to assess the individual's work personality. Occupations are suggested as they relate to work tasks involving those four dimensions. The user's work style personality is also described in the computerized report. In addition, the sections on work personality styles help the user gain a greater appreciation for differences among workers. The MBTI also enhances the user's appreciation of individual strengths and growth areas. The MBTI is helpful in that it uses a different classification for assessing the client's work personality and sometimes generates lists of career options that may differ from the options defined by the Strong Interest Inventory (Hammer et al., 1994) or the Self-Directed Search (Holland, 1985b).

- **Career Maturity Inventory (CMI).** Different aspects of career maturity may be assessed through the Career Maturity Inventory (Crites, 1978), the Career Decision Scale (Osipow, 1987b; Osipow, Carney, Winer, Yanico, & Koschier, 1980), My Vocational Situation (Holland, Daiger, & Power, 1980), the Career Development Inventory (CDI) (Super, Thompson, Lindeman, Jordaan, & Myers, 1981), and the Assessment of Career Decision Making (Harren, 1980).

- **Career Beliefs Inventory and Survey of Career Attitudes.** Irrational career beliefs may be assessed through use of the Career Beliefs Inventory (Krumboltz, 1988). In addition, the Survey of Career Attitudes (Woodrick, 1979) measures the career development myths that clients may have. Those irrational career beliefs linked to sexual orientation are not explored in these inventories.

World of Work Resources

It is especially helpful for clients to understand the world of work, or the full range of career options. That is, by locating specific subgroups of occupations in the world of work, clients can sometimes discover feasible occupations not specified by formal interest inventories. As clients read about specific job requirements or job duties, they can further define their vocational interests. These resources can be helpful in enhancing clients' understanding of specific job tasks, career options, requisite training, and job opportunities. Through a greater understanding of specific work requirements, clients can further clarify their own interests and develop solid options for a good fit between themselves (the person) and occupations (the environment). A number of resources are helpful in providing information about the world of work:

- *The Dictionary of Occupational Titles (DOT)* (U.S. Department of Labor, 1991). The *DOT* describes and defines more than 20,000 jobs. These jobs all require different combinations of skills, interests, and experiences. The numerical system used to organize this resource places similar occupations next to each other. Thus clients can find similar careers adjacent to each other in the *DOT*. Clients should explore the two- or three-digit number index at the front of the *DOT* in order to find which of the general fields are of primary interest. (Or clients can use the alphabetical index to locate a particular occupation.) Clients can then browse through that entire *DOT* section to locate other occupations that utilize similar skills. The middle three digits in the *DOT* code tell of required worker skills in three areas: data, people, and things. This information helps to further clarify clients' interests in particular jobs.

- *The Dictionary of Holland Occupational Codes* (Gottfredson & Holland, 1989). The dictionary utilizes Holland's system to group hundreds of jobs into categories based on the client's work personality type.

- *Guide for Occupational Exploration* **(GOE)** (Harrington & O'Shea, 1984). Occupational Exploration Worksheets help the user locate careers in the *GOE* that match the client's interests, values, leisure activities, home activities, school subjects, and work experiences. Careers are organized into 12 work groups: artistic, scientific, plants and animals, protective, mechanical, industrial, business detail, selling, accommodating, humanitarian, leading-influencing, and physical performing.

- *Occupational Outlook Handbook* (U.S. Dept. of Labor, 1994). This resource helps clients learn more about the employment outlook for a variety of occupations. In addition, information about the nature of the work, places of employment, and similar occupations is provided for each occupation.

- *Chronicle Occupational Briefs* (Chronicle Guidance Publications, 1989). The occupational briefs are organized using the same classification system as the *Guide for Occupational Exploration. DOT* numbers are also used to classify these briefs. Descriptions are provided about specific working conditions, work duties, earnings, education/training, licensing/registration/certification, personal qualifications, social and psychological factors, place of employment, employment outlook, entry methods, advancement, and related occupations.

- **The World of Work Map** (Prediger, 1976, 1981). This system classifies more than 450 ACT Job Families (groups of similar jobs) into 12 regions of the world of work. From the location on the map, the user can see the degree to which the occupations involve the four work tasks of data, ideas, people, and things. The World of Work Map is used in the ACT Interest Inventory (UNIACT) (Lamb & Prediger, 1981) and the DISCOVER computer programs. It also corresponds to the Holland classification system.

- **DISCOVER and SIGI-PLUS** modules contain occupational information that is updated yearly. This information includes information about the kinds of vocational interests, abilities, and values that characterize particular occupations. Occupations in DISCOVER and SIGI-PLUS have all been classified by interests, values, experiences, and abilities. Users get feedback on how well a specific occupation matches their characteristics on these dimensions, thus facilitating an immediate analysis of the degree of match between the person and the occupation. In addition, educational requirements, occupational descriptions, and employment outlooks are provided.

- **Informational interviews** may also be used to provide information about clients' interests. Informational interviews differ from interviews that are part of the job search process. That is, informational interviews have as their function the gathering of information about a specific career, versus applying for a specific position. This information is gathered from people rather than from written sources and thus supplies different types of career information. In conducting informational interviews, clients should discuss specific jobs with people who enjoy, excel in, and are stable in a particular occupation, and they should speak with more than one individual about a particular field if possible. If clients are able to interview a worker who is gay, lesbian, or bisexual, additional information about diversity in the workplace may be gathered.

Critically important to g/l/b persons is the degree of heterosexism and homophobia in work environments. Assessment of this is not available in the traditional resources just described. (See chapter 5 for a discussion of resources to assess workplace homophobia.)

Critical Issues in Existing Career Inventories and Assessment Procedures

We have noted two critical issues—or major problems—in current career inventories and methods of assessment. The first is that most fail to account for factors linked to sexual orientation. Thus the inventories may be biased and incomplete in assessing g/l/b client's interests, values, experiences, and skills. The second problem is that in existing g/l/b career counseling models, the full repertoire of career counseling techniques is not considered. Implications of these two problem issues, which are summarized in this section, are that we must be cautious in using traditional career assessment approaches with g/l/b persons. We recommend that practitioners consider the unique factors of sexual orientation in adapting career counseling assessments and approaches.

Problem Issue: Career inventories and assessment procedures fail to consider factors linked to sexual orientation

A major problem with all career inventories and assessment procedures is the fact that sexual orientation factors are not considered during the process of assessment. Thus such factors as the client's stage in the coming-out process, the client's level of self-esteem as a g/l/b person in the workforce, the degree to which the g/l/b person has internalized negative stereotypes about sexual orientation (internalized homophobia), the amount of societal homophobia experienced, and the availability of social support systems for that individual are not typically assessed in career inventories (Pope, 1992). The impact of such factors on career interests, values, experiences, and skills is unclear due to the lack of research in this area.

Because demographic data regarding sexual orientation are not gathered during the norming process when developing these inventories, the interaction among the factors linked to sexual orientation and the development of an individual's work personality is unclear. The reliability or validity of these inventories with g/l/b clients needs empirical research, and these inventories cannot be automatically assumed to be completely accurate for g/l/b persons. Pope (1992) commented that there is little research on the impact of sexual orientation on assessment and test interpretation, and he discussed his perceptions about the use of the Strong Interest Inventory, California Psychological Inventory (CPI), Myers-Briggs Type Inventory (MBTI), and Minnesota Multiphasic Personality (MMPI). Pope noted that clients taking these inventories may be concerned about revealing their sexual orientation (or masculinity or femininity) through their responses. There is some historical basis for this concern, as previous masculinity-femininity scales (e.g., earlier versions of the MMPI and CPI) were sometimes used as a way to try to differentiate heterosexuals from g/l/b persons. Although it is no longer a practice to use these tests to identify g/l/b persons, some clients may still fear self-disclosure when responding to these inventories.

Career counseling assessment approaches fail to consider fully the role of the client's perception of homophobia and heterosexism of the professional helper/helping environment on the assessment process. Individuals in the early stages of coming out may not self-disclose their sexual orientation to career counselors or to other professional helpers because of a fear of encountering homophobic helpers or helping agencies (Hradsky & Comey, 1992). Individuals may also have a fear of having their sexual orientation identified through a psychological test or career inventory (Pope, 1992) because the identification could have an adverse impact on the job search process.

Problem Issue: Gay, lesbian, and bisexual career counseling models fail to consider the full range of career developmental tasks and processes

G/l/b career counseling research, models, and approaches (e.g., Belz, 1993; Chung, 1994; Croteau & Hedstrom, 1993; Elliott, 1993; Fassinger, 1994; Hetherington, 1991; Hetherington et al., 1989; Hetherington & Orzek, 1989; Prince, 1994; Schmitz, 1988; Strader & Bowman, 1993) could be used to develop tools for the assessment of career and life planning (e.g., the assessment of an individual's work personality), but current models do not integrate relevant information from traditional career counseling models. For example, research on such factors as self-efficacy (Betz & Hackett, 1981, 1986; Lent & Hackett, 1987; Lent, Larkin, & Brown, 1989), career maturity (Betz, 1988; Jepsen, 1984), career decision-making processes (e.g., Gati, 1986; Gati, Fassa, & Houminer, 1995; Gati & Tikotzki, 1989; Harren, 1979; Krumboltz & Hamel, 1977), career decision-making style (Phillips & Pazienza, 1988), occupational aspirations (Gottfredson, 1981), and vocational interests, values, experiences, and skills has not been fully synthesized into existing models of career counseling with g/l/b persons, and no assessments based on this synthesis have been created.

G/l/b identity development assessment models do not incorporate the full range of career issues into the assessment process. Ideally, identity development assessment models could include a greater number of career issues into the assessment of g/l/b identity. D'Augelli (1991), for example, developed a Life Course Questionnaire to measure a number of identity developmental processes of gay men: (a) the development of gay identity status, (b) relationship with family members, (c) social relationships, (d) gay community involvement, (e) management of public identity, and (f) personal concerns such as depression and anxiety. Although this questionnaire was designed to measure psychological identity, rather than to assess the specific vocational concerns of g/l/b persons, vocational concerns are sometimes viewed as an aspect of self-identity (Super, 1963). Thus career assessment questions could be more routinely added to measures of g/l/b identity. Items from such taxonomies as Campbell and Cellini's (1981) diagnostic taxonomy of adult career problems could be incorporated into g/l/b identity assessment models.

4

Assessing the Person: The Role of Adult Development in Career and Life Planning

For effective career and life planning, it is important to assess a wide variety of person variables. These variables include the individual's work personality—vocational interests, values, experiences, and skills. These variables also include the individual's psychosocial development—level or stage of g/l/b identity development, adult life-span development, and career development. Other variables that can impact career and life planning for g/l/b clients include gender, age, physical health, cultural background, and ethnicity.

The preceding chapter has discussed the assessment of the individual's work personality variables. This chapter examines the assessment of the individual's psychosocial development variables. It first considers models of g//b identity development, provides a scale for assessing an individual's placement on a sexual orientation continuum, and discusses developmental differences among lesbians, gay men, and bisexual persons. The chapter then describes models of general adult life-span development, stressing the importance of determining the client's developmental or life stage and exploring appropriate developmental tasks, and models of adult career development. Finally, the chapter discusses a range of person variables important to consider and assess in career and life planning. Among these are morality/spirituality, minority status, social supports, health, employment/financial/education history, critical life events, and current life situation. Throughout the chapter, vignettes are provided to illuminate many of the issues being considered.

Gay/Lesbian/Bisexual Identity Development

As they progress through the stages of coming out, g/l/b persons have different thoughts, feelings, and behaviors. Models of g/l/b identity development and related issues are discussed by a number of researchers (e.g., Cass, 1979, 1984a, 1984b; Chapman & Brannock, 1987; Coleman, 1985; D'Augelli, 1991; Faderman, 1984; Hetrick & Martin, 1987; Minton & McDonald, 1984; Myers et al., 1991; Sophie, 1986; Troiden, 1989; Zinik, 1985). Levine and Evans (1991), in reviewing many of these g/l/b identity models, wrote that Cass's (1979, 1984a, 1984b) Sexual Identity Formation (SIF) model "provides an exceptionally comprehensive description of gay identity development" (p. 8). Levine and Evans further noted that Cass had "conducted extensive research on her theory, something which is lacking in several of the other models" (p. 9). We use Cass's (1979, 1984a, 1984b) model of identity development, which is not only comprehensive but also has empirical support, to illustrate the impact of identity development on career and life planning. Her model proposes six stages: *Identity Confusion*, which is marked by a growing awareness of the possibility that one may be gay, lesbian, or bisexual; *Identity Comparison*, during which individuals begin to gather additional information about sexual orientation issues and to seek contact with other g/l/b persons; *Identity Tolerance*, which is associated with greater feelings of empowerment; *Identity Acceptance*, which is marked by strong conflict with heterosexism; *Identity Pride*, which is marked by strong pride in identity as a g/l/b person; and *Identity Synthesis*, which reflects an integrated identity in which people see themselves as having many sides to their character, only one part of which is related to g/l/b elements.

Self-statements g/l/b persons may make at the end of each stage of the model include the following (adapted from Anthony, 1985[1]):

- Stage I—**Identity Confusion**. "Maybe the information I'm hearing about g/l/b persons pertains to me."
- Stage II—**Identity Comparison**. "My feelings of sexual attraction and affection for my own gender are different from my peers, family, and society at large."
- Stage III—**Identity Tolerance**. "I am probably g/l/b, but I'm not sure I'd like being g/l/b."
- Stage IV—**Identity Acceptance.** "In relating to other g/l/b persons and learning more about the g/l/b subculture, I feel validated in my sexual orientation. I try to fit into the main culture by trying to pass, to limit contacts with heterosexuals, and to keep my personal life to myself."
- Stage V—**Identity Pride.** "I feel a strong sense of belonging to the g/l/b community. I want to work toward its more equal treatment."

---

[1]From "Lesbian Client—Lesbian Therapist: Opportunities and Challenges in Working Together," by B. D. Anthony, 1985, in *A Guide to Psychotherapy With Gay and Lesbian Clients* (pp. 46–47), edited by J. C. Gonsiorek, New York: Harrington Park Press. Copyright 1985 by Haworth Press. Adapted with permission.

- Stage VI—**Identity Synthesis.** "My identity as a g/l/b person is one very important aspect of myself, but not my total identity. I feel comfortable in both g/l/b and heterosexual worlds."

Cass's (1979, 1984a, 1984b) model is useful to helpers because it increases awareness of individual differences in the process of coming out, in stages of identity development, in strategies for dealing with homophobia, in feelings about being g/l/b persons, and in relationships with heterosexuals. These differences are likely to impact career concerns (Chojnacki & Gelberg, 1994). New instruments are being developed that provide assistance in measuring g/l/b identity formation (e.g., Brady & Busse, 1994), but the only instruments that currently assess g/l/b identity development are research instruments. Thus Cass's model is particularly helpful in that it can be used as a framework for career and life planning assessment and information gathering.

In applying Cass's model to the g/l/b persons with whom we have worked, we have made several observations. First, some g/l/b persons seem to cycle through the model more than once as they encounter new work-related or personal challenges. Second, some g/l/b persons move through these stages more quickly than others and in a different order, thus indicating that there may be even more variety in identity development than Cass's model suggests. (For an in-depth discussion of these issues, see Fassinger & Schlossberg, 1992, who discuss a number of adult development models that question the view of adult development as involving a single invariant sequence through developmental stages.) Third, a number of g/l/b models show variety in the stages of identity development for gay men versus lesbians versus bisexual persons (e.g., Coleman, 1985; D'Augelli, 1991; Fox, 1991; McDonald, 1982; Minton & McDonald, 1984; Plummer, 1975; Pope & Reynolds, 1991; Raphael, 1974; Sang, 1989; Sophie, 1986; Zinik, 1985). Because of this variety, practitioners should be educated about the developmental differences of g/l/b persons and adapt their interventions to reflect those differences. Fourth, in addition to variation in development as a function of type of sexual orientation, there is a great deal of variation in individual development regardless of sexual orientation. Thus, for example, lesbians may differ substantially from other lesbians, and the same is true for gay men and bisexual persons. Despite these observations, Cass's model provides an important framework helpful in considering how out and strongly developed the identity is for a particular individual.

Assessment of Sexual Orientation

Although we may talk of g/l/b persons as if they are distinct groups of persons, it is helpful to consider people's sexual orientations as falling on a spectrum rather than as being within distinct and separate categories. In assessing sexual orientation, seven factors are suggested by the Klein Sexual Orientation Grid (Klein et al., 1985):

- Sexual Attraction (Who is the individual sexually attracted to?)
- Sexual Behavior (Who is the individual sexually active with?)
- Sexual Fantasies (Who does the individual fantasize about?)
- Emotional Preference (Who does the individual love, like, or feel emotionally close to?)
- Social Preference (Who does the individual spend time with?)
- Self-Identification (What is the self-image of the individual?)
- Straight/Gay Lifestyle (Does the individual prefer to live exclusively in the heterosexual world, the gay world, or in both worlds?)

Klein (1993) used the following 7-point scale to assess the first five factors—Sexual Attraction, Sexual Behavior, Sexual Fantasies, Emotional Preference, Social Preference:

1	2	3	4	5	6	7
Other sex only	Other sex mostly	Other sex somewhat	Both sexes equally	Same sex somewhat	Same sex mostly	Same sex only

To assess the last two factors—Straight/Gay Lifestyle, Self-Identification—Klein used the following scale.

1	2	3	4	5	6	7
Heterosexual only	Heterosexual mostly	Heterosexual somewhat more	Heterosexual and gay equally	Gay somewhat more	Gay mostly	Gay only

For these scales or continua, Klein (1993; Klein et al., 1985) adapted the 7-point rating scale developed by Kinsey (Kinsey et al., 1948). (The Kinsey Scale used a scale of 0 to 6; Klein relabeled the scale 1 to 7.)

Sexual orientation can thus be considered through use of seven factors, and a 7-point continuum can be used to reflect the continuous nature of each of these factors. For example, an individual can decide that for the sexual behavior factor or variable he or she is "heterosexual only" (thus receiving a score of 1), "heterosexual mostly" (receiving a score of 2), "heterosexual somewhat more" (receiving a score of 3), "gay and heterosexual equally" (receiving a score of 4), "gay somewhat more" (receiving a score of 5), "gay mostly" (receiving a score of 6), or "gay only" (receiving a score of 7).

The assessment scale presented in Table 1 is based on these seven factors and the 7-point continuum and can be used for career counseling purposes. The table is adapted from both the Klein Sexual Orientation Grid (Klein et al., 1985) and the Kinsey Scale (Kinsey et al., 1948). (In the table and elsewhere, for the final factor we use the term *Straight/Gay Lifestyle*—as in Klein et al., 1985—instead of the term *Heterosexual/Homosexual Lifestyle*—as in Klein, 1993.)

In using Table 1's scale for assessment, the individual records a number ranging from 1 to 7 for each of the factors of sexual orientation. In our experience, both heterosexuals and g/l/b persons show much variety in their responses to the factors. That is, heterosexuals may endorse some 6s and 7s, and some g/l/b persons may endorse a number of 1s or 2s.

The coming out process and g/l/b identity development may involve differing amounts of time. In one study of psychologists, the process of coming out as a g/l/b person took up to 18 years from the first awareness of g/l/b feelings to the disclosure of identity in a professional setting (Task Force, 1977). Caution must be used in generalizing the results, however, because the study was conducted almost 18 years ago and was limited to psychologists.

The age during which certain stages of g/l/b identity development occur may affect career development (Fassinger, 1994; Prince, 1994). For example, an individual who has only recently come out to himself or herself may have more difficulty with career assessment due to a lack of clarity about identity as a g/l/b person or as a worker. A g/l/b person may thus have to deal with career uncertainty because of a limited self-awareness (Prince, 1994).

Developmental Differences Among Lesbians, Gay Men, and Bisexual Persons

As already noted, all three populations (bisexual persons, gay men, and lesbians) have unique developmental issues and career concerns. It is important for helping professionals to understand that individual variations

TABLE 1

Assessment of Sexual Orientation Factors as Adapted From the Klein Sexual Orientation Grid

	1	2	3	4	5	6	7
Sexual Attraction							
Sexual Behavior							
Sexual Fantasies							
Emotional Preference							
Social Preference							
Self-Identification							
Straight/Gay Lifestyle							

Note. From "Sexual Orientation: A Multivariable Dynamic Process," by F. Klein, B. Sepekoff, and T.J. Wolf, 1985, *Journal of Homosexuality, 11*(1/2), pp. 35–49. Copyright 1985 by Haworth Press. Adapted with permission.

occur not only within but also among each type of sexual orientation. For example, some aspects of lesbian identity development differ from gay identity development (Sophie, 1986), and these differences have an impact on such career issues as self-disclosure and on feelings about integrating with lesbian communities or heterosexual communities, which then may affect opportunities important to career development (Hetherington & Orzek, 1989). In addition, lesbians face a double minority status as workers because they experience the impact of both sexism and heterosexism/homophobia in the workplace (Hetherington & Orzek, 1989), and thus they may have a lower projected earning power compared with gay men (Elliott, 1993). Further, more lesbians have their children residing with them than do gay men (Harris & Turner, 1986).

In exploring the impact of sexual orientation on career decision-making, Etringer, Hillerbrand, and Hetherington (1990) considered factors that included anxiety about making a career choice, indecisiveness about the choice, the need to acquire information about a particular career, uncertainty about the choice, and career choice dissatisfaction. These researchers found that lesbians showed less uncertainty in the career decision-making process than gay men and heterosexual men and women. Lesbians also showed greater satisfaction with their career choices then gay men and heterosexual men. These findings suggested that "the degree of uncertainty regarding one's career choice and degree of dissatisfaction with that choice vary by sex and by sexual orientation" (p. 107). The authors speculated that uncertainty may be due to such factors as employment discrimination or to difficulties in predicting reactions to self-disclosure of sexual orientation. They also recommended that further research be conducted to assess whether the specific nature of anxiety experienced by heterosexual men and women may vary with gender and sexual orientation.

In using models of g/l/b identity development, Fassinger (1991) suggested that some developmental models may be androcentric (based on male norms); insensitive to diversity factors such as age, class, race/ethnicity, locale, and occupations; and may fail to distinguish between the g/l/b self-identification processes and the g/l/b group-membership identification processes during identity development. Fassinger also noted that models of g/l/b identity development may have political or prescriptive overtones incorporated into their developmental sequences. Despite these limitations, she viewed these models as important in helping professionals and clients understand, predict, and normalize the experiences of g/l/b persons.

Bisexuals may have fewer supportive communities than lesbians or gay men (Fox, 1991; Klein, 1993; Shuster, 1987). The lack of support systems may create an increased feeling of isolation, and difficulty in dealing with *biphobia*, a prejudice based on the fear or distrust of bisexual persons (Wittstock, 1990). Bisexuals may experience this fear from heterosexuals as well as from the gay community (Klein, 1993) and from lesbian communities

(Shuster, 1987). Thus because bisexual persons do not limit themselves either to same-gender or opposite-gender relationships, they may not be fully accepted either by the gay and lesbian communities or by heterosexuals (Pope & Reynolds, 1991; Shuster, 1987). This lack of acceptance occurs in part because there is less educational programming concerning bisexuality than there is programming addressing gay and lesbian issues (Pope & Reynolds, 1991). In addition, there is less research on bisexuality, and theory-building efforts rarely address bisexual issues (Klein, 1993). Thus bisexuals must address a number of issues that are quite different from those faced by gay men or by lesbians.

Models of General Adult Development

Cass's (1979, 1984a, 1984b) model is helpful in providing a model of g/l/b identity development in considering the impact of sexual orientation on career and life planning, but the assessment of career behaviors involves not only characterizing g/l/b identity development but also understanding the client's overall psychosocial development. Chickering (1969; Chickering & Reisser, 1993), Erikson (1950, 1968), Gilligan (1982), Levinson (1986), and Perry (1970) are among those who have developed theories to consider when working with g/l/b clients. In applying these theories to career and life planning needs, it should be remembered that most psychosocial development theories do not emphasize the impact of sexual orientation on adult life-span development (Wall & Evans, 1991), with the exception of Chickering, who in his later work (Chickering & Reisser, 1993) emphasized the need to consider the impact of sexual orientation and gender role development in looking at adult development.

A thorough and comprehensive review of major adult development theories is beyond the scope of this book, but counselors and other helping professionals should familiarize themselves with these theories in order to facilitate good career counseling. The validity and reliability of adult life-span developmental theories for g/l/b persons have been examined in the literature (e.g., Kimmel, 1978; Vargo, 1987), and developmental differences have been noted between g/l/b persons and heterosexuals (e.g., D'Augelli, 1994; Golden, 1987; Shuster, 1987). Further, Wall and Evans (1991) have summarized studies that addressed the validation of adult life-span development theories for use with g/l/b persons, and Sang (1989) has highlighted the need to develop new theories of g/l/b adult development. In this section, we provide brief examples of utilizing several of the adult development models and applying their theoretical concepts in career and life planning.

One part of assessing psychosocial development involves identifying the client's current developmental tasks. The term *developmental task* refers to the set of problems that persons must master at particular points during their lives. These tasks differ at each life stage. Mastery of these tasks leads to happiness; failure creates unhappiness and difficulty with later tasks (Jepsen, 1990).

A failure to understand a client's cognitive, affective, and behavioral developmental levels can create a mismatch between a specific career intervention and the client. Schmidt and Davison (1983) discussed the importance of using "plus-one staging" interventions—or N + 1 interventions, with N representing the client's developmental level—in order to challenge the client to move to a slightly higher development level. That is, they advised planning an intervention that is one developmental level higher than the client's current developmental stage in order to provide the optimal level of challenge and support. If the developmental level of intervention is too high (e.g., the intervention is two developmental stages beyond the client's level—N + 2 or more) the challenge may be too great, and the client may not grow or develop in a particular way. If the client's development level is underestimated, and the intervention is at or below the client's current development level, there may be too little challenge and no subsequent client growth (Jepsen, 1990).

To illustrate the effect of the failure to match career counseling with the client's level of maturity:

> Clara wanted the counselor to tell her the occupations in which it was "safe" to be a lesbian and which of those occupations she should enter. Clara's counselor felt that it was her role to provide information about homophobic work environments but not her role to decide which was the "right" occupation for Clara. Instead, the counselor tried to facilitate Clara's own exploration and decision making. Clara did not respond well to counseling and failed to return for follow-up appointments. Her failure to return for counseling was probably because she wished to be told what to major in rather than be helped to make her own decision. Her psychosocial development reflects an early cognitive stage (Perry, 1970). In treating her as though she were thinking at a more advanced level, the counselor's career intervention was not at an N + 1 level, but probably N + 3 or 4, which was too discrepant from Clara's psychosocial development. Clara's counselor should have provided more direction to this client while at the same time encouraging Clara to become more active in the decision-making process.

To illustrate an N + 3 intervention:

> Ann, a senior who had only recently come out to herself, asked Jon, a university career center staff member, for help in enhancing her résumé. Jon, a bisexual staff member who was out both personally

and professionally, noticed that Ann had not mentioned in her résumé her activities in the g/l/b student organization. He felt that these activities could demonstrate Ann's leadership style, so he revised Ann's résumé to include her leadership and programming activities with the g/l/b student organization as well as her activities with an AIDS task force. Jon became confused when Ann strongly rejected his recommendations. Ann told him that she did not wish to have potential employers note those activities. She also told Jon that she had not disclosed her sexual orientation to anyone outside of the g/l/b student group members. Ann's counselor failed to note that Ann was at an early level of coming out. His recommendation was more appropriate for an individual who was further along in the process of identity development. Thus this counselor was at an N + 2 or N + 3 intervention—that is, he was several stages ahead of Ann in the recommendation he made for this client. Because Jon's intervention did not consider Ann's level of identity development, she not only failed to use Jon's suggestions but also began to see the career center as not fully valuing her current career needs or values.

One well-known theory of adult development that we have integrated into career counseling with g/l/b clients is the work of Chickering (1969; Chickering & Reisser, 1993). Chickering focused on developmental tasks, including competence, autonomy, identity, a sense of purpose, positive interpersonal relationships, integrity, and the management of emotions. For some g/l/b persons, the process of establishing a g/l/b identity may be impacted by the level of homophobia of the workplace. Or the g/l/b person's management of emotions related to coping with external oppression may develop in a different way because of the stressors of homophobia. Thus each of Chickering's developmental tasks may be influenced and shaped by sexual orientation.

Sexual orientation was not a research variable in Chickering's earlier work, described in 1969 in the first edition of *Education and Identity*, but in the second edition (Chickering & Reisser, 1993), sexual orientation is briefly discussed, and the general issues explored are relevant to the career needs of g/l/b persons. Thus to apply Chickering's developmental task model to the career needs of g/l/b persons, career counselors or other professional helpers should explore their g/l/b client's

- competence in the work environment as a g/l/b worker,
- level of development as an g/l/b worker who is autonomous and able to work in a self-directed manner,
- progress in establishing a positive personal identity as a g/l/b person,
- development of a sense of purpose in work and in personal life,

- quality of interpersonal relationships both at work and in the worker's personal life,
- the degree to which the client has developed a sense of integrity as a g/l/b worker and who thus uses her or his core values and beliefs as a foundation for "interpreting experience, guiding behavior, and maintaining self-respect" (Chickering & Reisser, 1993, p. 235), and
- skill in managing emotions in coping with such stressors as societal homophobia.

To illustrate the relevance of Chickering's (1969) set of developmental tasks:

Janet, a 43-year-old lesbian mother of three, has recently ended her marriage because of a romantic relationship with Sandra, age 38. Janet has only recently come out to herself, although Sandra has been out personally and professionally for a number of years. Because Janet's sense of identity is changing, she is addressing two developmental tasks: the establishment of identity as a lesbian and the development of interpersonal (romantic) relationships. Sandra, on the other hand, is seeking to develop a purpose in her job tasks at work. Thus her developmental stage is job related rather than interpersonal. Noting that both Sandra and Janet are addressing different aspects of development enables the helping professional to better understand each partner's conflicts as the two women strive to address different needs. Chickering's model also helps explain the fact that each woman has different priorities at a particular point in time.

Erikson (1968) provided another adult developmental approach that may be incorporated into career counseling. His eight stages of adult development (trust versus mistrust; autonomy versus shame and doubt; initiative versus guilt; industry versus inferiority; identity versus identity confusion; intimacy versus isolation; generativity versus stagnation; ego integrity versus despair) have application to g/l/b career development. Erikson believed that each stage involves psychological conflicts and a number of developmental tasks. He proposed that the healthy resolution of these tasks leads to the development of trust, autonomy, initiative, industry, identity, intimacy, generativity, and ego integrity.

Homophobia and heterosexism may influence each of the stages proposed by Erikson (1968) in different ways. For example, trust in others may be more difficult to establish after experiences with homophobia. G/l/b workers may find it difficult to develop a g/l/b support system at work after they have observed homophobic reactions to other g/l/b workers because they do not trust that others will act affirmatively toward them. Or because of problems in meeting other g/l/b persons, the development of intimacy may be difficult for some g/l/b persons. The ways in which g/l/b persons progress through these stages could have subtle impacts on career planning. As with Chickering's theories (1969; Chickering & Reisser, 1993), the impact of sexual orientation on the validity of these theories has not been studied in depth, and the nature/ordering of the stages may differ for g/l/b persons.

To illustrate how Erikson's (1968) developmental stages can be applied:

> *Carl recently told his father that he was gay. His father's response was dramatic and intensely negative. He threatened to disown Carl. In part because of his family's extreme homophobia, Carl is now addressing trust issues in his relationships. He finds it difficult to trust that others will value him as a gay male, and he has issues that relate to the developmental task of intimacy versus isolation. Other developmental tasks (e.g., career issues) are difficult for Carl to face because of his current mistrust of others. He seeks to develop a sense of trust in a romantic relationship and better relationships with peers. Carl's counselor sought to help him understand the importance of addressing relationship developmental tasks as well as career developmental tasks.*

Another set of developmental tasks was proposed by Gilligan (1982), who theorized that adult development research, normed on men, distorts the conception of the adult developmental tasks of women. She believed that some developmental processes (e.g., the development of attachment, interdependence, responsibility, and caring) differ for men and women. She suggested that women's development includes an increasing sense of connectedness and proposed a relational model of women's identity. Gilligan's developmental tasks highlight important differences between the development of men and women.

To illustrate Gilligan's (1982) model:

> *Laura, a 24-year-old lesbian, seeks to develop a set of friends who will value her as a lesbian. Her strongest wish is to learn to become more responsive and more caring with others, rather than to become increasingly independent or autonomous. Gilligan's model of development places Laura's behaviors within a normal relational model of identity development. Laura's behaviors could be negatively interpreted, however, if the counselor viewed her development through the lens of theories that propose independence as the primary development task of adulthood (e.g., Levinson et al., 1978). Gilligan's model enables the helper to view Laura as showing development that is following a normal adult developmental path.*

Gender issues are the focus of *Women's Growth in Connection: Writings From the Stone Center* (Jordan, Kaplan, Miller, Stiver, & Surrey, 1991), in which the authors proposed a number of new developmental perspectives for understanding women's psychological development. These perspectives also question previous models that use male norms and concepts such as separation and autonomy to define health and maturity. The proposed self-in-relation theories emphasize relational growth and highlight the primacy of relationships. Empowerment, work inhibitions in women, conflict management, empathy, mutuality, and self-esteem are discussed within self-in-relation frameworks. Familiarity with these perspectives will enable professional helpers to avoid viewing women from models that highlight such alternate concepts as autonomy and separation as the definitions of maturity and mental health. One helpful client resource that deals with gender issues in the workplace is *Talking From 9 to 5: How Women's and Men's Conversational Styles Affect Who Gets Heard, Who Gets Credit, and What Gets Done* (Tannen, 1994). Tannen, a professor of linguistics, focused on how gender differences in communication may influence factors such as job evaluations, promotions, conflict resolution, and coworker responses to authority.

In assessing a client's cognitive maturity, Perry's (1970) theories are helpful. This hierarchical model of cognitive development posits stages that include dualism, which is characterized by black/white thinking; multiplicity, in which all values are seen as equal; relativism, in which values are contextual; and commitment, which is characterized by a commitment and affirmation of values, despite lack of absolute certainty about those values.

To illustrate how Perry's (1970) concepts may be applied:

Tim, age 24, is a sales manager who always classified people at work as being either "totally supportive of his gay lifestyle" or as being "totally homophobic." This dichotomous thinking is characteristic of the dualistic stage, in which there are no relative or multiplistic perspectives. For dualistic thinkers, the world is only one extreme or another, without shades of gray. The professional helper should help Tim understand how his dualistic thinking may produce distorted perceptions of his workplace relationships. The professional helper could point out to Tim that there are rarely just two camps of people (us versus them) by showing Tim examples of times that people who Tim classified as "they" behaved in a supportive manner, or vice versa. Or the professional helper might have Tim see how the same person may vary in his or her support of g/l/b issues, depending on the particular issue. For example, there may be differing levels of support for health benefits, partner benefits, legal rights, or the invitation of partners to workplace social functions. Thus Tim could be encouraged to be less reflexive in his interpretations of persons, and to instead evaluate each person's level of support through consideration of both the current specific issue and through consideration of the consistency of that person's behavior across time. He could be encour-

aged to view people more multiplistically versus taking an either-or, reflective stance.

Models of Adult Career Development

There are a number of models of adult career development (Gottfredson, 1981; Super, 1963, 1980, 1983; Astin, 1984a, 1984b). Super's model, which proposes a set of career developmental tasks for each of five life stages, is used in this section to illustrate the application of a model of adult career development to the career planning needs of g/l/b persons. Super's stages are labeled *growth*, or childhood; *exploration*, or adolescence; *establishment*, or young adulthood; *maintenance*, or middle adulthood; and *decline*, or old age. Super (1980, 1992) also proposed nine adult life-span roles that include child, student, leisurite, citizen, worker, spouse, homemaker, parent, and pensioner.

The consideration of multiple life roles is helpful because it reminds counselors to encourage their clients to see beyond the role of worker. The impact of sexual orientation is not, however, considered in Super's (1963) theories, and there are heterosexist assumptions in this model. For example, because g/l/b couples cannot have legal marriages, the role of spouse is not an option in the legal sense. Despite this heterosexism, the language and concepts behind Super's model can be modified in order to reduce heterosexism. For example, the term *partner* could be substituted for the term *spouse*.

To illustrate how the worker role may be influenced by other roles:

Brad and Rob have recently been married in the Unitarian church. They want to adopt children but have been encountering resistance from adoption agencies. In addition, their family members are less than supportive about their efforts to adopt. Brad and Rob are finding it difficult to become parents because of heterosexism and homophobia in the legal system, in adoption procedures, and in their family support systems; their obstacles are societal, not personal. These events have put a strain on each of them, and this has impacted their on-the-job performance. Their difficulty in fulfilling the role of parent is affecting their ability to focus on other roles, such as that of worker.

Several theories of career development attend to gender-based factors. One is Astin's (1984a) need-based sociopsychological model of career choice and work behavior that proposes women and men make different choices because of differences in early sex-role socialization and structure of opportunity. According to Astin, work behaviors are motivated to satisfy three basic drives or needs: survival, pleasure, and contribution. She theorized that men and women differ in their work expectations, which relate to people's perceptions of their capabilities and strengths, available options, and the types of work that can best satisfy their needs. Astin viewed work expectations as being shaped by sex-role socialization and the perceived "structure of opportunity," a construct that includes the distribution of jobs, the sex typing of jobs, discrimination, job requirements, the economy, family structure, and reproductive technology. Astin's model has been critiqued and further developed by Bernard (1984), Farmer (1984), Fitzgerald and Betz (1984), Gilbert (1984), Hansen (1984), Harmon (1984), Kahn (1984), and Nevill (1984). Astin (1984b) responded to the comments of the reviewers and has proposed designs for future research. Her proposals included operationalization of the model's concepts and empirical research of the model.

In *The Career Psychology of Women*, Betz and Fitzgerald (1987) have reviewed research and theoretical contributions to the vocational psychology of women. They proposed that four groups of factors facilitate women's career development: individual variables, background variables, educational variables, and adult lifestyle variables. In summarizing theories and research in this field, they wrote that "there is as yet no satisfactory theory of the career development of women" (p. 27). They viewed Farmer's (1985) multidimensional model of career and achievement motivation for women and men as especially promising, however. Their own model, tested by Fassinger (1985), considered variables such as ability, instrumentality, feminist orientation, and family orientation, all of which influence career orientation, mathematics orientation, and, ultimately, career choice. Betz and Fitzgerald recommended that those who provide career counseling with women

- become knowledgeable about women's career development,
- become sensitized to sexism in career counseling and sex-restricted vocational interest inventories,
- encourage the development of nontraditional interests and competencies in order to facilitate free choices,
- counteract restrictive stereotypes, and
- provide assistance in responding to discrimination and sexual harassment.

Other Person Variables

We examined many of the traditional person variables considered in career counseling in chapter 3. Thus far in this chapter, we have discussed the use of developmental models to appreciate the many factors impacting upon the career and life planning of a g/l/b person. We turn now to considering other important person variables—morality/spirituality, double/triple minority status, social support, health, employment/financial/educational history, critical life events, and current life situation—that can impact g/l/b career and life planning.

Morality/Spirituality

Views about morality and diversity of sexual orientation differ among religions, religious denominations, and individuals within a particular religious denomination. Because of this variation, the assessment of spiritual issues must be on an individual basis.

To illustrate the impact of morality/spirituality on career and life decisions:

> *Sharon, a lesbian who wished to do church missionary work in another country, had been told that the culture she wished to enter viewed g/l/b lifestyles as immoral. She was afraid that if she chose to live in that particular area, she would be killed if she self-disclosed her sexual orientation. She stated that she was committed to do missionary work and would seek to pass as a heterosexual in order to be safe in her work. She was distraught over this dilemma, especially because her life history reflected other experiences with religious homophobia. (She had been expelled from her church when her sexual orientation was discovered.) It had been difficult and painful to come out personally and professionally, and she felt a spiritual loss at having to make the difficult choice between doing the religious work, about which she felt strongly, and living an open lesbian lifestyle. Sharon sought assistance in prioritizing her career and life planning values, which included prioritizing her values associated with being out as a lesbian or passing as a heterosexual.*

The morality of sexual orientation issues as viewed by traditional Christian religious communities has been addressed in a number of works. For example, in *Amazing Grace*, Boyd and Wilson (1991) have provided a collection of stories of the life experiences of lesbian and gay Christians. For another example, in *Heterosexism: An Ethical Challenge*, Jung and Smith (1993) have suggested that current Christian theological ethics reflect heterosexism and are biased regarding sexual orientation, and they advocated the reformation of Christian ethics as it relates to sexual orientation.

In considering the experience of gay men and lesbians from both Judeo-Christian and non-Judeo-Christian spirituality perspectives, Ritter and O'Neill (1989) focused on the kinds of spiritual losses experienced by g/l/b persons in response to traditional religions. They offered suggestions for reframing these losses into opportunities for spiritual integration.

Brooke (1993) investigated the relationship between Christianity's views on homosexuality and the level of moral development of churches, according to Kohlberg's (1981) theory. (Kohlberg described moral development as becoming less concrete and less based on self-interest with greater maturity.) Based on the results of questionnaires and literature reviews, Brooke postulated that the higher the level of the moral development of the church, the more accepting a church was of g/l/b persons. She found situational variants within individual churches in their level of moral development, and she reported that churches displayed different levels of reasoning for different moral situations. Brooke's work can be used to help evaluate the degree of homophobia expressed in particular religions.

A useful resource for clients who request brief g/l/b-affirmative readings about spirituality is *Is It a Choice? Answers to 300 of the Most Frequently Asked Questions About Gays and Lesbians* (Marcus, 1993). The publication presents the author's personal viewpoints about such questions as "What do different religions say about gay men and lesbians?" and "How have religious institutions and clergy been involved in the gay rights effort?" Another useful resource is *Is Homosexuality a Sin?*, which is available from the Federation of Parents and Friends of Lesbians and Gays (see Appendix 3's list of career center materials for gay, lesbian, and bisexual career clients). This booklet answers a number of questions about spirituality based on the views of prominent religious leaders (e.g., Lutheran, Mormon, Roman Catholic, and Jewish—Reform Reconstructionist, Independent). The views stated by these religious leaders are personal and do not represent the opinions of their formal religious affiliations.

Double/Triple Minority Status

Such factors as age, gender, physical characteristics, health, religion/spirituality, race, ethnicity, and geographic background are associated with such isms as ageism, sexism, ableism, racism, and ethnocentrism. Each ism carries with it unique career concerns, (e.g., Blank & Slipp, 1994; Gelberg et al., 1993; Hawks & Muha, 1991; Hoyt, 1989). Clients who have a double minority status have compounded concerns (Boden, 1992; Caballo-Diéguez, 1989; Chan, 1989, 1992; Dunker, 1987; Espin, 1987; Garcia, Kennedy, Pearlman, & Perez, 1987; Greene, 1994; Gutiérrez & Dworkin, 1992; Loiacano, 1989; Morales, 1992; Wall & Washington, 1991).

Most resources suggest that double or triple minority status makes actualizing life and career plans much more difficult. For example, Hetherington (1991) wrote that lesbian women may experience double negative stereotypes due to gender and sexual orientation. That is, lesbians must not only face the stereotypes or myths that surround being a women in the work force but also deal with g/l/b stereotypes. In addition, an individual with a double or triple minority status may find it difficult to find support groups sensitive to all of the minority statuses held by that individual.

Greene (1994) discussed relevant cultural variables that should be considered when working with g/l/b ethnic minority group members. These include exploration of cultural gender roles and gender stereotypes, the impact of the individual's family of origin, the culture's view of the importance of procreation and continuation of the family line, religious values, the importance of ties to the ethnic community, acculturation/assimilation factors, the history of discrimination or oppression by the dominant culture, group members' understanding of their oppression, and group members' coping strategies. Greene (1994) summarized mental health treatment issues for Latin Americans, Asian Americans, African Americans, and Native Americans.

Counseling Gay Men and Lesbians: Journey to the End of the Rainbow (Dworkin & Gutiérrez, 1992) also focuses on cultural considerations in counseling Asian American lesbians and gay men (Chan, 1992), Latino gay men and Latina lesbians (Morales, 1992), African American gay men and lesbians (Gutiérrez & Dworkin, 1992), and physically disabled lesbians (Boden, 1992).

Although double minority g/l/b issues are not considered in *Career Development and Vocational Behavior of Racial and Ethnic Minorities* (Leong, 1995), this resource is helpful in outlining theoretical and empirical career development issues for African Americans, Hispanic Americans, Asian Americans, and Native Americans. Assessment and intervention strategies are provided, and a multicultural theory of career development is proposed that includes variables such as self-concept, expression of self, life-stage development, ethnic identity developmental stage, worldview, person-environment interactions, environmental factors, and self-efficacy.

One resource especially helpful for career clients is *Voices of Diversity: Real People Talk About Problems and Solutions in a Workplace Where Everyone Is Not Alike* (Blank & Slipp, 1994). This book discusses the career concerns of African Americans, Asian Americans, Latinos, recent immigrants, workers with disabilities, younger and older workers, gay men and lesbians, women, and White men.

The primacy of sexual orientation and ethnicity may vary according to level of ethnic identity development as well as g/l/b identity development (Chan, 1992). Counselors should thus be educated about the interactive effects among such characteristics as sexual orientation race, gender, age, and able-bodiedness.

An example of the interaction between culture and sexual orientation concerns self-disclosure of sexual orientation. Languages can facilitate or hamper choices associated with self-disclosure. For example, in English, the term *partner* is often used to describe a person's significant other without indicating gender. Because *partner* may refer to either a male or female, the listener will be unable to determine whether the relationship is same gender or opposite gender. In contrast to English, some languages may make it more difficult to speak about one's partner without disclosing gender. For example, in Spanish, most nouns are either masculine, thus ending in an *o*, or feminine, thus ending in an *a*. Thus there are two words for the Spanish equivalent of *partner*: *compañero*, which refers to a male partner, and *compañera*, which refers to a female partner. The gender must be specified when using this word. Although some Spanish words are gender neutral, (e.g., the word *amante* means lover in Spanish without specifying gender, more often gender must be specific: for example, *esposa* or *esposo*; *mi querida* or *mi querido*; *mi amada* or *mi amado*; and *cariña* or *cariño*. Thus it may be more difficult for Hispanic workers to discuss (in Spanish) their personal lives at work without indicating that they are in a relationship with an individual of the same gender.

Social Support

Self-assessment can be influenced by the views others have about that person. Sometimes the two views may be the same. That is, the individual and others may believe that person is "skilled in sports" or "good with people." Sometimes the view the client has of her or his skills may differ from the perspective others have of that person. The career client, for example, may not think he or she is good enough to be a professional artist, but others may feel that the person does indeed have the talent to succeed in that field. Alternatively, the client may feel that, given the training, she or he could succeed in a specific field, although others are less sure about that person's capabilities.

When the view an individual has differs from the view others have of that person's capabilities, the difference may be because others see personal attributes the individual does not see. Or different views may result because the person is more aware than others are of her or his potential.

Sometimes other people's view of what careers the person may be successful at are more linked to what other people feel they are good at themselves—or to what field they themselves would like to enter. Thus recommendations or views about the person may be based more on the needs of others rather than on observations of that individual's needs, values, experiences, or interests. Counselors and other professional helpers must remain objective and help clients determine what the client feels is best in light of all interacting factors.

Because of these factors and because social support systems are crucial in helping people grow personally and professionally, career assessment should include an evaluation of the social support system. Without a strong social support system (e.g., friends who are gay, lesbian, bisexual, or allies), it is more difficult to cope with work-related or interpersonal stressors. Assessment should include analyses of support at work (to determine whether g/l/b peers, mentors, and supervisors are available) and of the career options the social support system encourages for that person (to determine any differences between the g/l/b person's self-estimate and the support system's suggested career options for the person).

Assessment should also be made of support at home. Assessment of romantic relationships is important in order to determine any dual career issues that may exist for g/l/b couples. The career decision-making skills and styles of the partners as well as their work personalities need to be assessed, as should each partner's level of investment in career and life planning issues. Are the partners at different stages in the process of coming out—which could affect the level of support each has at work and home? Are there financial concerns? What about parenting issues, such as coparenting, deciding about parenthood, or dealing with blended families? Are there problematic children or differences in parenting styles? (For a discussion of the challenges gay and lesbian families face, see Ariel Stearns, 1992.)

The assessment of romantic relationships also includes understanding the developmental history of the couple, or the couple's family life-cycle stage. McWhirter and Mattison (1985) have described six stages for gay couples. In stage one, *Blending* (during year 1 of the relationship), there is high sexuality and an equality in the partnership. Stage two, *Nesting*, (during years 1 through 3), involves greater homemaking and a greater sense of ambivalence. Stage three, *Maintaining* (during years 3 through 5), marks the beginning of individualization, greater risk-taking, dealing with conflict, and a greater reliance on the relationship. Stage four, *Collaborating* (during years 5 through 10), marks greater productivity, independence, and interdependence of the partners. Stage five, *Trusting* (during years 10 through 20), is marked by greater trust, merging of money and possessions, and taking the relationship for granted. Stage six, *Repartnering* (at 20 years and beyond) is marked by the attainment of goals, an expectation of permanence of the relationship, an awareness of the passage of time, and the emergence of personal concerns. This model is useful for counselors and other helping professionals because it shows how development of the romantic relationship changes over time. It also highlights the fact that it may take decades for a gay couple to achieve the final stage of expected permanence and commitment in the relationship.

McWhirter and Mattison's (1985) model was developed for gay men. Other issues with which male couples struggle are discussed by Hawkins (1992). Murphy (1992) noted that "homophobia, heterosexism, and sexism affect male and female couples differently" (p. 63) and highlighted issues with which lesbian couples are struggling. McCandlish (1985) also addressed issues faced by lesbian couples. Peplau (1982) presented an overview of research on same gender couples.

Health

Health factors and other physical attributes are also important person assessment factors. It is critical to separate health issues such as HIV/AIDS from sexual orientation and to avoid heterosexist assumptions that HIV/AIDS affects mainly g/l/b persons. HIV and AIDS occur across sexual orientations, ethnicities, socioeconomic classes, gender, and age.

To illustrate these stereotypes:

Elaine had lost her job as a nurse in a college infirmary. She had been told by her supervisor that she was judgmental with patients and had failed to screen patients fully for a number of health concerns. Elaine told her counselor that she felt that people who were "good Christians" would never get AIDS. In reflecting on her own at-risk behaviors, she believed that she was protected because she was "too young to get AIDS." She also felt that she was protected because she was aware of the sexual backgrounds of her partners. Elaine indicated that she was heterosexual and from a middle-class background, and she believed that her sexual orientation and background would protect her from health risks. Because of the stereotypes she had about AIDS/HIV, she was very ineffective in her job as a nurse at a college infirmary. She failed to screen patients for at risk–behaviors based on whether she believed them to be young, Christian, from certain socioeconomic backgrounds, and heterosexual. One goal of career counseling was to address the stereotypes Elaine held about HIV/AIDS.

Although AIDS is not a "gay disease," counselors should be aware that the g/l/b community has been affected physically and emotionally by this disease. It is important for helpers to be comfortable, knowledgeable, and empathetic—and to stay current on AIDS issues. Hoffman (1991) presented a conceptual framework for assessing a client's resources as he or she attempts to deal with the psychosocial issues that may occur as the result of HIV. The components of the model include special characteristics (e.g., the progressive nature of HIV infection, stigma, the time in life when the individual becomes ill), social supports, situational characteristics (e.g., role change, stage of HIV infection), and client characteristics (e.g., psychosocial competence, gender role identity, race, ethnicity, social class). A number of intervention guidelines address each of these components.

The impact of AIDS-related grief among gay men was studied by Schwartzberg (1992), who addressed the adverse effects of multiple loss, the relevance of "gay grief," the shortcomings of grief models, and existential issues linked to AIDS-related grief. Martin (1988) also studied psychological consequences of AIDS-related bereavement among gay men. Stress, demoralization, sleep problems, and use of psychological services were some of the symptoms directly related to the number of AIDS-related bereavements. Counseling and clinical issues linked to HIV infection and the gay community were also discussed by Martin (1988) as well as by Croteau and Morgan (1989), who further discussed ways to integrate antihomophobia elements into AIDS education.

Bradford, Ryan, and Rothblum (1994) surveyed 1,925 lesbians in the National Lesbian Health Care Survey. They gathered statistics on factors such as current psychological concerns, depression and anxiety, suicidal thoughts and suicide attempts, sexual abuse or other physical abuse, rape and sexual attack, experiences with discrimination, the impact of AIDS, alcohol and drug use, eating disorders, counseling, community and social life, and "outness." Similarities to and differences from heterosexual women were discussed. The authors found that over half of the persons in the sample had considered suicide, and 18% had made a suicide attempt. Nearly 37% reported physical abuse, and 32% had been raped or sexually attacked. About three fourths had sought counseling, many for feelings of sadness and depression. The psychosocial difficulties reported by the women in this survey should be viewed as stemming in large part from experiences and stigma and should not be used to pathologize lesbians. In fact, the authors of this study discussed the strong coping and survival skills of these individuals in responding to issues of low socioeconomic status, discrimination, and stigma. Clinicians should consider that many "lesbian problems" arise from societal hatred and oppression (Boston Lesbian Psychologies Collective, 1987, p. 2). Treatment recommendations based on this survey include the exploration of relationships, assistance in special issues such as substance abuse and depression, and attention to how low income level acts as a barrier to prevent comprehensive mental health care.

Helping professionals should be knowledgeable about health issues such as drug use and HIV infection, HIV testing, and toll-free HIV hotlines. Other health-related issues such as insurance problems linked to HIV, legal services, and housing discrimination should be considered as relevant person factors for all career clients, regardless of their sexual orientation.

One important variable to consider in focusing on health care for g/l/b persons is the prevalence of homophobia or heterosexism in the medical profession. Schwanberg (1990) analyzed a sample of health care literature from 1983 to 1987 in order to assess attitudes toward gay men and lesbians in health sciences literature and to determine the impact the AIDS epidemic has had on the images of gay men and lesbians in health sciences literature. In a content analysis of 59 articles, Schwanberg found that the majority included negative images about gay men and lesbians. Schwanberg noted that g/l/b persons must cope with stereotyping, stigmatization, other negative reactions, and the possibility of inferior care because of these negative attitudes toward g/l/b persons.

Boden (1992) addressed the impact of a disability on the psychological adjustment of lesbians and discussed such common themes as parental or social abandonment, social inclusion/exclusion, anger, depression, reduced self-awareness, and entitlement through use of case examples. Intervention guidelines were also provided.

Curnow (1989) explored issues of general vocational development of persons with disabilities. Misconceptions of disability that limit the application of vocational development theory to persons with disabilities as well as vocational development special needs of persons with disabilities were discussed. Limitations in early experiences, decision-making ability, and self-concept issues are included in the discussions.

Employment/Financial/Educational History

Assessment of employment factors involves consideration of the person's current position, employment history, and financial status. Maslow's (1970) hierarchy of human needs proposes that a person's needs can be classified in a ranked fashion and that needs lower in the hierarchy (e.g., safety needs) must be satisfied before needs higher in the hierarchy (e.g., self-actualization needs). Thus if an individual's current employment is such that basic safety needs such as food, clothing, and shelter are not met, higher needs such as self-actualization will not typically be addressed until those safety needs are satisfied.

To illustrate:

> Jay is a gay man who has been unable to perform his usual work as a tennis instructor due to a chronic lung condition. Jay is HIV positive but does not yet qualify for financial assistance. Because he expects to be able to do less physical work in the future, he has begun to train for a more lucrative position. In order to pay current bills while undergoing retraining, he also works as a telemarketer. Through this plan, Jay has addressed his health needs, safety needs (for food, clothing, and shelter), and self-actualization needs.

Professional helpers who ignore such factors as safety do their clients a disservice in that economic reality factors are ignored. Assessment calls for creativity and flexibility, tempered with common sense.

Critical Life Events

People's life experiences and personal histories affect their specific work priorities, interests, values, experiences, and skills (Jepsen, 1990; Vondracek et al., 1986). Embedded in a person's history, development, and current life circumstances are potential issues and unique circumstances. It is critical for the helping professional to be aware of these issues and circumstances because they can greatly impact career decision making. For example, an individual who is the survivor of a life-threatening illness may choose to enter the health professions or may be attracted to a particular work environment (e.g., a hospice, nursing home, or hospital) because of this experience. Alternatively, another individual may wish to avoid medical environments because of that past experience. Peoples' responses to their personal histories are unique and difficult to predict without a full knowledge of the perspectives they have as a result of their personal histories.

To illustrate the impact of life experiences on career choices:

Christopher was assigned to work with elderly patients in a hospital unit. These patients were unable to live at home due to their medical situations. Although Christopher appeared well suited for this assignment, he requested a change in his work duties. He indicated that he had been a caregiver for both of his parents, and he expected that working with the elderly would, at this time, be too difficult for him. In contrast, Barry, who had a similar background, specifically requested this particular work experience because of a belief that this job would enable him to apply a difficult family background experience productively to a work situation.

Approximately 92% of lesbians and gay men have experienced some form of verbal abuse because of their sexual orientation (Herek, 1989). Being subjected to such negative life events as antigay remarks and other forms of harassment or violence often has a strong impact on adult development in general (Savin-Williams, 1994) and on the career and life planning process.

Positive life events can have an equally powerful impact on career and life planning. For example, one career client's fondest childhood memories were the weekly outings she took with her family to the movies. She later entered the field of film production. Another client chose to work in the field of gerontology because of an early close relationship with her grandmother.

Thus life backgrounds shape work interests, values, experiences, and skills in both subtle and obvious ways. By asking career clients to describe their histories, including discussions of both positive and difficult life history events, the professional helper gains a better understanding of the career and life planning needs of that individual (Crites, 1974; Okiishi, 1987). In assessing psychosocial histories, the professional helper should be careful to avoid heterosexist interpretations (e.g., the notion that sexual abuse leads to a g/l/b orientation). Wall and Evans (1991) discussed a number of other heterosexist assumptions commonly made when assessing the psychosocial history of g/l/b persons. These include the fact that researchers often fail to consider alternative lifestyles and do not explore the full impact of negative experiences in a hostile environment on psychosocial development.

Current Life Situation

An individual's current life situation also influences her or his career interests, values, experiences, and skills. For example, a g/l/b person in a romantic relationship may have dual career needs that shape her or his interest in, or avoidance of, certain work environments. Thus that individual may choose to remain in a particular position because his or her partner enjoys a particular job or geographic location. Additionally, the fact that domestic partner benefits are offered by a particular organization may take precedence over either person's career interests, values, experiences, or skills if one partner is unemployed.

A recent experience with violence, heterosexism, or homophobia may also influence an individual's work priorities. Factors such as personal safety at work may make an individual less interested or more willing to enter a particular work environment.

To illustrate:

Don, a clothing store salesman who was gay, became uncomfortable at work because he felt that he had been harassed by Brenda, a wealthy customer. Brenda called him frequently at work, asked to meet with him after work, and refused to make purchases from any other individuals in Don's sales department. When he rejected her approaches, she became very angry and verbally abusive. When Don sought assistance in dealing with this harassment, his supervisor indicated that Brenda was a very good customer, and the store needed her business. Because Don received no support from his supervisor, he wanted to leave his job. His work performance also suffered because of the stress he experienced in being ordered to ignore his own needs for a comfortable work environment.

5

Assessing the Work Environment

Assessing the work environment can be one of the most empowering aspects of career counseling with g/l/b persons. It increases people's knowledge of what is out there and what issues they may face. It empowers people to make informed choices about employment and to begin to plan for the environmental forces that may be present in their choices. Indeed, assessment of environmental heterosexism is critical for helping g/l/b persons navigate through a heterosexist, homophobic society.

Traditional resources for assessing work environments, which are briefly described in the World of Work Resources section in chapter 3, should certainly be used with g/l/b persons. These resources include the *Dictionary of Occupational Titles* (U.S. Department of Labor, 1991), *The Dictionary of Holland Occupational Codes* (Gottfredson & Holland, 1989), and the *Guide for Occupational Exploration* (Harrington & O'Shea, 1984). Other instruments for assessing the environment, such as the Social Climates Scale (Moos, 1986), have been developed but are used more often for research than for career counseling. (For a complete review of environment assessment instruments, see chapter 11 of *Tests and Instruments*—Walsh & Betz, 1990.)

In assessing work environments for g/l/b persons, heterosexism and homophobia add significant new dimensions, however. Societal heterosexism (a belief in the superiority of heterosexuality) and homophobia (the manifestation of irrational fear, prejudice, hatred, and intolerance of g/l/b people) permeate the workplace (Obear, 1991). There are no federal laws that prevent overt discrimination based on sexual orientation (Hunter, Michaelson, & Stoddard, 1992). In many organizations, g/l/b persons can be fired without cause, harassed, and excluded from initial employment.

Even in jurisdictions or organizations with antidiscrimination laws or policies, prejudice and discrimination often exist. Just as the civil rights legislation of the 1960s did not result in the end of prejudice for oppressed populations such as African Americans, the existence of an antidiscrimination policy that includes sexual orientation does not guarantee that heterosexism and homophobia will not occur in a specific work environment. Thus it is crucial to help g/l/b persons assess workplace homophobia and heterosexism in all potential work environments. Although helping individuals investigate, discover, and assess workplace heterosexism can be disheartening, it can ultimately be empowering to the client, for with this knowledge comes the ability to make more informed career decisions.

This chapter begins with a discussion of how workplace environments may vary in levels of heterosexism and homophobia. Resources (recent publications, g/l/b professional organizations, and networking and informational interviewing) for assessing levels of discrimination or affirmation in companies and organizations in the United States are described. Assessment variables outside the workplace that should also be considered are briefly discussed. The chapter concludes with an illustrative example that demonstrates the importance in career and life planning of considering both person and environment variables.

Heterosexism in Workplace Environments

Work environments differ in the amount of discrimination or affirmation of g/l/b individuals. For example, Mickens (1994), in a review of heterosexism in the workplace, wrote that "high tech industries and higher education are moving faster than most" in becoming affirmative (p. 132). This stands in contrast to the U. S. military, which has discharged persons because of their sexual orientation (Shawver, 1995).

Chojnacki and Gelberg (1994) developed a description of various levels of workplace heterosexism. At the first level, *overt discrimination*, the organization has formal policies that discriminate based on sexual orientation. At the second level, *covert discrimination*, no formal discrimination policy exists, but discrimination occurs in hiring, firing, and promotion procedures. At the third level, *tolerance*, a company has a formal antidiscrimination policy, but there is little other support given to g/l/b employees. At the fourth and final level, *affirmation*, there is support for g/l/b employees through such agency actions as the extension of benefits for domestic partners, employee sensitivity training on diversity issues, and the facilitation of g/l/b employee groups.

This description of the levels of workplace heterosexism is not meant to provide discrete categories of work environments but rather to provide a language for marking various points along a continuum. Environments may be between levels or in a state of transition. The levels of workplace heterosexism can also be used to demonstrate the developmental stages through which organizations may pass as they move from being discriminatory to affirmative of g/l/b persons.

Descriptions of two corporations can demonstrate the extremes of the continuum. On one end is Cracker Barrel Old Country Stores, an organization that has gained recognition in the media for its overt discrimination of g/l/b persons. In 1991, all restaurant managers received a memo indicating that it was inconsistent with company values to employ g/l/b persons. Managers complied and quickly fired a number of persons because of their sexual orientation. After media attention, the company rescinded the policy but did not reinstate those employees who had been fired. One stockholder attempted to draft an antidiscriminatory policy and asked that it be put to the stockholders for a vote. Management blocked that effort. A federal court eventually forced the company to allow stockholders to vote on an antidiscrimination policy, but the policy was voted down. As Baker, Strub, and Henning (1995) noted, "Cracker Barrel is obviously not a safe place for lesbian and gay workers to seek employment" (p. 108).

On the opposite end of the continuum is Apple Computer. Apple enacted an antidiscrimination policy in 1988. In 1992, it provided partner benefits that included child care, relocation, and family leave, and in 1993, it extended partner benefits to include health insurance. In addition, Apple provides corporate training on diversity issues that include sexual orientation. Apple also has a gay and lesbian employees group and has taken an active, affirmative stance on a number of g/l/b political issues. It is rated as one of the top companies for g/l/b employees (Baker et al., 1995; Mickens, 1994).

Resources for Assessing Work Environments

Helping g/l/b persons learn about various work environments is critical for good career decision making. Although little formal systematic assessment of workplace heterosexism has been made, two recent publications (Baker et al., 1995; Mickens, 1994) have begun to fill this void and can serve as valuable resources for career counselors and their clients. Other resources include g/l/b professional organizations, which help in gathering information about work environments relevant to each profession; and networking and informational interviewing, for which g/l/b organizations provide starting points, to examine structural, human relations, political, and cultural/symbolic factors as well as to explore critical structural, human relations, political, and cultural/symbolic factors as well as to explore critical perspectives (the political, moral, and ethical implications of organizational decisions).

Recent Publications

Two books are on the cutting edge of workplace assessment and are immensely helpful in assisting persons to make informed choices about the companies for which they might work: *Cracking the Corporate Closet* (Baker et al., 1995) and *The 100 Best Companies for Gay Men and Lesbians* (Mickens, 1994). The publications are well researched, illuminate key aspects of corporate America relevant to g/l/b persons, and are a must for career counselors, career resource libraries, and other professional helpers.

Both publications use several key criteria in determining whether an organization is gay affirmative, tolerant, or discriminatory.

The first criterion is the existence of an antidiscriminatory policy that includes sexual orientation. As the result of federal legislation (e.g., the Civil Rights Act) all companies must have antidiscrimination policies. These protections were most recently extended to cover the physically challenged with passage of the Americans With Disabilities Act. No such legislation exists concerning sexual orientation. A handful of states and several progressive large cities do, however, have antidiscrimination laws (Baker et al., 1995). This patchwork of legislation has resulted in some companies drafting antidiscrimination policies, but other companies have not drafted such policies. The first corporation to do so was IBM in 1974.

A second criterion is whether the organization offers domestic partner benefits, "the real cutting edge today for companies on lesbian and gay issues" (Baker et al., 1995, p. 5). Often the most significant of these benefits is the extension of health insurance to domestic partners. According to Baker et al., the extension of domestic partner benefits is often indicative of organizations that provide generally affirmative environments for g/l/b persons. Many municipalities began providing domestic partner benefits in the early 1980s, including Seattle, San Francisco, and Santa Cruz. In 1991, Lotus was the first large publicly held company to extend domestic partner benefits to its employees.

Other criteria used to assess heterosexism in the workplace include the existence of g/l/b employees groups, diversity training that includes sexual orientation issues, and the active marketing of products and services to the g/l/b community.

In *Cracking the Corporate Closet*, Baker et al. (1995) used a number of different sources to rate American corporations. One was a survey of the Fortune 1000 companies conducted by the National Gay and Lesbian Task Force (NGLTF) Policy Institute Workplace Project (1994) that includes inquiries about antidiscrimination policies and domestic partner benefits. Another was a survey developed by Baker et al. to provide further follow up with the Fortune 1000 companies and which included additional private and foreign-owned companies. Additional sources were media reports over the past years and responses solicited from employees. The information in

Cracking the Corporate Closet is organized by industry. Comparative charts of companies within each industry amplify the text and rate the company's survey responsiveness, the existence of antidiscrimination policies, the extension of benefits to domestic partners, diversity training, AIDS education, and the existence of g/l/b support groups.

For *The 100 Best Companies for Gay Men and Lesbians*, Mickens (1994) also used the NGLTF survey, together with a separate survey conducted by the Society for Human Resource Management in 1993, anecdotal information, and media reports. In the book, the top 100 companies are rated in terms of antidiscrimination policies, domestic partner benefits, g/l/b diversity training, and the existence of g/l/b employee groups. The companies are also rated on a scale from 1 to 5 for overall "gay friendliness."

Corporate America is the focus of these two books, but g/l/b clients are also often interested in noncorporate work sites. As yet there are only a few useful written resources. One of these, published by the National Gay and Lesbian Task Force (1994), is a list of organizations that have domestic partner benefits. The list includes nonprofit groups, municipalities, educational institutions, and unions.

Another resource for information on noncorporate work sites is the national edition of the *GAYELLOW PAGES* (Green, 1994). This book is published yearly and provides a list of businesses, services, networks, and associations for g/l/b persons. Listed organizations are likely to be g/l/b affirmative. Resources similar to the national *GAYELLOW PAGES* are sometimes also available for local geographic areas. For example, in the Chicago area the *Lesbian and Gay Pink Pages* (Cohen, 1994) and *Out! Resource Guide* (1994) provide information about specific regional workplaces or communities.

G/L/B Professional Organizations

Professional organizations for g/l/b persons that can be useful in gathering information about work environments include the Lesbian and Gay Teachers Association, Lesbian and Gay People in Medicine, and the American College Personnel Association Standing Committee for Lesbian, Gay, and Bisexual Awareness. (See Appendix 3 for addresses of these and other organizations/agencies.) Extensive listings of g/l/b professional organizations, and their addresses and telephone numbers, are provided in *Counseling Gay Men and Lesbians: Journey to the End of the Rainbow* (Dworkin & Gutiérrez, 1992) and a resource list by Brooks (1991).

These organizations address issues uniquely relevant to each profession. One example is the ACPA Standing Committee for Lesbian, Gay, and Bisexual Awareness (SCLGBA). The committee, which is compiling data assessing the levels of heterosexism for those working at American colleges and universities, has information on issues such as domestic partner benefits and antidiscrimination policies as well as on concerns unique to higher education professionals, including whether domestic partners can live in faculty and married student housing, and whether on-campus residence hall coordinators can cohabitate with a partner of the same gender. The SCLGBA also publishes the newsletter *Out on Campus*.

Another example is the American Psychological Association's Public Interest Directorate. The directorate's booklet, *Graduate Faculty Interested in Lesbian and Gay Issues* (1993), reports the results of a survey of graduate departments on their available courses, research, and training opportunities in g/l/b areas. The booklet also discusses the number of openly identified lesbian and gay faculty and/or graduate students present in the program, and provides information about whether a lesbian or gay student organization is available within the institution.

Newsletters are provided by many g/l/b professional organizations. Some of these are included in Appendix 3. Free or inexpensive materials may be obtained by writing to these organizations and requesting materials regarding g/l/b career issues. These materials have enabled us to make easily accessible to g/l/b career clients a variety of information on site.

Networking and Informational Interviewing

G/l/b professional organizations also serve as a resource for networking and informational interviewing, that is, for talking to those people in and around an organization or profession to find out how an organization, corporate or noncorporate, responds to g/l/b issues and concerns. Mc-Naught (1993) listed seven main concerns in describing what gay employees want to have—and thus want to find out about in considering employment: an antidiscrimination policy, an environment free of heterosexist behaviors, awareness training on gay issues and AIDS, domestic partner benefits, support of g/l/b employee groups, full participation in all aspects of corporate life, and public support of g/l/b issues.

We have suggested resources that are helpful in assessing many of these concerns, but for many organizations, this information may not yet be available. Further, other concerns, such as the prevalence of heterosexist behaviors at the workplace and the ability to participate fully in corporate life, are not easily assessed by formal methods.

Through networking and informational interviewing, however, people can learn not only whether there is an antidiscriminatory policy but also if there is more subtle workplace intolerance: Do all people feel equally welcome at organizational social functions? Do people make homophobic jokes at the workplace? Does a "glass ceiling" (an invisible barrier of unstated prejudice that prevents people from reaching the top levels of an organization) exist in hiring and promotion? These and other more subtle indicators of heterosexism in the workplace may be best learned by talking to persons who are working in, or are knowledgeable about, an organization.

People can start the process of networking and informational interviewing by making contacts through g/l/b professional organizations or through g/l/b social networks and organizations. Talking with friends, family, colleagues, and instructors often produces the name of someone knowing someone else who knows about the organization of interest.

What kind of questions can be asked in an informational interview or when networking informally with others? We have generated a list of possible questions that are based on five organizational frameworks or perspectives and related to issues discussed in this chapter. Four of the five organizational frameworks or perspectives concern structural, human relations, political, and cultural/symbolic factors, as described by Bolman and Deal (1991). Each of the four frameworks is helpful in understanding a particular aspect of a particular organization; using all four together provides important insights into work environment characteristics. The fifth framework or perspective is based on Foster's (1986) "critical perspectives theory" and concerns the political, moral, and ethical implications of administrative decisions. Some of the questions in the list are also based on surveying resources that focus on gay issues in the workplace (e.g., Baker et al., 1995; McNaught, 1993; Woods, 1994) and from reviewing literature that focuses on general corporate assessment (e.g., Furnham & Gunter, 1993).

Possible informational interview questions for assessing homophobia and other work environment characteristics, grouped by organizational framework or perspective, are as follows:

1. **Structural factors.** This framework considers organizational goals, formal roles and relationships, policies, and management hierarchies (Bolman & Deal, 1991; Weick, 1976). Sample informational interview questions include the following:
   - What is the formal hierarchy of management power within the organization? Is it clear who has the formal decision-making authority?
   - Are there any individuals who are out in the organization who are in positions of power in the organization?
   - Are there opportunities for personal development, career progression, and advancement of g/l/b workers?
   - What are the stated formal organizational goals? Do any of the organizational goals relate to diversity issues (e.g., affirmation of diversity)?
   - Are organizational rules and policies spelled out? For example, are there written rules and policies that protect against discrimination (e.g., that add the words *sexual orientation* to nondiscrimination policies)? Are there equitable benefits programs (e.g., benefits for domestic partners)?
   - Do employment policies comply with federal, state, and local law (McNaught, 1993)?

- Does the organizational structure make sense, given the organizational goals? That is, do company goals "provide a useful context for the everyday functioning of this organization" (Furnham & Gunter, 1993, p. 141)?
- Does the company advertise employment opportunities in g/l/b presses (Baker et al., 1995)?
- Do the organization's search committees consider sexual orientation as a desirable characteristic in diversifying its work force, along with race, ethnicity, age, and gender?
- Do committees exist that focus on enhancing the company's diversity, and do these committees value sexual orientation as a type of diversity?
- Does advertising and marketing of products or services include consideration of g/l/b markets?
- Is there any evidence of homophobia in the formal and informal communication channels among individuals or units of the organization?
- Is there a grievance procedure for worker complaints, including complaints about sexual harassment or discrimination based on sexual orientation?
- Is there confidentiality in the company policy about employee records (e.g., health records)?
- Do company audits include an assessment of the corporate climate for g/l/b workers?
- Does manager diversity training include consideration of sexual orientation?
- Are organizational formal and informal policies consistent throughout the hierarchy of the organization?

2. **Human relations factors.** This framework emphasizes the interdependence of people and the organization (Barnard, 1981; Bolman & Deal, 1991; Miles, 1965). Sample informational interview questions include the following:
   - Is the psychological climate shaped by homophobia or heterosexism? Is there a positive, friendly atmosphere prevailing among the people in the organization?
   - Are there informal norms and roles that differ from the formal organizational structure? How affirmative are these norms toward diversity?
   - Are the needs, skills, and values of g/l/b workers of this organization valued and utilized by the organization?
   - How does the work environment atmosphere seem to affect g/l/b identity development? That is, does the work atmosphere seem to facilitate or block the professional development of g/l/b persons?

- Does the management seem to view the employees as being self-directed? Or is management more guarded about peoples' ability to self-direct?
- Is there company education about diversity issues (including gay issues) in the workplace (McNaught, 1993)?
- Are there any g/l/b associations or support groups within the organization?
- Is staff morale high in most departments? Is it high among g/l/b workers?
- How does the organization handle conflict around sexual identity issues?

3. **Political factors.** This framework considers political dynamics in the workplace. Under the political view, conflicts are natural, inevitable, and dealt with openly in the workplace (Bolman & Deal, 1991; Pfeffer, 1981). Sample informational interview questions include the following:
   - Do g/l/b persons fully participate in all aspects of corporate life, including jobs involving interactions with the public (Blank & Slipp, 1994; McNaught, 1993)?
   - Is the company nondiscrimination policy supported by management?
   - Is there a scarcity of resources in the organization? How does this affect conflict within the agency?
   - Do resources seem to be equitably distributed? Or are there concentrations of resources in one part of the organization and deficits in another part?
   - How have coalitions formed in the organization? Are coalitions affected by work tasks, gender, age, experience, socioeconomic class, or sexual orientation?
   - How are networks built? Are there networks of g/l/b workers within the organization?
   - Are conflicts constructively resolved? Is there open discussion of conflict?
   - Is power concentrated in certain places in the organization?
   - How much conflict is built around worker needs, perspectives, lifestyles, preferences, or values? Is heterosexism evident in conflict around these factors?
   - How level is the playing field for g/l/b workers who are out?

4. **Cultural/symbolic factors.** This framework focuses on the importance of the role of symbols in instilling a sense of purpose and meaning in work. Ceremonies, metaphors, and organizational practices are viewed as influential in building a culture (Bolman & Deal, 1991; Greenfield, 1980; Meyer &

Rowan, 1977; Sergiovanni & Corbally, 1986). Sample informational interview questions include the following:

- Are the organizational ideology, values, and beliefs homophobic or heterosexist?
- Does the organizational history (e.g., organizational stories) include heterosexist or homophobic elements?
- Is organizational humor homophobic or heterosexist? For example, are stereotypical jokes or demeaning terms used in the workplace (Blank & Slipp, 1994)?
- What is the best way for a g/l/b person to enter the organization as a new worker? How out should she or he be, given the present level of organizational homophobia or heterosexism?
- Does the organization use language that is inclusive of different sexual orientations and does not imply that everyone is heterosexual (Blank & Slipp, 1994)?
- Are organizational ceremonies and social events respectful of diversity of lifestyle? For example, are unmarried partners invited to company events?
- Are stereotypes or myths about sexual orientation endorsed by employees or by management?
- Are g/l/b persons penalized for their failure to conform to heterosexual gender roles? For example, are they penalized for differences in styles of behavior or dress (Blank & Slipp, 1994)?

5. **Critical perspectives.** This framework emphasizes the political, moral, and ethical implications of administrative organizational decisions. Using this perspective, the organization is examined for the degree to which the organization works toward the improvement of society. According to this framework (Foster, 1986), social conditions of inequity or disempowerment should be addressed by organizations. Sample informational interview questions include the following:

- Does the company publicly support gay issues (McNaught, 1993)?
- Do the company's charitable foundations give to relevant causes (e.g., to civil rights organizations or to charitable groups that serve the gay community)?
- Does the leadership of particular groups within the organization (e.g., fraternities, country-club social sets, fundamentalist religious groups, or athletic groups) perceive of g/l/b lifestyles as being contrary to the goals of that group? Do respected members of the group challenge antigay bias (McNaught, 1993)?

- Is there company support for individuals with HIV/AIDS (Baker et al., 1995)?
- Does the organization have a sick leave pool?

One complicating factor in networking and informational interviewing is that it may be difficult to ask people direct questions about the level of homophobia in a particular work environment without actually outing one-self during the discussion. This self-disclosure issue may be viewed differently by different people. That is, self-disclosure may be influenced by such factors as the stage of g/l/b identity development, the particular geographic area in which the interview is conducted, and local, state, and national laws regarding protection against discrimination linked to sexual orientation.

Assessment Variables Beyond the Workplace: Legal and Geographical Considerations

We have focused thus far on the assessment of variables in the immediate workplace environment. Variables beyond the immediate environment are also likely to play an important role in the quality of life and work for a g/l/b individual. As already noted, laws that protect g/l/b persons from discrimination vary by state and by region. On the one hand are states that have enacted antidiscrimination legislation, including Connecticut, Hawaii, Massachusetts, New Jersey, Vermont, Wisconsin, and the District of Columbia (Baker et al., 1995). On the other hand are states like Colorado, which in 1992 approved an amendment to the state constitution that prohibited legislation protecting gay men and lesbians. The constitutionality of this amendment is currently being debated in the courts (Blank & Slipp, 1994).

On the local level, more than 100 municipalities have passed antidiscrimination laws (Blank & Slipp, 1994). Many of these municipalities are large cities and college towns (Baker et al., 1995). A recent study suggested that there are a greater proportion of self-identified g/l/b persons living in urban areas than in rural areas (Michael et al., 1994). Thus the presence of protective laws may be linked to differences in population distribution. A good resource not only for coverage of workplace issues but also for legal concerns such as family issues, housing, and free speech is *The Rights of Lesbians and Gay Men: The Basic ACLU Guide to a Gay Person's Rights* (Hunter et al., 1992). Another resource, which details the legal rights of workers, is *Power on the Job: The Legal Rights of Working People* (Yates, 1994).

Geographic regions vary not only in terms of legal protection but also in the availability of g/l/b-affirmative medical, counseling, and other services as well as of g/l/b-affirmative spiritual groups and social opportunities. This can greatly impact the quality of life and may impact career decisions.

The national *GAYELLOW PAGES* (Green, 1994) can be helpful in finding what support might be available in various geographic locations.

There are many potential variables that can become salient in individual career counseling cases. Some of the most important variables are touched upon in this chapter. Still others are alluded to in chapter 8. The variables are numerous, and the importance of each factor shifts from individual to individual. Career helpers need to appreciate how any number of these can become salient in counseling a particular individual.

The Importance of Considering Both Person and Environment Variables: An Illustrative Example

We have considered person variables (chapters 3 and 4) and environment variables (chapter 5) separately. In career counseling, however, these variables are usually intertwined and need to be considered simultaneously. Furthermore, these variables are often dynamic over time. Person variables can interact with, and sometimes impact, environmental variables and vice versa.

The example of Colonel Margarethe Cammermeyer demonstrates the interdependence of person and environment variables and illustrates many of the points made in chapters 3, 4, and 5. Her story has received national attention. She has written about her life in *Serving in Silence* (1994), and a made-for-television movie of the same name has aired on NBC.

> *Colonel Margarethe Cammermeyer had a distinguished military career. She was chief nurse of the Washington State National Guard. She was named Veterans Administration nurse of the year, and she received a Bronze Star for her duty in Vietnam. Her career goal was to become chief nurse of the entire national guard. She was married and had four children.*
>
> *During the late 1980s, Cammermeyer was depressed and sought counseling. With her counselor, she reviewed her life events and explored her relationships in order to gain understanding about her depression. It was within this counseling relationship that Cammermeyer first considered aloud the possibility of not being heterosexual. In reviewing her life, she found hints about her sexual orientation, such as remembering crushes on female teachers, the absence of desire in high school to get married, and distance in her relationship with her husband, including a lack of a desire to be physically intimate.*
>
> *Cammermeyer and her husband were eventually divorced. Although she had done some thinking about her sexual orientation, Margarethe Cammermeyer was not ready to accept that she might be lesbian. She wrote about not wanting to be lesbian: "In my ignorance*

I had only negative images of them, they were taunted, beaten up, fired from jobs, rejected by friends. I didn't want to be part of that group" (Cammermeyer, 1994, p. 219).

It was not until meeting a female friend, Diane, that Cammermeyer's self-identity began to shift further.

> *Meeting Diane and experiencing the rightness of being with her made me realize I am a lesbian. Finally, being able to acknowledge that gave me the last, connecting piece to the puzzle of my identity. It was a puzzle I had tried to solve since my adolescence. At the age of 46, I finally had to face the fact that being straight wasn't a choice I had. (pp. 218-219)*

To further her career, she applied for admission to the Army War College and was interviewed. She wanted to be honest and trustworthy during this interview. Cammermeyer reflected, "Of course I'd tell the truth. Even though it was a truth I'd given a name to less than a year before" (p. 3). When asked about her sexual orientation during the interview, she replied, "I am a lesbian" (p. 3). Cammermeyer was given multiple opportunities to recant her statement, but as she wrote, "There is no choice, I'd rather sacrifice my uniform than my integrity" (p. 5).

Cammermeyer's case attracted media attention as she pursued legal action. Her case and others brought the issue of gays in the military to national attention. Soon afterward, the military changed the policy with respect to sexual orientation and moved from an outright ban on g/l/b persons in the military to a "don't ask, don't tell" policy. Although Colonel Cammermeyer won her case against the military in federal court, appeals by the military have kept her from returning to duty.

This example illustrates the dynamic interaction between the person (Cammermeyer) and the work environment (the U.S. military). Cammermeyer's long and successful career in the military suggests a good match on traditional variables, such as vocational interests, values, and abilities. However, in a key variable, sexual orientation, there is a mismatch because of homophobia in the military. For a number of years, Cammermeyer was unaware of her sexual orientation. She probably then entered the first sexual identity development stage, Identity Confusion, in which she began to question her sexual orientation and experienced considerable bewilderment and confusion about the actions, feelings, and thoughts she was having (Cass, 1979, 1984a, 1984b). Her cognitive, behavioral, and affective responses to g/l/b work issues were influenced by this early developmental level.

Cammermeyer's work environment was initially overtly discriminatory and was thus at the most extreme level of environmental heterosexism.

Military regulations specifically banned g/l/b persons from the service. This did not overtly impact Cammermeyer early in her career because her identity development was at an earlier level.

Developmental/life events, including a divorce, allowed Cammermeyer to explore other types of relationships. By developing an intimate relationship with Diane, her sexual identity changed. She now experienced more overt conflict with workplace environmental heterosexism. As the result of her relationship with Diane, Cammermeyer solidified her identity. She felt strongly enough about being lesbian that she was willing to disclose its existence in the workplace and risk severe consequences to her career. Her level of sexual identity development had shifted. She wrote, "Up to a few years before. . . I would have affirmed my heterosexuality and the interview would have proceeded without a hitch. But I had changed, I had painfully and slowly come to terms with my identity" (p. 3). Because of a stronger, more positive identity, she refused to recant her statement. This shift in her sexual identity development (a person variable) and the workplace's reaction to it (an environment variable) permanently affected her life and her career.

Cammermeyer (the person) has also had the opportunity to affect the military (the environment). Her legal actions, along with the legal actions of other military personnel, have been catalysts in the small shift of the military's level of discrimination from a total ban on gays in the military to the "don't ask, don't tell" policy.

6

Career Decision Making and Goal Setting

Approaches to career decision making and setting short- and long-term goals can be both rational and nonrational. Rational models provide steps to take in a particular order and may have strongest relevance to the career needs of g/l/b persons. For example, a g/l/b person who is seeking to generate a list of career options based on her or his work interests, values, experiences, and skills may benefit most from using a rational decision-making process to gather more data before making any decisions. Nonrational models are more intuitive and may be most useful when alternatives, goals, and preferences are not clear. For example, an individual who is deciding whether to come out at work may benefit most from using a nonrational decision-making process based on hunches about the work environment's attitude toward diversity.

Effective career decision making may sometimes require using both rational and nonrational approaches. It may be beneficial, for example, for an individual first to go through the rational six-step model presented in this chapter to generate career options and then reflect on how he or she feels about the options. Or a person may benefit by picking a career option that he or she simply likes and then justifying it by going through the rational model.

In the literature on career decision-making models and processes, sexual orientation has been little considered. Thus career counselors and other professional helpers should strive to integrate g/l/b identity development factors (see chapter 4) into any model or sequence of steps to ensure relevance for g/l/b clients. Only when g/l/b persons are helped to understand both themselves and specific work environments, and to develop good decision-making skills, are their chances of selecting meaningful careers maximized. It is crucial to attend to the unique decision-making issues linked to sexual orientation (Croteau & Hedstrom, 1993) as well as to help g/l/b persons attend to the career decision-making issues that all individuals address, regardless of sexual orientation.

This chapter first reviews what rational decision-making models typically include, discusses the importance of clarifying the specific career questions that clients are asking before starting the career decision-making process, and describes the six career decision-making steps we find most relevant for use with g/l/b clients. Nonrational decision-making models, which also have important relevance to the career needs of g/l/b persons, are also examined. The impact that g/l/b identity development and sexual orientation factors may have on the career decision-making process and g/l/b identity development is then explored, and examples of integrating identity development factors into the decision-making steps are provided. The chapter concludes with a discussion of other factors—self-efficacy, career maturity, and locus of control—that may particularly affect the career decision-making process for g/l/b clients.

Rational Career Decision-Making Models

Among available rational career decision-making models are Tiedeman's (1961) sequence of steps that includes the enhancement of self-awareness, information gathering, the development of career options, the selection of one career alternative, and the development of a career plan. Another is Krumboltz and Hamel's (1977) DECIDES model that includes the steps of Defining the problem, Establishing an action plan, Clarifying values, Identifying alternatives, Discovering probable outcomes, Eliminating alternatives, and Starting action. Gati (1986) has also suggested a sequential process of evaluation and elimination of career alternatives.

These and other models of rational career decision making typically include variants of the following actions:

- Assess personal traits and work-related interests, values, experiences, and needs.
- Gain an awareness of the wide number of options available in the world of work or education.
- Generate a more specific list of those career or educational options that are suggested by specific personality traits as well as by work-related interests, values, experiences, and skills.
- Gather additional information about one or more of the career or educational options that are suggested by interests, skills, values, and experiences.
- Based on the additional information gathered about specific careers or educational programs, develop a tentative general long-term action plan and begin to think about specific ways to start working toward these goals.

- Discuss with the client potential barriers to implementing the action plan and develop strategies for overcoming those barriers.
- After doing some initial work on implementing the short-term action plan, reassess thoughts and feelings about that particular plan and make decisions accordingly.

Clarifying Career Needs

Individuals have different career needs at different points in their lives. At one point, they may wish simply to understand their strengths and skills as workers. Later they may wish to move beyond self-assessment into determining which careers could best utilize their potentials as workers. At a still later point, they may wish to advance in their present job or develop a different career objective. Individuals may need assistance in responding to job stressors such as time management problems, assertiveness difficulties, or coping with homophobia in the work environment. Thus career needs vary over the life span, depending on personal or environmental factors.

To assist g/l/b clients most effectively, it is important to clarify the specific career questions being asked before focusing on career decision-making steps. That is, why does the client want career counseling? What are the client's specific career needs?

Clients seeking the help of a professional typically have one or more of the following concerns:

- **Self-assessment.** Clients wish to learn more about their unique interests, values, experiences, and skills.
- **Generation of career options.** Clients need to learn about what educational majors or careers would make good use of their interests, values, experiences, and skills.
- **Provision of information.** Clients would like to find information about specific careers or educational majors.
- **Decision making.** Clients wish to make a tentative decision about a particular major or career.
- **Action planning.** Clients seek to develop a plan to implement educational and career goals.
- **Job search training.** Clients want to improve their job search skills (e.g., résumé writing and interviewing skills).

These concerns have some parallels to career decision-making steps. Some, for example, relate to early self-assessment, and others relate to the job search, which occurs later in the process of making a career decision.

Activities and materials that facilitate the initial definition of the person's career needs include a tour of the career facility or helping them make use of computer-assisted guidance systems such as DISCOVER (Modules 1 and 2) or SIGI-PLUS (Introduction section). Clients may also benefit from browsing in the career section of the career agency, bookstores, or libraries. Resources such as *What Color Is Your Parachute?* (Bolles, 1995), *The New Quick Job Hunting Map* (Bolles, 1990), *I Could Do Anything if I Only Knew What It Was: How to Discover What You Really Want and How to Get It* (Sher, 1994), and *Wishcraft: How to Get What You Really Want* (Sher & Gottlief, 1986) can help clients get a better sense of the career and life planning process.

The Six Career Decision-Making Steps

The decision-making steps described here for optimizing career decisions by g/l/b persons are a compilation of approaches based on a review of career counseling literature (e.g., Betz & Fitzgerald, 1987; Harris-Bowlsbey et al., 1991; Phillips, 1992) and our own clinical career counseling experiences.

1. **Help clients explore their work-related interests, values, experiences, and skills.** (*Assessment*) Chapters 3 and 4 present guidelines for assessing the client's vocational personality and stage of adult development.

2. **Help clients better understand the world of work and their career or educational options.** (*Information gathering*) Chapter 3 describes world of work resources, and chapter 5 provides a framework for the assessment of work environments.

3. **Help clients develop their decision-making skills.** (*Decision making*) Without good decision-making skills, it is of little use for clients to have an awareness of their interests, values, experiences, and skills or to understand the organization of the world of work. That is, if clients make decisions based more on the opinions of others—or if they make decisions in a state of panic—they are less likely to make a decision that will result in an optimal match between themselves and a particular job. If clients understand the role of clear thinking, pay attention to their intuition, and proceed through a rational set of decision-making steps, they are more likely to make optimal career and life planning decisions.

   To enhance and develop decision-making skills, it is important to help clients

   - learn about decision-making principles, decision-making styles, the six steps in making career decisions, and the impact of sexual orientation on the decision-making process;
   - locate educational majors or careers that best fit their personalities;
   - identify information sources to be used in making career decisions;

- narrow and prioritize occupational and educational alternatives; and
- make a tentative decision about a major or career to pursue.

Individualized professional assistance can also help clients better analyze their own decision-making style and facilitate their movement through the six career decision-making steps more effectively.

4. **Help clients learn how stereotyping, bias, and discrimination may limit their career choices, opportunities, and achievement.** (*Explore biases*) All career clients are influenced by, for example, ageism, sexism, heterosexism, ableism, ethnocentrism, and racism (Gelberg, Foldesi et al., 1993). Sometimes the influence of these isms is so subtle that clients do not see how isms may be affecting the career goals they set for themselves. Without a conscious exploration of their own internal stereotypes, as well as an understanding of the role of society in shaping their career goals, clients may set goals that are either too low or unrealistic for their individual work personalities.

In addressing stereotyping, clients should learn to
- understand stereotyping as it relates to work and education,
- identify limitations placed on people by stereotyping,
- identify opportunities, regardless of past stereotyping or discrimination,
- understand how their own stereotypes or the stereotypes of others influence their career and life planning, and
- understand how societal homophobia and heterosexism affect the decisions that they make.

Because there is little current practical written material addressing these issues, it is important for clients to discuss stereotyping concerns with others rather than simply read about stereotypes or address stereotypes through a computerized guidance system. Clients should thus be encouraged to locate g/l/b-affirmative agency resources, talk with someone working in a field of interest about stereotyping issues, and/or consult with professional helpers or with work mentors. Individuals may also read about homophobia and heterosexism to educate themselves about possible barriers and to develop plans for addressing these issues. In addition, career or personal counseling may help individuals reduce the impact of stereotyping on their own career and life planning. (See chapter 2's discussion of stereotyping and discrimination.)

5. **Help clients develop a long- and short-term career plan.** (*Action plan*) Setting long- and short-term goals helps clients

begin to implement the career goals they have set for themselves. Without a plan of action, clients are more likely to become overwhelmed by their career goals. Or clients may procrastinate and thus put off working toward their goals. Clients can develop action plans through securing individual career counseling, enrolling in a career choice class, or finding a career coach or mentor to help them develop professionally and personally as g/l/b persons.

In developing action plans, individuals should

- develop long- and short-term educational and occupational goals to implement their choices,
- develop an alternate plan,
- develop a plan for periodic reevaluation of career decisions, and
- develop a support system to enhance motivation to implement career plans.

In making career and life planning decisions, it is important to have more than one career action plan because self-assessment and decision making continue even after an individual has entered a new work environment. Some information is simply not available to the career client before the job search stage, or the stage in which career objectives are implemented. Thus individuals can do a good job of gathering information before they start to look for jobs, but they may not fully understand how well a job may fit their work personality until they near the final stage of the job search or actually begin to work in a specific job. Having more than one action plan takes into account the potential for a change in career goals based on information gained either during the job search or during the early stages of work in a new work environment.

Multiple action plans thus help individuals remain open to the information and feedback gathered in the job search process or implementation stage. Multiple plans also prevent clients from continuing to work toward career goals that seem to be less appropriate or less feasible given the additional information gained during the job search process or the stage in which career objectives are implemented. Counselors and other professional helpers should encourage g/l/b persons to build reevaluations of career goals into every stage of their career decision making in order to utilize effectively the new information gained at every stage of the decision-making process.

6. Help clients develop their employability skills. (*Job search*) Even with the best formulated career plans, clients may fail to realize their career objectives if they are unskilled at writing resumés, or if their job interview skills are poor. If clients fail to understand the role of networking or the hidden job market in locating job openings, they may fail to land the job of their choice. Similarly, if clients do not have good self-presentation skills, such as the ability to demonstrate assertiveness or self-confidence, they may be underestimated by the interviewer, whose job it is to assess potential in a very short period of time. Thus sharpening job search skills and employability skills can lead to improving the client's chance of landing a job that utilizes her or his potential.

It is important for clients (as more fully explored in chapter 7) to

- develop positive work attitudes and behaviors;
- prepare resumés that are consistent with career interests, values, experiences, and skills;
- effectively complete job applications;
- learn how to gather information about the level of homophobia and heterosexism in the particular work environment under consideration;
- develop interviewing techniques, resulting in successful job interviews;
- understand legal and illegal job interview questions, especially as they relate to sexual orientation;
- understand how to ease the transition from school to work; and
- learn to manage heterosexism and homophobia in the job interview and work environment.

The assessment of decision-making processes may be facilitated through use of inventories such as Harren's Assessment of Career Decision Making (ACDM) (Harren, 1985) or the decision-making scale of the CDI (Super et al., 1981). These inventories do not, however, synthesize information about gay/lesbian/bisexual identity development into the assessment and may thus miss critical information.

Nonrational Decision-Making Models

Although the six steps of the rational decision-making model just described have strong relevance to the career needs of g/l/b persons, nonrational types of decision making also have significance. Robbins (1993), for example, emphasized the importance of nonrational factors in optimal decision making. Alternatives to rational decision-making models include the *satisficing model*, in which the first solution that is "good enough" (i.e., satisfactory and sufficient), rather than optimal, is selected; the *implicit favorite model*, in which a preferred alternative is selected early in the process and other choices are biased by the first alternative; and the *intuitive model* of decision making, which relies on unconscious processes and intuition on career decisions. These models may be useful in making decisions in which all of the alternatives are unlikely to be known, and when goals and preferences are not clear or consistent. They are also useful when it is cognitively impossible to process all of the information necessary to use a rational decision-making process. (For a more detailed description of these models, see Robbins, 1993.) In addition, nonrational models are helpful when one or more of the following conditions is present: ambiguity, uncertainty, lack of a particular precedent, less predictability, fewer facts or fewer analytical data, more than one plausible solution, time limitations, and pressure to make the right decision (Agor, 1986; 1989). Further, individuals tend to apply intuitive processes during the early stages of decision making, or at the end of the decision-making process.

To illustrate:

> *John interviewed for a position at three major universities. During one interview, he learned that one university had secured a grant for research on sexual orientation issues. In addition, there were two out staff members as well as a group for faculty and staff who were gay, lesbian, and bisexual. Because of the appreciation of diversity, John intuitively felt that this university was right for him. Although he gathered information and had job interviews at both other universities, his evaluations about such factors as promotion opportunities were biased toward the first university because that institution was perceived to be more gay/lesbian/bisexual affirmative than the other two universities. He used the implicit favorite model of decision-making.*

Gelatt (1989) also favored a nonrational decision-making framework. According to Gelatt, rational decision-making approaches were more relevant in the past, when the future was more predictable. Today, because the job market is changing so quickly, counselors should encourage clients to tolerate uncertainty and inconsistency and use nonrational and intuitive processes in making decisions. His proposed decision-making strategy is called *positive uncertainty* and emphasizes helping clients to feel positive about ambiguity in a constantly changing world.

In addition, Gati et al. (1995) have proposed a practical, nine-step sequential elimination model of decision making that considers it unrealistic or improbable to imagine that individuals will gather comprehensive information about all available career options because of natural cognitive limitations or limited resources and time. Their model, which helps clients deal with a large number of alternatives, may be especially suitable for career counseling with g/l/b persons because information about how g/l/b affirmative a particular work environment is often limited.

Career Decision Making and Gay/Lesbian/Bisexual Identity Development

The impact of individual differences, developmental aspects, and contextual factors on the process of making career decisions was emphasized by Harren (1979). Although he did not specifically mention gay/lesbian/bisexual identity development factors, or contextual factors linked to homophobia or heterosexism, his discussion of the relevance of adult development provides support for the proposal that sexual orientation factors have an impact on the career decision-making process.

Some decisions that g/l/b persons make involve decisions not faced by heterosexuals. For example, g/l/b persons must make the decision to "pass" or to "not pass" as heterosexual in the work environment due to environmental barriers such as job discrimination (Elliott, 1993; Hetherington, 1991). As another example, g/l/b persons must make decisions about how to handle the homophobia or heterosexism they may encounter should they decide to come out in the work environment. Other questions that g/l/b persons may need to ask include

- "What is the best way for me to handle gay/lesbian/bisexual discrimination in the workplace?"
- "How should I handle relationship issues at work?"
- "How should I approach gender role issues when making career decisions?"
- "In the job search process, how do I decide about self-disclosure as I gather information about the level of homophobia in a particular work environment?"
- "As I make a career decision, how do I gather information about the level of gay/lesbian/bisexual affirmation of a particular geographic region?"

In studying the influence of sexual orientation on career decision making, Etringer et al. (1990) investigated factors that included anxiety about making a career choice, indecisiveness, the need to gather information about the career of choice, uncertainty about the choice, and career choice dissatisfaction. These researchers found that the degree of uncertainty about career choice and the degree of dissatisfaction with that choice varied by gender and sexual orientation. Gay men had the highest level of uncertainty, and lesbians had the lowest level of uncertainty. Heterosexual women and gay men showed higher levels of dissatisfaction about their career choices, relative to heterosexual men and lesbians. In addition, both career choice anxiety and uncertainty about career choice were associated with career choice dissatisfaction and a greater need to gather career information. The authors cautioned that their findings were correlational and not causal.

In responding to questions linked to job discrimination, g/l/b persons indicated their decision making reflects different coping mechanisms. Some decide to enter homophobic environments and not disclose their sexual orientation. Others choose to avoid certain environments altogether because of homophobia. Still others enter hostile environments and selectively self-disclose their orientation, although other individuals openly self-disclose their orientation in the workplace (Orzek, 1992).

A number of dual-career questions relevant to g/l/b persons are discussed by Hetherington and Orzek (1989). Among these are how to present the relationship to coworkers, introduction of one's partner to coworkers, dealing with professional or social events, dealing with child care issues, and social isolation because of limited self-disclosure. These questions all involve the utilization of effective career and life planning decision-making skills.

G/l/b persons face unique decisions during the job interview process. Most heterosexuals do not have to concern themselves with discussing their sexual orientation during an interview in order to determine whether the work environment would be affirmative of those relationships. Many g/l/b persons want to gather that information so they can evaluate the level of workplace heterosexism and make a better career decision about entering or avoiding a particular work environment. It may be difficult for these individuals to obtain that information during the job interview without facing self-disclosure of their sexual orientation. For some persons, especially those who are in the initial stages of coming out as gay, lesbian, or bisexual, the timing and degree of self-disclosure may be problematic. For other individuals who are already out personally and professionally, early and complete self-disclosure may be an important part of the job interview.

Some geographic areas seem to have larger gay and lesbian populations than others (Hillerbrand, Hetherington, & Etringer, 1986; Michael et al., 1994). Thus geography may be especially important for g/l/b persons during the process of career decision making (Hetherington, 1991).

Cass's (1979, 1984a, 1984b) model (or other models of gay/lesbian/bisexual identity development such as those described in chapter 4) is helpful in consideration of the six career decision-making steps. For example, individuals who are at Stage I of identity development may have different responses to Step 3, Decision making (understand and develop decision-making skills), than do people who are at Stage VI of identity development. Or compared with individuals who are at a later stage of g/l/b identity development, individuals who are at Stage I of identity development may find it especially difficult to discuss sexual orientation issues with a helper when going through career decision-making Step 1, Assessment (explore career interests, values, experiences, and skills).

Table 2 may be used to conceptualize the impact of the stages of identity development on an individual's progress through the six decision-making steps.

To illustrate:

James has just begun to network with other males in order to address the low self-esteem he is experiencing as a gay male. He is uncomfortable with self-disclosure issues, and he finds it difficult to value his own sexual orientation. He is currently trying to gather information about an opening in a particular agency. Because of his own internalized homophobia and because he perceives the agency as heterosexist and homophobic, he finds it difficult to ask direct questions about the level of affirmation of diversity in that particular work environment. He is also unable to gather information about the level of benefits for his partner, and he is unsure about how many social or networking opportunities that particular community has for g/l/b persons. He is at Cass's Stage III. (Cass, 1979, 1984a, 1984b).

Lenore, in contrast, is out professionally and personally. She is able to ask these questions directly when applying for a particular job and has developed positive coping skills for dealing with any homophobia or heterosexism she may encounter. She is at Cass's Stage VI.

For all six career decision-making steps, there are differences between James and Lenore because the two individuals are at different levels of identity development, and their career decision-making behaviors differ. Table 2 graphically conceptualizes the interaction between Cass' stages of identity development and the six stages of career decision making described earlier in this chapter.

Because James is at Stage III, Identity Tolerance, his career self-assessment on Step 1 is affected by self-esteem issues such as his inability to value himself fully as a g/l/b worker. The fact that James may devalue g/l/b issues should be considered while assessing his vocational interests, values, experiences, and skills. James' ability to gather information about specific work environments on Step 2 may be affected by self-disclosure issues. For example, he may avoid asking about homophobia in the work environment because of a desire to pass as heterosexual. When prioritizing his vocational interests, needs, and values on Step 3, James' current or immediate decisions about meeting his needs as a g/l/b worker may differ from decisions made at a later stage of development. Exploring biases on Step 4 may be especially difficult due to internalized homophobia or heterosexism. James' action plan on Step 5 may not include strategies for confronting homophobia in the work environment due to his need to pass as heterosexual, and his job search on Step 6 may be affected by his need to pass and difficulty in fully valuing his sexual orientation.

TABLE 2

The Interaction Between Career Decision Making and Identity Development

		Decision-Making Steps					
		Step 1	Step 2	Step 3	Step 4	Step 5	Step 6
Identity Development		Assessment	Information gathering	Decision making	Explore biases	Action plan	Job search
Stage I	Identity Confusion						
Stage II	Identity Comparison						
Stage III	Identity Tolerance						
Stage IV	Identity Acceptance						
Stage V	Identity Pride						
Stage VI	Identity Synthesis						

Lenore seems to be at Stage VI of Cass's (1979, 1984a, 1984b) model. The professional helper might observe that during career assessment on Step 1 Lenore is more comfortable than James in exploring issues of sexual orientation as they impact her career and life planning. Lenore is also more comprehensive in gathering information on Step 2 about work environments due to her greater comfort in self-disclosure of g/l/b issues. Because Lenore has come to integrate her identity as a lesbian into other facets of her personality, her decision making on Step 3 may reflect (relative to James) a more balanced consideration of issues of adult development, career development, and g/l/b identity development. Lenore may have a greater awareness of her own internal and societal biases on Step 4 because of her level of g/l/b identity development, and her ability to develop an effective action plan on Step 5 might include the development of healthy strategies for coping with homophobia in the work environment. Finally, Lenore's job search on Step 6 might be characterized by effective interviewing skills due to her greater comfort with her sexual orientation and greater sense of clarity in her value system as her values relate to sexual orientation.

Other Factors Affecting Career Decision-Making

Self-Efficacy

Self-efficacy (Bandura, 1977; Betz & Hackett, 1981, 1986; Hackett & Betz, 1981) refers to an individual's belief that she or he will be able to take the actions required to meet a specified set of goals. Self-efficacy can be low while potential as a worker can be high, or vice versa. If self-efficacy is low, a person may eliminate possible career options, even though that individual's actual ability may be high. Self-efficacy, therefore, can impact the career decision-making process.

Some self-efficacy problems can be related to gender, with women having more difficulties in showing high self-efficacy. Self-efficacy may also be related to sexual orientation. Because of societal homophobia and heterosexism, self-efficacy as a g/l/b person may be weak for individuals who are at the beginning stages of g/l/b identity development.

To illustrate:

Jamie, who is bisexual, works in the media department of a large corporate agency. She has always found it difficult to utilize her full potential, in part because of her family's failure to accept her bisexuality. She is not out at work and has no social support system aside from a partner who lives in a nearby town. Despite her high artistic talent, she rarely seeks challenging assignments and does not enjoy hearing praise about her work. She has low self-efficacy as a worker, and she is failing to fulfill her potential because of this low self-efficacy. It is important for her to address her low self-efficacy so that she is better able to utilize her work potential and to enjoy success in her work.

Self-efficacy may be related to stereotyping factors. For example, some careers are viewed as being stereotypically gay professions. For example, in one study, college students thought that careers such as photographer, interior decorator, and nurse would be most interesting to gay men, but that auto mechanic, plumber, and truck driver would be most interesting to lesbians (Botkin & Day, 1987). Thus a gay male who chooses to become a photographer may have higher self-efficacy in his work than a gay male who enters the military because stereotypes have led him to believe that gay men work and succeed in this field.

Career Maturity

The concept of career maturity includes

- the individual's ability to be planful in addressing career and life planning issues (Super, 1983),
- the person's level of knowledge of occupational information (Crites, 1965),
- the ability to effectively incorporate information about oneself and the work environment into an effective action plan (Phillips, 1992),

- decision-making skills and the ability to make realistic and consistent choices (Super, 1983),
- the presence of positive work attitudes that help in the planning and exploring of occupational futures (Crites, 1965), and
- the degree of self-awareness of career-related needs, values, interests, and skills (Phillips, 1992).

Career maturity has been linked to career satisfaction, occupational advancement, and attained status (Super, Thompson, Lindeman, Myers, & Jordaan, 1985). Career maturity has also been linked to such factors as intellectual activity, gender, and ethnic background (Westbrook, 1983). Although career maturity has not been studied as it relates to sexual orientation, career maturity has been correlated with some aspects of self-concept (Osipow, 1983). Because g/l/b identity development includes self-concept components (Cass, 1979, 1984a, 1984b), g/l/b identity development may influence some aspects of career maturity. Individuals who are in different stages of coming out as g/l/b persons may be at varying levels of career maturity.

Career maturity may be assessed through use of tools such as the Career Development Inventory (CDI) (Super et al., 1981) or the Career Maturity Inventory (CMI) (Crites, 1978). The CDI assesses factors such as planning, exploration, information about the world of work, decision making, and knowledge of specific occupations. (For an exhaustive review of methods of assessment of vocational maturity, see Betz, 1988, and *A Counselor's Guide to Career Assessment Instruments*, Kapes et al., 1994. Note that sexual orientation is not a primary focus of most inventories of career decision-making factors, nor is sexual orientation a major focus when decision-making inventories are reviewed. Thus the impact of gay/lesbian/bisexual identity development on career maturity is not considered in most standardized measures of career maturity.)

Locus of Control

The concept of *locus of control* (Friedrich, 1987; Rotter, 1966) refers to peoples' cognitive responses to their own successes or failures. People with an internal locus of control believe that they have some control over their own successes and failures, and they feel that they can take actions to influence the likelihood that their performance will be successful. These people also respond to their own failures with a positive mindset, and they are likely to be effective at problem solving even in the face of disappointment. People with an external locus of control tend to respond to failures with a strong sense of helplessness or hopelessness, and they feel that they have less control over their own successes and failures. These individuals often suffer from low self-esteem and are at greater risk for depression.

These people often view failures as reflections of some negative character-istics about themselves. This belief system may inhibit the use of helpful career decision-making approaches.

Locus of control may be independent of skill level, capabilities, or potential. That is, people can be quite gifted yet not see their own potentials or their own roles in their successes. Individuals with an external locus of control are most likely to set lower career goals for themselves, compared with individuals with an internal locus of control.

Locus of control may be confused with homophobia and heterosexism factors. That is, homophobia may, in fact, take some career options out of the control of a g/l/b worker (e.g., through the impact of discrimination based on sexual orientation factors). Counselors and other professional help-ers should be careful not to label g/l/b workers as showing an external locus of control because of discrimination experiences that are, in fact, at-tributable to external factors of homophobia or heterosexism rather than to individual locus-of-control factors.

7

The Job Search

Sexual orientation influences a number of aspects of the job search. G/l/b persons who are in the process of writing resúmés, locating jobs, conducting job interviews, evaluating homophobia in the work environment, negotiating offers, and transitioning into the work environment can benefit from counselors and other professional helpers who can appreciate the complex interactions between sexual orientation and these job search factors.

This chapter focuses on the final step of the career decision-making process: on the development of employability skills that can help to ensure job search success. This chapter discusses preparing effective resúmés, conducting electronic job searches, and sharpening interview techniques, and then briefly considers guidelines for negotiating job offers. The chapter concludes with an examination of personal characteristics that may affect an individual's ability to conduct an effect job search, including self-efficacy, assertiveness, time management skills, and stress management skills.

Preparing Resúmés

Most libraries and career centers have books and computer programs that help individuals prepare effective resúmés and cover letters (e.g., Fry, 1995b; Parker, 1988). However, even though these resources provide an in-depth coverage of resúmé writing, most do not cover how gay/lesbian/bisexual career and life planning issues can affect resúmés. Thus g/l/b persons have choices about when, how, and if they should come out during the job search process.

To illustrate:

Alan was an officer in a g/l/b student organization. During his job search, he was faced with the decision about whether or not to come out in his resúmé. That is, he had to make a decision about whether to cite the name of the student organization or to simply describe his leadership skills without specifically naming the organization.

G/l/b persons may decide to come out in the resúmé, during an initial interview, after a job offer has been made, soon after beginning the job or later, or after experience has been gained in the job and work relationships established. Some individuals may decide not to come out at all at work. If self-disclosure is a goal at work, that self-disclosure may occur in a one-time, full-disclosure communication; or a trial balloon may be floated to test the level of affirmation present in a particular organization or agency.

A recent study of disclosure levels of g/l/b college student affairs professionals illustrated the various decisions a person can make during the job search process about if, when, and how to come out. Croteau and Destinon (1994) used a sample of 249 g/l/b student affairs professionals, half of whom were female, and half of whom were male. Of this sample, 7% disclosed their sexual orientation in initial correspondence or cover letters, 31% disclosed during the interview process, 4% disclosed after an offer was made but before accepting the position, 38% disclosed after entering the position, and 21% reported that they never disclosed their orientation.

In helping g/l/b persons make decisions about how much to come out in the resúmé, four factors should be considered.

1. **The stage of g/l/b identity development.** Individuals in different stages of coming out may have different levels of comfort about coming out in a resúmé.

2. **The level of work environment heterosexism.** Assessing the job environment will help individuals come to more informed decisions about what information linked to sexual orientation should be included in the resúmé. Some g/l/b individuals choose to write more than one resúmé, depending on the work environment. That is, they may have one resúmé in which they are out for use with affirmative work places and one resúmé in which they are not out for use with more homophobic work environments.

3. **The importance of sexual orientation self-disclosure at work relative to other job values.** In some situations, individuals may see safety needs (such as housing or food costs) as taking priority over self-disclosure issues, but others who are more secure financially may have different job value priorities.

4. **The partner's level of comfort with self-disclosure.** The fact that one partner in a romantic relationship may feel more or less comfortable about being out may influence the other partner's degree of self-disclosure at work.

For these four factors, there is likely to be a great deal of individual variation. Counselors and other professional helpers should be careful not to make assumptions about how a particular client feels about any of the factors, nor should professional helpers project their own feelings or values in assisting g/l/b persons in making decisions about the level of self-disclosure of sexual orientation in the resúmé.

Counselors should also help g/l/b clients see the complex nature of the decision to come out. Some clients may view this process somewhat simplistically. For example, some individuals decide to avoid coming out at work, and they expect that this will be an easy option. Clients may not be aware of the time, energy, and emotional endurance it takes to keep such a large part of their lives from being known. Failure to come out may lead to poor self-concept and other emotional problems (Berger, 1982; Elliott, 1993). Career counselors should help clients weigh the positive impacts of coming out at work with the possible homophobia that may follow self-disclosure. Negative consequences of self-disclosure were seen in the results of Croteau and Destinon's (1994) study, which found that those persons coming out during the job search process reported significantly higher levels of discrimination.

Although resúmé resource books usually have sample resúmés, most do not provide examples of coming out or not coming out on a resúmé. (We have found that some career counselors have even been unaware of the need to consider these issues in writing a resúmé.) It is very helpful for counselors to have sample resúmés available that illustrate varying levels of self-disclosure in a resúmé.

Locating Jobs: The Electronic Job Search Revolution

Jobs may be located through use of a number of resources: position openings, networking, and newspaper announcements. These resources have been described in most traditional career books such as *What Color Is Your Parachute?* (Bolles, 1995).

An exciting new development is the impact of information technology on the job search process. The electronic job search revolution now makes it possible for job seekers to connect with employers electronically. For example, resúmé database services can now give employers access to an individual's resúmé anywhere in the world. Employer databases allow people to get company names and profiles through the computer. Many companies use applicant tracking systems to scan resúmés, and on-line job ads are available through a number of communications network services. These and other electronic resources (including the names, addresses, and telephone and fax numbers of electronic job search services) are discussed in *Electronic Job Search Revolution* (Kennedy & Morrow, 1994) and *Hook Up, Get Hired!* (Kennedy, 1995).

The On-Line Job Search Companion (Gonyea, 1995) also gives the names of career planning and job search resources that are available via the computer. Topics discussed include electronic career planning, on-line education, the electronic job search, the Internet, commercial on-line network services, bulletin board systems, and a resource index.

A list of gay/lesbian/bisexual/transgender computer resources is available from the American College Personnel Association Standing Committee for Lesbian, Gay, and Bisexual Awareness (SCLGBA). This list includes resource directories, gophers, e-mail addresses for gay/lesbian/bisexual/transgender organizations, general mailing lists (e.g., GayNet), diversity-based mailing lists (e.g., glbpoc—gay, lesbian, bisexual people of color), user net news groups, and commercial subscription services (e.g., the Gay and Lesbian Community Forum available from America On-Line).

Career centers are beginning to utilize this new technology to enhance career assessment, intervention, and evaluation services. These include on-line services with Internet access, resúmé databases, job announcement databases, employer information databases, user net news groups (bulletin-board-style discussion groups), telnet services (which connect the user to other computers on the Internet), gopher services (the software development at the University of Minnesota that supports a worldwide network of university and organization information systems), campus-wide information systems (CWIS; any local campus networks), Listserves (electronic discussion groups that enable the user to network with people who share the user's interests), FreeNets (metropolitan networks with computerized information such as lists of community organizations), and the World Wide Web (WWW), a hypertext system that allows browsing and searching on the Internet (Hradsky, Waldrep, Hill, & Paul, 1995; Youngblood, Nichols, & Wilson, 1995).

One result of having resources available on the information superhighway is that resource information management is now viewed as a primary purpose of career centers. Thus it is important for career clients and their professional helpers to become more educated in computer technology in order to help career clients use the full scope of services available through the emerging technology.

Some individuals find themselves less comfortable becoming educated about these new technologies. The vocational personality of the career client or the professional helper may influence his or her comfort in becoming educated about the electronic job search technology. Vocational personality type has been found to be predictive of computer anxiety (Gelberg, 1990). Artistic and realistic personality types, as defined by Holland's (1985a) schema, are associated with high levels of computer anxiety.

To illustrate these fears about technology:

A college sophomore with an artistic personality type who was thinking about a teaching career in English wrote the following response

to an unstructured question about feelings about computers and vo-
cational interests: "I am personally scared by computers and know I
don't want any part of them in my career." Another individual with
both artistic and social personality types wrote, "I think that people
who are interested in more analytical type jobs (such as engineers,
chemists, any scientific fields) would be more apt to use computers and
feel more comfortable about using them." Finally, another person, also
with an artistic personality type, wrote, "I wish I knew more about
computers. It scares me that I'm so uneducated about them. It seems
everything is computers nowadays." (Gelberg, 1988, p. 114)

The influence of vocational personality type and comfort with technology is highlighted by a study (Gelberg & Harnisch, 1988) in which
students were classified as having majors that were "congruent with computers" or "incongruent with computers." The congruent group of students
perceived of computers as offering more occupational and educational benefits, showed a greater preference for using computers, were more familiar
with computers, and showed more positive feelings about computers compared to students in majors that were classified as being incongruent with
computers. Gelberg and Harnisch concluded that principles of congruence
and incongruence (Holland, 1985a) should be applied to the teaching of
computer literacy in order to accommodate to the variety of individual differences in vocational interests, skills, and values. In addition, because career
counselors and other professional helpers need to assist individuals with a
variety of vocational interests learn to make use of electronic job search
technologies, and because the vocational personalities of career counselors,
psychologists, or others in different helping fields may be less congruent
with computer technology (Gelberg, 1990), professionals in the helping
fields should also use principles of congruence and incongruence to better
understand their own anxieties or lack of experience with computer technology.

As computer technology becomes more commonplace in educational
settings, the differences in comfort and experience with computers as experienced by individuals of differing personality types are likely to be reduced, and with time there will probably be a more universal comfort with
computers and technology. There are still large segments of society, however, that have had less access to the information superhighway. Older individuals, persons from lower socioeconomic classes, and individuals from
rural areas may have fewer opportunities for exposure to this technology.
Age, gender, socioeconomic class, and geographic region may still have an
impact on the level of comfort and experience with technology. Thus career
counselors and other professional helpers should remember to consider not
only individual personality types in helping g/l/b persons become educated
about the information superhighway job search services but also variations

in peoples' feelings and willingness to enhance their computer/technological literacy.

Fortunately, a number of resources are now available to help educate people about such resources as the Internet. Many computer resources are now more user friendly than they were a decade ago. For example, *The Internet Guide for New Users* (Dern, 1994) provides an easy-to-follow guide for new users of the Internet, and *The Internet Yellow Pages* (Hahn & Stout, 1995) is a directory that facilitates finding and accessing what is on the Internet. "Margaret Riley's Employment Opportunities and Job Resources on the Internet," available on the World Wide Web, is an excellent, comprehensive listing of Internet job search resources.

Although it is beyond the scope of this book to evaluate specific electronic career resources, note that not all on-line resources are of high quality (Elmer-Dewitt, 1995). Counselors and other professional helpers should personally evaluate specific on-line resources before endorsing them.

Sharpening Interviewing Techniques

Career libraries, book stores, and career centers usually have a number of resources on enhancing interviewing skills (e.g., Fry, 1995a; LaFevre, 1992). These materials stress the importance of self-awareness of vocational interests, values, experiences, and skills during the job interview. With this awareness comes a more positive self-presentation during the interview. However, most interview resources, like the resources for preparing resumés, do not cover issues linked to sexual orientation. Career counselors and other professional helpers should become aware of these issues in order to best advise g/l/b persons.

One of these interview issues linked to sexual orientation is self-disclosure. Unlike race or gender, sexual orientation is not readily apparent. Thus self-disclosure is an option—but an option that creates career issues different from those related to race, age, culture, or gender (Eldridge & Barnett, 1991; Hetherington, 1991).

Self-disclosure may be subtle, as when individuals wear necklaces or clothing with pink triangles, rainbows, or a lambda. Such symbols may not be understood by some heterosexuals, but they serve to help g/l/b individuals network with each other. For example, we once observed a cotton belt that had been decorated by a male nurse, who worked in a nursing home, with a lambda carefully integrated into a landscape. This lambda, probably not observed by most heterosexuals, was a clear symbol to other g/l/b persons who worked in that nursing home.

The issue of self-disclosure is closely related to the assessment of homophobia in the work environment. Networking and informational interviewing are important tools for gathering information about how affirmative a particular organization is to g/l/b persons (see chapter 5). Thus when a g/l/b person is reluctant to ask certain questions because of fear concerning the impact of self-disclosure too early in the interview process, that person can use networking and informational interviewing with local, state, or national professional organizations to gather the needed information. Career counselors and other helping professionals should maintain lists of as many local networking names as possible in addition to knowing about professional g/l/b state and national networks.

Because self-disclosure is a complex issue involving such variables as the level of the g/l/b person's identity development, the person's career needs (e.g., safety needs versus self-actualization needs), possible concomitant self-disclosure needs of the individual's partner, the level of homophobia of the agency, and geographic factors, counselors and other helping professionals should be sensitive to—and nonjudgmental about—the client's need to avoid self-disclosure or, conversely, to come out early in an interview.

Other interview issues linked to sexual orientation are legal issues. It should be remembered during an interview that discrimination against workers on the basis of their sexual orientation is not outlawed in most places, as is discrimination based on race, color, religion, sex, national origin, or disability. There is no federal law that prohibits private employers from discriminating against employees on account of sexual orientation (Yates, 1994). In the public job arena, local, state, or federal departments and government agencies are mandated to provide "fair treatment of all individuals." Despite this general guideline of fair treatment to all individuals, there are still some government agencies that continue to discriminate against g/l/b persons (e.g., the military) (Hunter et al., 1992).

Some states and large cities have outlawed discrimination based on sexual orientation. Information about these states and cities that have legal protection against discrimination should be made available to g/l/b persons who are conducting a job search. Note, however, that it is difficult to document discrimination linked to sexual orientation, and that some forms of discrimination are so subtle that they may be difficult to observe (Hunter et al., 1992).

Career counselors or other helping professionals should help g/l/b persons become aware of g/l/b advocacy groups that can provide information about legal protection within some agencies. In addition, information about legal issues, as well as legal resources for discrimination, should be made available to g/l/b persons who are conducting a job search. Some legal rights and employment issues are covered in *The Rights of Lesbians and Gay Men: The Basic ACLU Guide to a Gay Person's Rights* (Hunter et al., 1992). The Lamba Legal Defense and Education Fund (see Appendix 3 for address) also provides information about legal employment issues.

Negotiating Guidelines

There is very little information available on negotiating for employment. Basic interpersonal skills, negotiation skills, the ability to manage stress, timing skills (i.e., the ability to make requests at the appropriate time in the job search), and communication skills are all factors that influence the willingness of the agency to meet the interviewee's demands. We have seen individuals who are skilled in these areas secure better job offers than others who are more qualified but lack one or more of the skills and abilities. Counselors and other professional helpers should use coaching, written materials, or role plays to enhance the negotiation abilities of g/l/b persons.

Transitioning Into the Job: Management of Homophobia in the Workplace

The job search process ends when an individual accepts a job offer, transitions out of the role of job applicant/interviewee, and enters into the role of worker. Some professional helpers may view the topic of transitioning into the role of worker as being separate from topics associated with the job search process. Because homophobic workplaces often stigmatize g/l/b persons, however, additional pressures may be placed on new g/l/b employees who are transitioning out of the job search. Although full treatment of this transitioning process is beyond the scope of this book, we describe here a few relevant studies that may be especially helpful to new employees who are coping with workplace stigma associated with sexual orientation.

Troiden (1989) and Humphreys (1972) discussed the ways in which gay males and lesbians respond in general to stigma associated with sexual orientation. Women and men who *capitulate* "avoid homosexual activity because they have internalized a stigmatized view of homosexuality" (Troiden, 1989, p. 61). *Minstrelization* refers to the actions of individuals who behave in stereotyped ways, along the lines etched out by the popular culture. *Passing* refers to the efforts to conceal sexual orientation to heterosexuals. *Group alignment* refers to active affiliation with the g/l/b communities. Applying Troiden's and Humphrey's coping strategies to g/l/b persons in homophobic work environments, individuals may respond to stigma through the rejection of gay/lesbian/bisexual identity or behaviors in the workplace, through the concealment of sexual orientation at work, or through greater affiliation with gay/lesbian/bisexual communities at work.

Croteau and Hedstrom (1993) also discussed the management of anti-gay stigma. They wrote that an *assimilation* or passing strategy (De Monteflores, 1986) may lead to a sense of self-betrayal in some g/l/b persons. The strategy of *confrontation* (De Monteflores, 1986) refers to the process of coming out. Confrontation may lead to a sense of "identity, acceptance, and affirmation in being gay" (Croteau & Hedstrom, 1993, p. 205). Croteau and Hedstrom wrote that a crucial factor in determining the success of particular strategies is the internal experience and perceptions of the g/l/b person. Thus there is the potential for a wide range of individual differences in how g/l/b persons respond to antigay stigma.

Personality Characteristics That Affect the Job Search

Self-Efficacy

Chapter 6 discussed self-efficacy (Bandura, 1977; Betz & Hackett, 1981, 1986; Hackett & Betz, 1981) as it influences the career decision-making process. Because self-efficacy relates to an individual's beliefs about his or her ability to take the actions required to meet a specific set of goals, self-efficacy is also likely to affect the job search. Low self-efficacy may result in poor interviewing and in poor job search strategies. It may thus reduce the number of job offers (Kanfer & Hulin, 1985; Stumpf, Brief, & Hartman, 1987).

Self-efficacy may also influence an individual's beliefs that he or she will be able to meet certain g/l/b-related needs. For example, because of low self-efficacy, a g/l/b individual may not feel that she or he will be able to ask questions effectively about domestic partner benefits during the job search. Thus addressing self-efficacy issues during the job search is crucial.

Self-efficacy linked to sexual orientation has not been explored. However, low self-efficacy linked to gender issues—and the modification of low self-efficacy—has been discussed by Hackett and Betz (1981). Further, Betz and Fitzgerald (1987) stated that female socialization "provides less access to the sources of information important to the development of strong expectations of efficacy with respect to career-related behaviors" (p. 116). These less accessible sources of information include "performance accomplishments, vicarious learning (modeling), and encouragement and support of achievement-related behaviors" (p. 116). Levels of self-efficacy for g/l/b persons may also be affected by reduced access to performance, learning, encouragement, and support of achievement-related behaviors. Thus counselors can help g/l/b persons enhance self-efficacy as it relates to sexual orientation by

- helping g/l/b persons actively pursue exploration of career options that challenge societal stereotypes,
- positively supporting, encouraging, and highlighting the strengths of g/l/b persons because their beliefs in their abilities may be diminished by homophobia and heterosexism,

- increasing g/l/b persons' exposure to g/l/b worker role models, thereby increasing vicarious learning,
- highlighting the positive value of diversity of sexual orientation in the workplace, and
- providing verbal encouragement of career pursuits that validate the positive aspects of sexual orientation in the workplace.

Assertiveness

Regardless of sexual orientation, assertiveness training benefits all individuals who are conducting a job search. For example, individuals who are passive during the job search may find that they cannot maintain the momentum and follow-through necessary to secure job offers that are good matches with their work personalities. In addition, because passive styles are often associated with low self-esteem, these individuals may not be able to describe clearly their vocational interests, skills, experiences, and strengths.

To illustrate:

Linda, a bisexual woman, had a quiet, reserved personality style. Although she was talented in her work, she was reluctant to apply for a supervisory position in her department. She stated that she would find it difficult to describe her strengths in an interview. (She felt that this would be "bragging.") She reported that in previous interviews she had answered each question as briefly as possible, without wishing to "embellish" her description of herself as a worker. Because she was relatively shy at work, her achievements were often unnoticed and her skills underestimated. She also lacked self-confidence because of her bisexuality. Counseling addressed her interview skills and self-esteem issues linked to her sexual orientation. Through learning to feel more confident about being assertive in a job interview, she was able to interview more effectively. She was eventually promoted to the supervisory position to which she had aspired. Her new skills in assertiveness also enabled her successfully to challenge her supervisees in productive, growth-enhancing ways. Although she decided to be selective in self-disclosing her sexual orientation at work, she did network with other bisexual workers in other agencies, and this strong professional support system further enhanced her self-confidence and assertiveness.

An aggressive communication style may also result in fewer job offers due to ineffective self-presentation. Aggressive communications are characterized by the intent to place one's own needs above the needs of others. When a speaker is aggressive, the listener does not feel that his or her needs or perspectives are being considered or respected. The intent of the speaker seems to be to dominate, rather than cooperate, and it becomes more difficult for the listener to avoid taking an aggressive stance. These intents and perceptions of aggressive interviewees may have a strong impact on the job interview.

Because of homophobia in the workplace, g/l/b persons may have a special need for assertiveness skills. Passive or aggressive individuals may find homophobia less effectively managed than do those individuals who are able to make assertive responses. However, other extenuating circumstances (e.g., safety needs) may make it necessary for individuals to adopt either an aggressive or passive style in responding to homophobia in the workplace. In general, during the job search, individuals who develop an assertive (rather than passive or aggressive) communication style are the most likely to conduct an effective interview. Client-centered resources are available that teach assertive communication skills (e.g., McKay, Davis, & Fanning, 1983).

Time Management Skills

Time management skills are especially crucial to conducting an effective job search. With poor time management, individuals may find it difficult to work steadily toward implementing their career goals and thus fulfill their career potentials. Procrastination and failure to address career needs can also result in high levels of stress.

Thus all individuals may benefit from assistance in prioritizing goals, developing realistic long-term and short-term action plans, reducing procrastination tendencies, and learning to anticipate future needs. Mancini (1994) offered a number of concrete strategies for the identification of time management strengths and weaknesses. Mancini also provided suggestions for the development of more effective time management strategies. These include dispelling myths about time management, assessing time management skills, understanding procrastination, prioritizing, creating more time through reducing "time wasters," learning to delegate, anticipating time management needs, developing assertiveness skills, and developing time management tools.

Sometimes time management is difficult because individuals have too many things to do or because they have assumed a number of life roles—such as partner, friend, worker—and are experiencing "role overload." Although most studies dealing with the management of role overload assume a heterosexual orientation, some coping methods described in these studies may be relevant to the role overload experienced by g/l/b persons. For example, in a discussion of role overload for married women, Epstein (1970a, 1970b) described a number of methods of coping with conflicting demands. The methods that may be relevant to g/l/b persons include

- eliminating social relationships that are negative or stressful,
- reducing the number of contacts in some social relationships (e.g., through socializing less with some individuals),
- reducing the number of obligations in a particular role (e.g., taking on fewer duties in one role),
- planning time so that some roles are emphasized at certain times more than other roles (most possible with individuals who have more flexible time schedules),
- compartmentalizing by scheduling so as to avoid role overlap (e.g., adopting a 9-to-5 schedule and avoiding evening activities in order to avoid role overlap),
- delegating tasks and roles (e.g., enlisting the help of the partner for household chores or hiring others to help out),
- increasing the visibility of role demands in order to reduce additional demands from others (e.g., through discussing more openly the demands of a particular role), and
- relying on rules or third parties for help in legitimizing role behaviors (e.g., referring to "outside work demands"—rules—to justify reduced participation in certain social activities).

Hall (1972a) summarized 16 coping strategies of women by categorizing them into three coping types: In Type I *structural role redefinition* strategies, roles were redefined in ways that distributed time and responsibility more equitably among family members. In Type II *personal role redefinition* strategies, the woman changed her own behavior and expectations. In Type III *reactive role behavior* strategies, the woman sought to meet all role demands and "please everyone." Hall (1972b) found that "satisfaction" was positively related to Type I strategies but negatively related to Type III strategies.

Gray (1980) found that career satisfaction was positively associated with the delegation of household tasks, the reduction of standards for certain roles, and consideration of personal interests as important. Gray (1979) also found negative relationships between satisfaction and overlapping roles, keeping roles separate, trying to meet all expectations, eliminating roles, and the lack of strategies for dealing with role conflict.

Although none of these studies focused on role overload as experienced by g/l/b persons, coping strategies may be adapted to the needs of these individuals. However, same-gender couples may have some unique gender role dynamics. For example, because of male socialization (such as the stereotype that men should be breadwinners), one or both men may find it difficult to assume responsibilities for household chores (Carl, 1990).

To illustrate:

Lee and Marty both disliked cleaning their large home, so they hired someone to do the majority of cleaning. Although they generally liked to work together, they disliked household tasks so much that they decided to delegate some of the remaining chores to each other. By delegating tasks, both would not have to do every job. Because Lee enjoyed yard chores more than Marty, he assumed those jobs and Marty took over the laundry. Marty did not mind doing laundry as much as Lee did because he could do it while watching television.

Thus the nature of the specific type of role overload as experienced by g/l/b couples may, at times, differ from the type of role overload experienced by heterosexual couples. In addition, because of homophobia, couples who could serve as role models to help g/l/b persons develop effective strategies for dealing with role overload may not be out or as highly visible as heterosexual couple role models.

Stress Management Skills

Stress management skills are needed, in part, because of homophobia and heterosexism in the workplace. In managing stress, it is helpful to consider two types of anxiety that may be experienced. *Debilitative anxiety* is the type of anxiety that is so strong that it "freezes" the individual and makes that person unable to function effectively in career and life planning. In contrast, *facilitative anxiety* tends to motivate individuals to move ahead in the career and life planning processes.

If stressors associated with homophobia create a high level of debilitative rather than facilitative anxiety, personal counseling or career counseling may be helpful in providing support to the g/l/b person who is dealing with the effect of homophobia or heterosexism in the workplace. It is also helpful for g/l/b persons to have role models of other g/l/b persons who are effectively managing either of these two types of anxiety.

Self-help resources for stress management are available (e.g., McKay, Davis, & Eshelman, 1995). Resources about workplace stress for professional helpers include *Job Stress in a Changing Workforce: Investigating Gender, Diversity, and Family Issues* (Keita & Hurrell, 1994), which focuses on the ways job stresses can affect individual workers, and *Controlling Work Stress* (Matteson & Ivancevich, 1987), which focuses on management of human resources. In addition, many organizational groups, some of which are listed in Appendix 3, provide suggestions for dealing with stress resulting from workplace homophobia.

Because the job search process is both stressful and time consuming, counselors and other professional helpers should encourage g/l/b persons to develop professional support systems during the job search process. These support systems, which may take the form of mentors or career coaches, serve to keep individuals motivated to implement their career plans. Mentors and career coaches can also help individuals deal with the homophobia and heterosexism that they will encounter during the job search process.

8

A Comprehensive Model of Career and Life Planning for Gay, Lesbian, and Bisexual Persons

A growing movement sees sexual orientation within the definition of *multiculturalism* (Fassinger, 1991; Pope, 1995). Thus multicultural career counseling includes consideration of sexual orientation along with race, gender, physical attributes, age, and ethnicity (Gelberg, Foldesi et al., 1993). Because an estimated 5 to 25 million g/l/b persons live in the United States (Henderson, 1984; Kinsey et al., 1948; Kinsey et al., 1953; Michael et al., 1994), the g/l/b community constitutes a significant part of the population.

This chapter integrates the material presented in this book into a comprehensive model for conceptualizing career and life planning factors and processes as they pertain to g/l/b persons. The model emphasizes the use of developmental career counseling principles (e.g., Super, 1980, 1983; Vondracek et al., 1986) and person-environment theories (e.g., Moos, 1987; Osipow, 1987a; Rounds & Tracey, 1990; Walsh, 1987). The model also incorporates principles from adult life-span development (e.g., Chickering, 1968; Chickering & Reisser, 1993; Erikson, 1968; Jepsen, 1984, 1990; Levinson, 1986; Levinson et al., 1978; Thomas & Chickering, 1984) and theories of gay/lesbian/bisexual identity development (e.g., Cass, 1979, 1984a, 1984b; Klein, 1993; Sophie, 1986; Zinik, 1985). In addition, principles are drawn from person-centered career counseling (e.g., Bozarth & Fisher, 1990) and person-centered counseling (e.g., Rogers, 1959), psychodynamic counseling (e.g., Watkins & Savickas, 1990), social learning theories (e.g., Krumboltz & Nichols, 1990), social psychological perspectives (e.g., Dorn, 1990), and computerized career counseling (e.g., Rayman, 1990).

This chapter first briefly describes and illustrates the basic components and principles of our model and how they are used: person factors, environment factors, career decision-making steps, person-environment interactions, and career counseling as a type of person-environment interaction. The chapter then concludes with a discussion and graphic presentation of the complete model.

Basic Components and Principles

Person Factors

The vocational personality of the individual should be assessed when helping clients make career decisions (Betz, 1992). This includes evaluation of the person's vocational interests, values, experiences, and skills (e.g., Holland, 1992). Chapter 3 and Appendix 1 suggest a number of factors to consider in gathering information about g/l/b persons' vocational work personalities and other person variables.

The client's overall psychosocial development should also be assessed. This includes consideration of the full range of the individual's thoughts, feelings, and behaviors. Helpful in the assessment of psychosocial development are theories of adult psychological development (e.g., Chickering, 1969; Chickering & Reisser, 1993; Fassinger & Schlossberg, 1992; Gilligan, 1982; Gottfredson, 1981; Levinson, 1986; Levinson et al., 1978), gay/lesbian/bisexual identity development (e.g., Cass, 1979, 1984a, 1984b; Chapman & Brannock, 1987; Coleman, 1985; D'Augelli, 1991; Faderman, 1984; Hetrick & Martin, 1987; Levine & Evans, 1991; Minton & McDonald, 1984; Myers et al., 1991; Sang, 1989; Sophie, 1986; Troiden, 1989; Wall & Evans, 1991; Zinik, 1985), adult career development (e.g., Jepsen, 1984, 1990; Super, 1980, 1983, 1992; Vondracek et al., 1986), and gay/lesbian/bisexual career development (e.g., Chojnacki & Gelberg, 1994; Croteau & Hedstrom, 1993; Elliott, 1990, 1993; Hetherington, 1991; Hetherington et al., 1989; Hetherington & Orzek 1989; Klein, 1993; Orzek, 1992; Schmitz, 1988).

In addition to the consideration of person factors such as vocational interests, values, experiences and skills, assessment should include consideration of double/triple minority status (e.g., Caballo-Diéguez, 1989; Chan, 1989; Loiacano, 1989; Wall & Washington, 1991), type of sexual orientation (e.g., Fox, 1991; Golden, 1987; Pope & Reynolds, 1991), social support/relationships (e.g., McCandlish, 1985), physical well-being (e.g., Bradford et al., 1994), employment status, financial and educational history, psychosocial history, spirituality (e.g., Boyd & Wilson, 1991; Brooke, 1993; Nelson, 1985), age (e.g., Browning, 1987; Kehoe, 1986a, 1986b; Kimmel, 1978), gender (e.g., Betz, 1989; Fassinger, 1994; Gilligan, 1982; Kaschek, 1992), and current life situation. Assessment of clients' cognitive development should include an evaluation of career maturity (e.g., Savickas, 1984) and self-efficacy (e.g., Bandura, 1977; Betz & Hackett, 1981). Chapter 4 and Appendix 1 focus on the assessment of these factors. Figure 1 summarizes person assessment factors relevant to career and life planning with g/l/b persons.

To illustrate the impact that a person characteristic—in this case double minority status—can have:

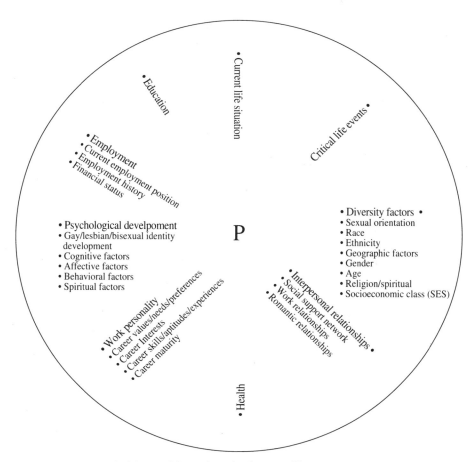

Figure 1. The gay, lesbian, or bisexual worker/person (P)

*José, a Mexican American, faces issues associated with a double mi-
nority status. As a Latino, he wants a work environment that has
close interpersonal relationships and feels like a family environment.
Thus his cultural background has shaped his expectations of his work
environment. His coworkers view him as unprofessional and are uncomfortable around him because of his need to know something about
his coworkers before he can work effectively around them. Because he
is gay, he has been kept out of high-exposure positions due to a fear
that exposure to the public will lead to negative attitudes from the
public. José's double minority status makes it more difficult for him
to have a sense of community. He finds some Latinos homophobic,
and finds that some g/l/b persons fail to understand or value his
Latino background. Because of these double minority status issues, he
finds it difficult to advance in his position, to develop positive work
relationships, and to focus on his job duties.*

Environment Factors

Person-environment theories (e.g., Dawis & Lofquist, 1984; Holland, 1992; Rounds & Tracey, 1990; Spokane, 1987) suggest a number of factors relevant to the assessment of environmental factors. In conducting an assessment, the workplace environment should be evaluated. Additionally, environments beyond the workplace, such as the local community environment and the national environment, need to be considered.

Agency, local, and national work environment factors are summarized in Figure 2, and some should be assessed in all three environments. For example, finances should be assessed as they relate to organizational finances, city or state finances, and national finances.

In assessing organizational work environments, it is important to examine factors that include the degree of organizational affirmation of diversity, work opportunities available within the organization, organizational

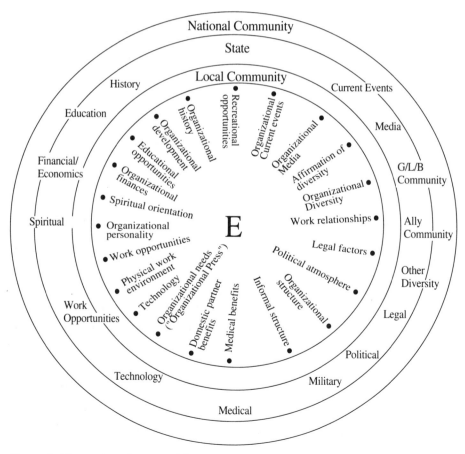

Figure 2. The work environment (E)

needs ("organizational press"), formal and informal policies regarding diversity, the organizational hierarchical structure, the physical work environment, the level/type of technology, status of organizational finances, the political atmosphere of the organization, types of benefits that are available (e.g., educational opportunities and medical benefits), organizational development factors (e.g., training in diversity), the history of the organization as it relates to diversity issues, the spiritual orientation of the organization (e.g., pastoral agencies), and the characteristics of the administrators, supervisors, and coworkers of the agency. A number of resources provide guidelines and information helpful in evaluating specific organizations (e.g., Baker et al., 1995; Bolman & Deal, 1991; Furnham & Gunter, 1993; Gerstein & Shullman, 1992; McNaught, 1993; Mickens, 1994).

In assessing community and national environmental factors, it is important to consider the presence of other g/l/b persons (gay/lesbian/bisexual community); the strength of the ally community; other types of diversity within the community; the spiritual characteristics of the community; community educational opportunities; the history of the community, state, and nation; local, state, and national current events that relate to diversity; the influence of the local and national media; political factors; legal issues; economic variables; financial factors; the level of technology available in the community; and the type of work opportunities available within the community (Bolman & Deal, 1991). Note that there are some local and national environment factors that parallel agency factors.

To illustrate the impact that an organizational characteristic—in this case the personal backgrounds of administrators—can have:

> *Maria joined an advertising agency that was very affirmative of sexual orientation, but her friend Barry worked in an organization that was very homophobic. Although the directors of both agencies had relatives who were gay, Maria's director had a very poor relationship with his brother while Barry's director had a strong, positive relationship with his cousin. Thus the personal histories of the two administrators influenced the level of organizational affirmation to diversity, the formal and informal policies relating to diversity, and even organizational programming. For example, Barry's agency had a strong organizational development emphasis on diversity, and his agency sponsored training sessions devoted to understanding and valuing diversity. In contrast, this topic was consistently ignored by Maria's agency. Thus the agencies differed in their approaches to diversity because of the personal background characteristics of each agency's administrator.*

Career Decision-Making Steps

Career decision-making research and literature on career choice (e.g., Etringer et al., 1990; Gati, 1986; Gati et al., 1995; Gati & Tikotzki, 1989;

Gottfredson, 1981; Krumboltz & Hamel, 1977; Phillips, 1992; Tiedeman, 1961; Tiedeman & O'Hara, 1963) are considered in applying career decision-making principles to career counseling with g/l/b clients. In chapter 6 the focus is on adapting career decision-making principles to help clients set long-term and short-term career goals. The six decision-making steps described in that chapter are as follows:

1. Help clients explore their work-related interests, values, experiences, and skills.
2. Help clients better understand the world of work and their career or educational options.
3. Help clients develop their decision-making skills.
4. Help clients learn how stereotyping, bias, and discrimination may limit their career choices, opportunities, and achievement.
5. Help clients develop a long- and short-term career plan.
6. Help clients develop their employability skills.

Decision-making is influenced by gay/lesbian/bisexual identity development. That is, clients at different developmental levels may make different decisions, depending on their stage in coming out as gay, lesbian, or bisexual.

To illustrate the impact of identity development on career decision making:

John is out professionally and personally. He wants to become a teacher, and he feels strongly about being out in his job, whatever the position. He has heard that gay men have commonly experienced homophobia when they work in the field of secondary education; however, he is firm about working in the field and about being out professionally. In contrast, Lyle has only recently come out to a few close personal friends. Although he, too, wants to be a teacher, he is unwilling to enter that field because he has heard that it is difficult for gay men to be accepted in the field of elementary education. John and Lyle are at very different stages in the process of coming out, and that has influenced their willingness to enter a homophobic environment and realize their top job priorities (especially as they relate to their feelings about self-disclosure of sexual orientation). Thus their decision making will differ for each career decision-making step.

Person-Environment Interactions

In order to facilitate career and life planning, it is important not only to understand the characteristics of people and their work environments but also to focus on the nature of the interactions between people and their environments.

When workers interact with their work environments (and thus have person-environment interactions), there are certain outcomes for the worker: job satisfaction, productivity, stability, performance, and motivation. When the interaction is poor, burnout, stress, or absenteeism may result, in addition to other psychological and social difficulties (Hackett & Lent, 1992).

Person-environment interactions also create outcomes for the work environment (Bolman & Deal, 1991). Possible organizational outcomes include changes in the organization's structure (e.g., new positions added), changes in administrators or coworkers (e.g., an administrator whose behaviors or values change because of being in contact with g/l/b workers), changes in current events, new educational opportunities, or changes in the financial or economic situation of an organization. In addition, there may be changes in the physical work environment, level of technology available, organizational needs, and organizational culture. Finally, the level of organizational affirmation of sexual orientation may change.

Thus, as Figure 3 indicates, people affect their work environments, and work environments are affected by people. Figure 4 lists major person and environment variables that are affected by the person-environment interactions.

To illustrate interactions between people and their environments:

> *Judy was a student in a small Southern community college. Because there was no gay/lesbian/bisexual student organization, she organized one. She eventually became president of the organization and developed leadership skills as the result of that experience. Because of her positive relationships with many staff members, the college began to include sexual orientation in its diversity programming. She began to develop interests in administration because of her success at this institution. Judy's career goals changed, and her resumé also changed through the addition of leadership qualities as well as gay/lesbian/bisexual programming activities.*
>
> *Had Judy gone to an institution in a different geographical region, or to an institution initially more affirmative, she might not have entered into a leadership role. Thus the institutional characteristics shaped her behaviors, goals, and experiences, and the college was also affected by this individual.*

Future career development and career behaviors are the result of continuous interactions between people and their work environments. That is, a person's feelings about his or her work environment will probably have an impact on future career decisions and behaviors. For example, an individual who is feeling valued by a particular organization may decide to stay

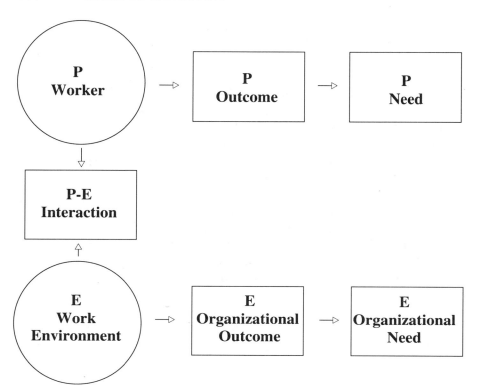

Figure 3. Person-environment (PE) interaction

within that agency, but another person who feels less valued may opt to leave that agency or may change work behaviors while in that agency (e.g., becoming less motivated at work).

Similarly, future decisions made by the agency are influenced by current worker relationships. For example, an agency that develops a positive relationship with a single worker who is gay, lesbian, or bisexual may feel more positive about hiring others who are gay, lesbian, or bisexual.

To illustrate how an individual worker can affect future organizational interactions and behaviors:

> *Jerry, who was out both professionally and personally, had joined a consulting firm that seemed to be negative toward him from the beginning of his employment. He was surprised by the agency's negative response toward him because in his previous jobs he had enjoyed the respect and warmth of his colleagues. Some time after he had started work at that consulting firm, a colleague told him in confidence that several years previously, Andy, a gay male, had joined the firm. Jerry was told that Andy had been dismissed from that particular consulting firm because of his negative interpersonal behaviors*

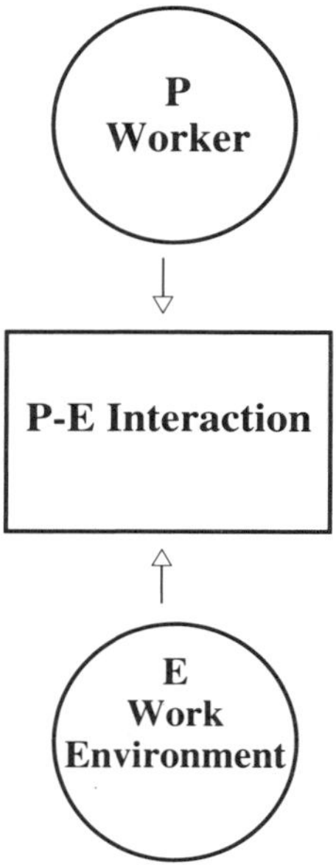

Outcome for Worker

Affects level of worker:
  • **Job satisfaction**
  • **Job performance**
  • **Job stability**
  • **Job motivation**

Affects degree of worker:
  • **Burnout**
  • **Stress**
  • **Absenteeism**

**Has psychological and social impacts
      on worker**
**Affects current career and life planning
      needs of worker**
**Has an impact on future career
      decisions made by worker**

Outcome for Work Environment

Affects future decisions about worker
Possible organizational impacts on:
  • **Formal ogranizational structure**
  • **Informal organizational structure**
  • **Administrators**
  • **Coworkers**
  • **Organizational history**
  • **Organizational current events**
  • **Organizational politics**
  • **Organizational educational opportunities**
  • **Organizational finances**
  • **Physical work environment**
  • **Technology**
  • **Organizational needs ("press")**
  • **Organizational culture**
  • **Future organizational hiring practices**
  • **Affirmation of diversity**

**P
Worker**

P-E Interaction

**E
Work
Environment**

Figure 4. Outcomes of person-environment interactions

(e.g., he was viewed as being inflexible, dogmatic, and domineering). Andy's dismissal was because of these interpersonal work behaviors, rather than because he was gay. Nonetheless, when Jerry joined the firm as a consultant who was out, the organizational history with Andy made it more difficult for the organization to welcome Jerry. Had Jerry's colleague not told him of the organizational history, he might have remained confused about the reason behind the firm's initial failure to welcome him into the organization. This illustrates the fact that an organization's history, one aspect of the work environment, can influence workers in subtle ways. Although he was frustrated to hear of the reason behind the cold responses he received from the agency, the information he was given helped him avoid person-

alizing the problem. With time, the agency was able to see that he was different from the previous employee, with a very different set of interpersonal behaviors.

Person-environment interactions continue throughout the worker's career and the organizational history. To illustrate how both people and their work environments affect each other across time:

Dan worked in an agency that did not resolve conflict well. When he entered the organization, there was a great deal of backstabbing, passiveness, aggression, and agitation. The workers found it difficult to do their jobs because they were overwhelmed by the poor interpersonal relationships at work. The agency was in disarray. Financial resources began to dwindle. Because Dan had good conflict management skills, he was able to take on a leadership role and help the agency develop healthier ways to deal with the conflicts that came with scarce organizational resources. As people began to work more effectively, they were able to develop better programming and eventually secured additional funding due to the quality of their work. With additional funding came new programming, and new staff members were hired. Within several years, the agency had become known for the quality of its programs and for the healthy way in which the agency solved conflict. In turn, Dan was promoted to a higher administrative position. Thus the agency was affected by Dan, and Dan by the agency. Had he not entered that institution at that particular time, both the organizational history and Dan's professional history would have evolved in quite different ways.

Career Counseling: A Type of Person-Environment Interaction

In providing career and life planning services for g/l/b persons, counselors and other professional helpers should consider the quality of the interaction between the client and the professional helper/helping agency. The personal qualities of both the professional helper and the helping environment's level of affirmation may impact the career decisions made by g/l/b clients. Thus during the career counseling interaction, the client may be viewed as the person and the professional helper and helping agency viewed as the environment.

Such factors as the professional helper's personal background characteristics, development as g/l/b-affirmative, and knowledge of gay/lesbian/ bisexual culture influence the helper-client interactions. In chapter 2, the General Counseling Issues and Considerations section focuses on some of these personal qualities of the professional helper. Similarly, the qualities and behaviors of helping agencies influence helper-client interactions.

Chapter 2's The Need for Affirmative Symbols section suggests a number of ways to communicate a positive regard for career issues linked to sexual orientation. In addition, the appendixes list a number of resources that enhance organizational services and programs.

We were sent an anonymous documentation of homophobic practices in an institution, with the comment that these institutional practices were ". . .a major reason we gay psychotherapists discourage the use of straight counselors. We can't tell the 'straight, but not narrow' people from the fanatics." The concerns that gay, lesbian, and bisexual persons have about working with heterosexual counselors and other professional helpers stem from repeated experiences with personal, agency, or societal heterosexism and homophobia (Herek, 1989, 1993).

The results of research on the role of the helping professional's sexual orientation in working with g/l/b clients are mixed (Rochlin, 1985). There does not seem to be universal preference among g/l/b persons. That is, some gay men and lesbians tend to prefer gay or lesbian counselors or other professional helpers, but other gay men and lesbians do not have a preference (e.g., McDermott, Tyndall, & Lichtenberg, 1989). Some of the issues about the sexual orientation of the helper may be linked to concerns about the degree of homophobia in heterosexuals (Obear, 1991). In addition, there is a strong concern about heterosexist biases in some counseling therapies (Garnets et al., 1991).

Whatever the sexual orientation of the professional helper, certain ethical issues should be addressed (Anthony, 1985). These include an awareness of the professional helper's level of internalized homophobia (Obear, 1991), knowledge of g/l/b culture, awareness of occupational stereotyping that g/l/b persons face (Botkin & Day, 1987), management of confidentiality and privilege issues about self-disclosure, avoidance of dual relationships, and maintenance of healthy boundaries between the professional helper and the client (Dworkin, 1992).

Some developmental theories predict differing responses to heterosexuals, depending on the stage of gay/lesbian/bisexual identity development (Cass, 1979, 1984a, 1984b). During some stages of coming out, g/l/b persons may benefit from interactions with g/l/b persons, but at other stages, exposure to heterosexual allies may be beneficial. It is important to have diversity in professional helpers' sexual orientations in order to accommodate these differing needs (Chojnacki & Gelberg, 1995).

The concept of *heterophobia* is also relevant to understanding the nature of some interactions between g/l/b persons and professional helpers. *Heterophobia* refers to the concerns that g/l/b persons have about interacting with heterosexuals (Triplet & Busher, 1994). Heterophobia is an inevitable consequence of homophobic societal teachings and values, just as concerns about racism are the natural consequences of experiences with racist attitudes. Counselors and other professional helpers should expect g/l/b clients to have varying degrees of heterophobia based on their previous experiences with heterosexism and homophobia.

A number of resources are available to sensitize helpers to these issues (Buhrke & Douce, 1991; Holahan & Gibson, 1994; Rudolph, 1988, 1989; Sobocinski, 1990). In addition, Appendix 4 presents a model of ally professional development. In order to provide career counseling that is not itself homophobic or heterosexist, counselors and other professional helpers are responsible for educating themselves about these issues when working with gay, lesbian, and bisexual persons.

Career and Life Planning With Gay, Lesbian, and Bisexual Persons: The Model

Our conceptual model for career and life planning with g/l/b persons integrates principles from g/l/b identity development, career development, and adult life-span development. Two specific approaches, developmental career counseling and person-environment career counseling, are highlighted.

Figure 5 illustrates the model and summarizes the complex factors and processes involved in career counseling with g/l/b persons. (The specific locations of these career and life planning factors in the figure are indicated by the numbers in parentheses in the text that follows.)

A client who seeks career counseling has a diverse set of vocational values, experiences, and skills. In addition, the client has a unique personality and personal history, which often includes homophobic experiences. Both vocational and psychological characteristics should be fully assessed (1).

A client who seeks career counseling is usually already in a particular work/educational situation, such as an educational institution or work environment, which also has a set of complex characteristics. These environment factors should be fully evaluated in order to help the client make optimal career decisions (2). In addition, the quality of the interaction between the client and the work/educational environment should be assessed (3).

Because of the current interactions between the client and the client's environment (3), the client develops a career and life planning need (4). For example, if the interactions have been positive, the client may have the need for a promotion. If the interactions have been negative, the client may wish to change jobs or choose a new educational field. This career and life planning need is the reason the client has sought career counseling.

After the assessment of the person (1), the environment (2), the person-environment interaction (3), and the client's current career needs

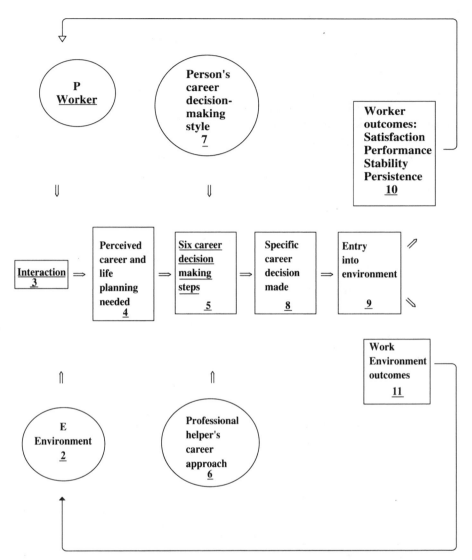

Figure 5. The model: Career and life planning with gay, lesbian, and bisexual persons

(4), clients are encouraged by the helping professional to proceed through one or more of six career decision-making steps (5), which begin with self-assessment and end with the development of career objectives and action plans.

In interacting with helping professionals during career decision-making, the quality of the client-helper interactions is critical. It is important for clients to be served by fully informed professionals who are educated about career issues linked to sexual orientation and who value sexual orientation as another type of diversity. Another factor that affects career decision making is the client's particular career decision-making style (7). The helper-client interactions are thus impacted both by the helping professional's career approaches (6) and by the personality of the client. At the end of career decision making, a specific career decision has been made (8), and the client enters the work environment (9). For some clients, this may be the previous work or educational environment, and for others, it may be a new job or educational environment.

The client then experiences a set of professional and personal outcomes (10). The organization is also influenced by the worker's professional behaviors (11—see also Outcome for Work Environment in Figure 4). Thus there is a person-environment interaction that leads to specific outcomes for both the worker and the work environment. Based on these personal and agency outcomes, the g/l/b person experiences reinforced or changed vocational interests, values, experiences, and skills (1). The client once again interacts with the work/educational environment (2 and 3), and new career needs may be experienced (4). The process thus begins once again. Similarly, future organizational decisions and behaviors are, in part, based on previous organizational outcomes that resulted from historical person-environment interactions.

This model of career counseling (Figure 5) integrates concepts presented in some of the previous figures. For example, the variables depicted in Figure 1, The Gay, Lesbian, or Bisexual Worker/Person, may be conceptualized as lying within the P/Worker section of Figures 3, 4, and 5. Similarly, the factors listed in Figure 2, The Work Environment (E), may be conceptualized as lying within the E/Environment section of Figures 3, 4, and 5. Some of the Outcome for Worker factors listed in Figure 4 appear in Figure 5 (10). Outcome for Work Environment factors as described in Figure 4 are omitted in Figure 5 (11) in order to simplify the model.

Our model takes into account the vocational personality of the individual. It emphasizes assessment of the whole person in its inclusion of sexual identity and adult life-span development characteristics. The model is interactional in that it emphasizes the continuous interactions between people and their work environments. In addition, it emphasizes the quality of interactions between clients and their professional helpers.

The model seeks to be comprehensive in that it stresses the full assessment of the work environment, local community, and national community. Thus it includes a full assessment of the individual but moves beyond by considering a number of environments (organization, community, state, and nation).

The model seeks to integrate a number of principles from gay/lesbian/bisexual identity development, gay/lesbian/bisexual career development, adult life-span development, and adult career development. The utility of the model lies less in the creation of new principles and more in its ability to integrate a number of fields that typically do not cross-pollinate. We believe that to omit consideration of any of the factors of adult development, career development, gay/lesbian/bisexual development, and person-environment match results in career and life counseling that lacks both depth and scope.

We hope that this model provides a practical, applied framework for working with gay, lesbian, and bisexual persons. We acknowledge that the overall model needs empirical validation. Many of the model's assumptions are based on empirical data. Where few empirical data exist, we have sought to do a comprehensive literature review of nonempirical writings. Although we acknowledge the lack of research in the field of gay/lesbian/bisexual career counseling, we hope that this model stimulates future research on its components. In addition, we enthusiastically endorse the comments made by Prince in *Career Development of Gay Men: Implications for Research* (1994) that are also relevant to the career and life planning needs of lesbians and bisexual persons:

> It is. . .important that as practitioners we do not wait for empirical studies to guide our initial interventions in this area. In fact, creative and sensitive interventions can often stimulate research interests. Promoting gay-friendly career settings and offering specific group interventions to gay men can provide immediate relief to the homophobia and isolation that interfere with the career development of so many men. Such exciting research possibilities abound in this area. My hope is that the energy of the "Gay 90's" that has captured the attention of the country's press and politics will also finally capture the attention of our peers working in the career development arena. (pp. 5-6)

Epilogue

We have found career counseling with gay, lesbian, and bisexual persons to be rewarding and challenging as we sought to become more proficient at addressing career and life planning issues with this population. With greater experience, we find that we continue to grow in this area, and we view our own professional and personal development in these areas as being a lifelong process.

We hope that this book enables others to enter the field with a greater awareness of the joys and struggles of gay, lesbian, and bisexual persons as they seek to integrate sexual orientation into career and life planning. As more individuals enter the field, either as gay, lesbian, and bisexual helping professionals or as allies who are helping professionals, there will come a stronger support network, more effective services, and better programming for gay, lesbian, and bisexual persons.

There is good news and bad news about career and life planning with gay, lesbian, and bisexual persons. Because of the stigma still associated with sexual orientation, this is not an easy field to enter. Homophobia and heterosexism still exist in the career counseling area and in the world of work. That is the bad news. The good news is that because of these deficits, there are wonderful opportunities to make important contributions for a much underserved population. Whatever one's professional identity—career counselor, adviser, student affairs administrator, therapist, psychologist, educator, employer, or employee—a wealth of opportunities exist in a number of areas, whether they be in service delivery, training, or theory development/research.

Gay, lesbian, and bisexual persons benefit greatly from the work of both the gay, lesbian, and bisexual community as well as from heterosexuals who join in addressing heterosexism and homophobia. Regardless of the helper's professional identity or sexual orientation, there are contributions to be made.

There is exciting work to be done. We hope that this resource gives you a head start on this important professional and personal journey.

APPENDIX 1:

Sample Career Counseling Form for Counselors

The sample form in this appendix offers practical suggestions for applying information contained in this book and should be used in conjunction with the material presented in chapters 1 through 8.

Our intent is to enable helping professionals to translate theories into practical discussion questions or interventions more effectively. Counselors and other professional helpers could use the form as the basis for a semi-structured interview in their work with gay, lesbian, or bisexual persons. Or the form might serve as a framework for reflecting upon the information gathered about the g/l/b career client. We have left spaces for entering material so that the form could also be incorporated into a client's records.

Initial Discussion of Confidentiality Issues

Notes regarding confidentiality parameters which were discussed and agreed upon (including issues of confidentiality of both intake discussion and written assessment): _____

_____

Demographics

Name: _____   Telephone: ___(Work/home)

Address: _____(Work/home)

E-mail: _____

Fax: _____

Employment status: __ Currently employed __ Unemployed __ Student __ Other

    Notes: _____

    Resúmé submitted: ____Yes ____No

Age: _____   ____Female ____Male

    Notes: _____

Marital status: ___Single ___Domestic Partner ___Married ___Divorced

    Notes: _____

Life roles (circle: worker, student, partner/spouse, parent, son/daughter, community worker, religious roles, friend, other _____):

    Notes: _____

Dual career issues: _____

Nationality: ___Hispanic

           ___Latino, Latina

           ___Caucasian

           ___Asian American/Pacific Islander

           ___African American

           ___Native American

           ___Other

    Notes: _____

Health/physical attributes relevant to career and life planning: _____

    Notes: _____

Religious issues relevant to career and life planning: _____

    Notes: _____

Double/triple minority status: _____

Person's perception of influence of diversity on career and life planning (e.g., race, cultural background, gender, sexual orientation, physical characteristics, age, socioeconomic class):

Notes: _____

_____

Gay/Lesbian/Bisexual Occupational Stereotyping

Does the person feel that there are certain occupations which are characterized as either "heterosexual" or "gay"? If so, what are those fields, and how does the person feel about those stereotypes?

Notes: _____

_____

Career Concerns

Presenting concern: _____

_____

Career Decision-Making Steps Relevant to Career Needs

_____**Self-assessment**—Person wishes to learn more about her or his unique interests, values, experiences, and skills: _____

_____

_____**Generation of career options**—Person needs to learn about what educational majors or careers would made good use of his or her interests, values, experiences, and skills: _____

_____

_____**Provision of information**—Person would like to find information about specific careers or educational majors: _____

_____

_____**Decision making**—Person wishes to make a tentative decision about a particular major or career: _____

_____

_____**Action planning**—Person seeks to develop a plan to implement educational and career goals: _____

_____

_____**Job search training**—Person wants to improve his or her job search skills (e.g., resúmé writing, interviewing skills): _____

_____

Educational Background

_____High school: _____Attended _____Completed Date: _____

_____College: _____Attended _____Completed
      Dates: _____Degree: _____Major field of study: _____

_____Master's degree
      Dates: _____Degree: _____Major field of study: _____

_____Doctoral degree
      Dates: _____Degree: _____Major field of study: _____

_____Other training: _____
Educational interests: _____
Educational skills: _____
Educational fields which are NOT main interests: _____
Weak areas or fields (vs. strengths): _____

Career History

Vocational Interests, Values, Experiences, and Skills

1. Current employment:
      Title and agency: _____
      Job tasks: _____
      Skills/strengths: _____
      Challenges/growth areas: _____
      Perceived match of job with person's interests, values, experiences, and
          skills: _____
      _____

2. Previous employment:
      Title and agency: _____
      Job tasks: _____
      Skills/strengths: _____
      Challenges/growth areas: _____
      Perceived match of job with person's interests, values, experiences, and
          skills: _____
      _____

3. Previous employment:
      Title and agency: _____
      Job tasks: _____
      Skills/strengths: _____
      Challenges/growth areas: _____
      Perceived match of job with person's interests, values, experiences, and
          skills: _____
      _____

4. Other: _____
_____

Person-Environment Fit

Current work agency: _____
Description of agency (e.g., organizational structure, politics, quality of work environment conditions, organizational culture): _____
_____

Level of homophobia of agency:

Officially	**Unofficially**
____Openly discriminatory	____Openly discriminatory
____No discrimination policy	____Discriminatory
____Nondiscrimination policy	____Discriminatory
____Nondiscrimination policy	____Nondiscriminatory
____G/l/b-affirmative policy	____G/l/b-affirmative practices

Community factors (e.g., city, county, state, region, nation): _____
_____

Degree of person-environment match: _____
_____

Previous agencies:
1. Agency: _____
        Description of agency (e.g., organizational structure, politics, quality of work environment conditions, organizational culture): _____
        _____

        Community factors (e.g., city, county, state, region, nation): _____
        _____

        Level of homophobia of agency: _____
        Degree of person-environment match: _____
        _____

2. Agency: _____
        Description of agency (e.g., organizational structure, politics, quality of work environment conditions, organizational culture): _____
        _____

        Community factors (e.g., city, county, state, region, nation): _____
        _____

        Level of homophobia of agency: _____
        Degree of person-environment match: _____
        _____

Formalized Assessment

Career Assessment Inventories:

- Self-Directed Search: _____

   _____

- Strong Interest Inventory: _____

   _____

- Myers-Briggs Type Inventory Career Report: _____

   _____

- DISCOVER or SIGI-PLUS: _____

   _____

- Gay/lesbian/bisexual identity questionnaires: _____
- Other inventories: _____

   _____

Summary: Vocational Personality

Vocational interests, values, experiences, and skills: _____

_____

_____

_____

_____

Attitude toward work: _____

Work habits and attitudes relevant to career and life planning (circle if issue is relevant to career and life planning): career maturity; self-esteem as a worker who is g/l/b; self-efficacy; stress management skills; time management skills: _____

_____

_____

Personal History

Positive and Negative Life Milestones

Positive and negative life milestones (circle): first job; significant achievements; beginning or ending of romantic relationship; graduation; loss of job; development of support systems; coming out; births; deaths; financial hardships; divorce; experiences with homophobia; illnesses; chemical abuse—self or family; major trauma; other _____:

   Notes: _____

   _____

Impact of milestones on person as a person and worker: _____

Notes: _____

_____

Timeline of milestones: Summary of milestones and age of occurrence:

_____

Past   Present   Future

Developmental Transitions

Times when person felt "anchorless," in a state of transition, or in a state of uncertainty about life or work: _____

How the situation or feelings were resolved: _____

_____

Possible unmet career and life planning factors that may have been linked to transition period: _____

_____

Sexual Orientation

Person's self-description of her or his sexual orientation: _____

_____

Use of the Klein Sexual Orientation Grid (Klein et al., 1985) and the Kinsey Scale (Kinsey et al., 1948) to consider the person's sexual orientation for the seven factors listed below:

	1	2	3	4	5	6	7
Sexual Attraction	___	___	___	___	___	___	___
Sexual Behavior	___	___	___	___	___	___	___
Sexual Fantasies	___	___	___	___	___	___	___
Emotional Preference	___	___	___	___	___	___	___
Social Preference	___	___	___	___	___	___	___
Self-Identification	___	___	___	___	___	___	___
Straight/Gay Lifestyle	___	___	___	___	___	___	___

Code: For the seven variables, use the Kinsey Scale to reflect the continuous (vs. dichotomous) nature of each of these aspects of sexual orientation:

1	2	3	4	5	6	7
Other sex only	Other sex mostly	Other sexes somewhat	Both sexes equally	Same sex somewhat	Same sex mostly	Same sex only

1	2	3	4	5	6	7
Hetero-sexual only	Hetero-sexual mostly	Hetero-sexual somewhat more	Hetero-sexual gay equally	Gay somewhat more	Gay mostly	Gay only

Gay/Lesbian/Bisexual Identity Development

Person's self-description of where he or she is in the process of coming out: _____
_____
_____

Cass's model. Gay and lesbian self-statements, as proposed by Cass's model, that best characterize the person's gay/lesbian/bisexual identity development (adapted from Anthony, 1985[1]):

_____Stage I—**Identity Confusion**. "Maybe the information I'm hearing about gay and lesbian persons pertains to me."
      Notes: _____
_____

_____Stage II—**Identity Comparison**. "My feelings of sexual attraction and affection for my own gender are different from my peers, family, and society at large."
      Notes: _____
_____

_____Stage III—**Identity Tolerance**. "I am probably gay or lesbian, but I'm not sure I'd like being gay or lesbian."
      Notes: _____
_____

_____Stage IV—**Identity Acceptance**. "In relating to other gay and lesbian persons and learning more about the gay subculture I feel validated in my sexual orientation. I try to fit into the main culture by trying to pass, to limit contacts with heterosexuals, and to keep my personal life to myself."
      Notes: _____
_____

---

1. From "Lesbian Client—Lesbian Therapist: Opportunities and Challenges in Working Together," by B. D. Anthony, 1985, in *A Guide to Psychotherapy With Gay and Lesbian Clients* (pp. 46–47), edited by J. C. Gonsiorek, New York: Harrington Park Press. Copyright 1985 by Haworth Press. Adapted with permission.

_____Stage V—**Identity Pride**. "I feel a strong sense of belonging to the lesbian and gay community. I want to work toward its more equal treatment."

      Notes: _____

_____

_____Stage VI—**Identity Synthesis**. "My identity as a gay or lesbian person is one very important aspect of myself, but not my total identity. I feel comfortable in both homosexual and heterosexual worlds."

      Notes: _____

_____

Alternate g/l/b identity development model used to characterize person's g/l/b identity.

      Model: _____

      Person's gay/lesbian/bisexual identity level: _____

      Notes: _____

_____

Influence of Others

Family Vocational Histories: Family Tree

Mother's career: _____

Father's career: _____

Sibling(s): _____

Careers of others in blended families: _____

Grandfather's career: _____

Grandmother's career: _____

Aunts and uncles: _____

Partners, Friends, and Peers

Careers of partner, friends, and/or peers: _____

What others have told person his or her career choices should be: _____

      Notes: _____

What others have told person his or her career choices should *not* be: ____

      Notes: _____

Occupational Daydreams

Childhood Daydreams

Careers person daydreamed about as a child, adolescent, or young adult:

      Person's current feelings about those jobs: _____

Factors influencing person's current perceptions (e.g., issues of prestige, homophobia, changed interests): _____

"Discarded" careers that person wishes to reconsider: _____

Current Occupational Daydreams: Visualization Activity

The visualization activity described here will help the g/l/b person set
career goals that maximize that person's potential, given his or her unique
career interests, experiences, values, and needs.

In a quiet setting, make use of peaceful music, progressive muscle
relaxation, and imagery to encourage the person to think about the ideal
career of her or his choice:

- "If you were to have the career of your choice, without wor-
  rying about whether you would be good at that job, or whether
  you could obtain the training to qualify for that job, what
  would that job be?"
  Notes: _____
- "Where would you live? What part of the country? Would you
  live in the city, the suburbs, or a rural area?"
  Notes: _____
- "What would your home look like, physically?"
  Notes: _____
- "Would you be living alone, or would someone be with you?"
  Notes: _____
- "When you woke up each morning, before work, what would
  you do before leaving for work?"
  Notes: _____
- "Would you spend time before work with anyone?"
  Notes: _____
- "How would you spend your work day?"
  Notes: _____
- "What activities would you be doing?"
  Notes: _____
- "Would you be working alone, or with others?"
  Notes: _____
- "What would the workplace look like? What would your office
  look like?"
  Notes: _____
- "What would the work environment be like, as far as organi-
  zational structure, politics, culture, and human relations?"
  Notes: _____

- "What kind of clothes would you be wearing at work?"
  Notes: _____

- "How would you spend your breaks? Your lunch times?"
  Notes: _____

- "What would the most enjoyable parts of your work be?"
  Notes: _____

- "What would be the challenges or 'growth areas'?"
  Notes: _____

- "When you returned home, what would your activities be?"
  Notes: _____

- "Would you spend time with anyone after work?"
  Notes: _____

- "Would you stay at home for part of the evening, or go out?"
  Notes: _____

- "What would your weekend activities be?"
  Notes: _____

- "Would you be spending time with someone during the weekend?"
  Notes: _____

- "Would you be doing any work at home?"
  Notes: _____

- "How out would you be at work? How out would you be in your personal life?"
  Notes: _____

- "How important is it for you to work in an environment which is gay-, lesbian-, and bisexual-affirmative? To live in a community which supports and appreciates diversity?"
  Notes: _____

- "What would be the optimal balance for you between your work and personal life?"
  Notes: _____

- "Who could help you reach these goals?"
  Notes: _____

- "Who or what is preventing you from living this lifestyle? How can you reduce the negative impact of these factors?"

Summary of Career and Life Planning Assessment

_____
_____
_____
_____
_____

_____
_____
_____
_____
_____
_____
_____
_____

Action Plan: Career Counseling Goals

Person's Perceptions

Next career counseling step: _____

_____

Notes on person's goals for additional career counseling: _____

_____

_____

Helper's Perceptions

Next career counseling step: _____

_____

Notes on helper's goals for additional career counseling: _____

_____

_____

_____

Helper: _____

Date of sessions: _____

Date of next scheduled session: _____

APPENDIX 2:

Sample Career Counseling Handout for Clients

This appendix presents a sample handout that could be given to a g/l/b person seeking career assistance. The handout describes the six decision-making steps (discussed in chapter 6) and then makes practical recommendations for actions to implement those steps. Although the handout was developed specifically for use with students at Illinois State University, it could easily be adapted for use beyond the college student population.

Career Decision-Making for Gay, Lesbian, and Bisexual University Students

Career decisions may be optimized by going through six decision-making steps. Those steps are as follows:

1. **Explore your work-related interests, capabilities, values, experiences, and skills.** Before you can select a job that will make good use of your potential, it is important to have a clear understanding of your needs, values, skills, and experiences. The *Dictionary of Occupational Titles* (U.S. Department of Labor, 1991), a resource book that career centers use, lists more than 20,000 jobs. These jobs all require different combinations of skills, interests, and experiences. A good way to find the right subset of the jobs that will match your personality is to find the category of jobs that uses your own unique set of values, interests, and needs. Without an awareness of your own uniqueness, it will be difficult to determine which of those 20,000 jobs is a good match for you. John Holland's classification system will help you organize and clarify your work-related interests and preferences.

2. **Understand the world of work and your career or educational options.** The same classification system that helps you clarify your interests also helps organize those 20,000 plus jobs that make up what career counselors call the world of work. That is, we can organize jobs according to how much they utilize realistic, artistic, investigative, social, enterprising, and conventional interests. Without use of Holland's classification system—or other systems that organize the world of work in different ways—we would be left to our own resources to try to find the smaller subset of those 20,000 jobs listed in the *Dictionary of Occupational Titles* (U.S. Department of Labor, 1991).

3. **Develop your decision-making skills.** Without good decision-making skills, it is of little use for you to have an awareness of your interests, needs, and values or to understand the organization of the world of work. That is, if you make decisions based more on the opinions of others—or if you make decisions in a state of panic, due to time pressures—you will probably not be as likely to make a decision that will make an optimal match between you and particular jobs. If you understand both the role of clear thinking and paying attention to your intuition, and if you proceed through a rational

set of steps, you are more likely to make optional career and life planning decisions.

4. **Learn how stereotyping, bias, and discrimination may limit your career choices, opportunities, and achievement.** We are all influenced by "isms" associated with diversity: ageism, sexism, heterosexism, ableism, ethnocentrism, racism, and "lookism." Sometimes the influence of these isms is so subtle that we do not see how they are affecting the career goals we set for ourselves. Thus without a conscious exploration of our own internal stereotypes—as well as an understanding of the role of society in shaping our career goals—we may set goals that are either too low or unrealistic given our work personalities.

5. **Develop a long- and short-term career plan.** Setting long- and short-term goals helps us begin to implement the career goals that we have set for ourselves. Without a plan of action, we are likely to become overwhelmed by the goals we set. Or we may put off working toward those goals and procrastinate, which will slow down the progression of our career paths.

6. **Develop your employability skills.** Even with the best-laid-out career plans, we may fail to realize our career objectives and fail to land the career of our choice if we are unaware of the art of writing a resumé, or of going through job interviews, or of understanding the role of networking or the hidden job market in locating job openings. Similarly, if we do not have good self-presentation skills, such as the ability to show assertiveness or self-confidence, we may be underestimated by the interviewer whose job it is to assess our potential in a very short period of time. Thus sharpening employability skills can lead to a better chance of landing a job that helps us utilize our potential, given our interests, values, needs, experiences, and skills.

*

Before starting to go through the steps—Determine the type of questions you want to address. Do you want to

- learn more about your interests, skills, and values?
- learn about what majors or careers would make good use of your interests, skills, and values?
- find information about specific majors or careers?
- make a tentative decision about a particular major or career?
- develop a plan to begin implementing your educational and career goals?

- improve your job search skills (e.g., resúmé writing and interviewing skills)?
- understand the impact of your sexual orientation on the career and life planning decisions you make?

Suggested activities and materials:
- Ask for a tour of a university career resources center.
- Use DISCOVER (computer-assisted guidance): Modules 1 and 2.
- Use SIGI-PLUS (computer-assisted guidance): Introduction.
- Browse in the career section of bookstores or libraries.
- Look through books that deal with gay, lesbian, and bisexual issues.
- Discuss career issues with someone who is out in a particular work environment.

*

As you go through the steps—

For Step 1—Explore capabilities and interests.
Do you know about your

- educational and career interests?
- work aptitudes and skills?
- career and life planning values?
- preferred job characteristics?
- preferred life roles?
- development as a g/l/b person, and how it affects your career and life planning?

Suggested activities or materials:
- DISCOVER: Module 3.
- SIGI-PLUS: Section II.
- Self-Directed Search (career assessment inventory), using the Majors Finder, the Occupations Finder, and *The Dictionary of Holland Occupational Codes* (Gottfredson & Holland, 1989).
- Discuss with a career counselor whether or not the career inventories you take are heterosexist.
- Take a career choice class through your university.
- Strong Interest Inventory (computerized inventory).
- Read books on gay, lesbian, and bisexual issues.
- Talk with someone in the work force about how his or her development as a g/l/b person or as an ally has affected his or her own career and life planning interests.

For Step 2—Understand the world of work and education. Find out about

- the organization of occupations (called the world of work),
- those interests and skills that characterize specific jobs or majors,
- educational requirements for specific majors or jobs,
- projected job outlooks,
- lifestyles associated with specific jobs,
- salary ranges, and
- the benefits and legal rights for gay, lesbian, and bisexual persons available in particular work environments.

Suggested activities or materials:

- DISCOVER: Modules 4 and 5.
- SIGI-PLUS: Section IV (Information).
- *Dictionary of Occupational Titles* (*DOT*) (U.S. Department of Labor, 1991).
- *Chronicle Occupational Briefs* (Chronicle Guidance Publications, 1989).
- *Guide for Occupational Exploration* (*GOE*) (Harrington & Shea, 1984).
- College catalogs.
- *Occupational Outlook Handbook* (U.S. Department of Labor, 1994).
- Conduct informational interviews.
- Consult the Standing Committee for Lesbian, Gay, and Bisexual Awareness (SCLGBA) Resource Clearinghouse for information on current issues and topics of concern for lesbian, gay, and bisexual people (e.g., the military, domestic partnerships): John Leppo, 907 Floyd Avenue, VCU Box 842032, Richmond, VA 23284-2032 (tel: 804-828-6500; email: jleppo @ cabell.vcu.edu).
- Gather information about organizational benefits and legal rights through books such as *Cracking the Corporate Closet* (Baker, Strub, & Henning, 1995), *The 100 Best Companies for Gay Men and Lesbians* (Mickens, 1994), *The Rights of Lesbians and Gay Men* (Hunter, Michaelson, & Stoddard, 1992), and the *GAYELLOW PAGES* (Green, 1994).

For Step 3—Understand and develop decision-making skills. It is important to

- learn about decision-making principles, decision-making styles, the six steps in making career decisions, and how sexual orientation influences the decision-making process,

- analyze the pros and cons for majors or careers that best fit your personality,
- identify where to obtain information for making career decisions,
- narrow and prioritize occupational and educational alternatives, and
- make a tentative decision about a major or career to pursue.

Suggested activities or materials:
- DISCOVER: Module 6.
- SIGI-PLUS: Section VIII (Deciding).
- Individual career counseling can help you analyze your decision-making style and help you go through the six decision-making steps more effectively.

For Step 4—Learn how stereotyping, bias, and discrimination limit choices, opportunities, and achievement.
It is important to

- understand stereotyping as it relates to work and education,
- identify limitations placed on people by stereotyping,
- identify opportunities, regardless of past stereotyping or discrimination,
- understand how your own stereotypes or the stereotypes of others influence your career and life planning, and
- understand how societal homophobia and heterosexism affect the decisions you make.

Suggested activities or materials:
- See readings on resource lists in Career Services Center "Pink Triangle" g/l/b books.
- Talk about these issues with someone who is working in a field of interest to you.
- Consult Resource Clearinghouse (American College Personnel Association Standing Committee for Lesbian, Gay, and Bisexual Awareness) about these issues (address listed in Step 2).
- Consult with Career Services Center staff member about these issues.
- Read books on homophobia or heterosexism to educate yourself about possible limitations imposed by homophobia or heterosexism, in order to develop a plan for addressing these issues as they impact you.
- Seek career counseling or personal counseling to help you reduce the impact of stereotyping on your own career and life planning.

For Step 5—Develop a career plan.
You should begin to

- develop long- and short-term educational and occupational goals to implement choices,
- develop an alternative plan if appropriate,
- develop a plan for periodical reevaluation of career decisions, and
- develop a support system to keep you motivated to implement your plan.

Suggested activities or materials:
- Individual career counseling.
- IDS 106: Career Choice Class.
- Find a career coach or mentor to help you develop professionally and personally as a g/l/b person.

For Step 6—Develop employability skills.
It is important to

- develop positive work attitudes and behaviors,
- prepare your resúmé in a way that is consistent with your interests, values, and skills,
- develop interviewing techniques and have job interviews,
- understand legal and illegal job interview questions, especially as they relate to sexual orientation,
- complete your job application,
- be able to manage heterosexism and homophobia in the job interview and work environment effectively,
- learn how to gather information about the level of homophobia and heterosexism in a particular work environment you are considering during the job search process, and
- understand the transition from school to work.

Suggested activities and materials:
- Attend Career Services Center workshops on resúmé writing and interviewing.
- Request an individual critique of resúmé by Career Services Center staff member.
- Use the computerized resúmé writing program at Career Services Center.
- Discuss with a Career Services Center staff member ways to find out how gay/lesbian/bisexual affirmative a particular work environment is.
- Discuss these issues with a g/l/b person who is already in the work force.

- Consult Lambda Legal Defense and Education Fund (LLDEF), Inc., 666 Broadway, Suite 1200, New York, NY 10012-2317 (tel: 212-955-8585; email: lldefny @ aol.com) LLDEF also has two regional offices: Midwest Regional Office, 17 East Monroe, Suite 212, Chicago, IL 60603 (tel: 312-759-8110; email: lldefmro @ aol.com); and Western Regional Office, 6030 Wilshire Blvd., Suite 200, Los Angeles, CA 90036-3617 (tel: 213-957-2728; email: lldefla @ aol.com).
- Use books such as *Cracking the Corporate Closet* (Baker, Strub & Henning, 1995) to help assess work environment heterosexism.

APPENDIX 3:

Career Counseling Resources

Resources are suggested throughout this book. However, given the vast literature in the fields of career development, gay/lesbian/bisexual identity development, and adult life-span development, it may be difficult for those new in the field of career and life planning with g/l/b persons to get started. To avoid information overload, this appendix suggests a few readings for each topic. This appendix's topical listings may also help career centers or other helping agencies in beginning to move toward developing more affirmative services and programs.

The resources listed are especially useful when used in conjunction with the career and life planning model proposed in this book. The resources include both applied and theoretical materials.

Career and Life Planning With Gay, Lesbian, and Bisexual Persons

Belz, J. R. (1993). Sexual orientation as a factor in career development. *Career Development Quarterly, 41*(3), 197–200.

Chojnacki, J. T., & Gelberg, S. (1994). Toward a conceptualization of career counseling with gay, lesbian, and bisexual persons. *Journal of Career Development, 21*(1), 3–10.

Croteau, J. M., & Hedstrom, S. M. (1993). Integrating commonality and difference: The key to career counseling with lesbian women and gay men. *Career Development Quarterly, 41*(3), 201–209.

Elliott, J. E. (1993). Career development with lesbian and gay clients. *Career Development Quarterly, 41*(3), 210–226.

Fassinger, R. E. (1994, January). *Identity and work: Issues in the vocational psychology of lesbians.* Paper presented at the annual conference of the National Career Development Association, Albuquerque, NM.

Hetherington, C. (1991). Life planning and career counseling with gay and lesbian students. In N. J. Evans & V. A. Wall (Eds.), *Beyond tolerance: Gays, lesbians, and bisexuals on campus* (pp. 131–145). Alexandria, VA: American College Personnel Association.

Hetherington, C., Hillerbrand, E., & Etringer, B. D. (1989). Career counseling with gay men: Issues and recommendations for research. *Journal of Counseling and Development, 67*, 452–454.

Hetherington, C., & Orzek, A. (1989). Career counseling and life planning with lesbian women. *Journal of Counseling and Development, 68*(1), 52–57.

Schmitz, T. J. (1988). Career counseling implications with the gay and lesbian population. *Journal of Employment Counseling, 25*, 51–56.

Strader, S. C., & Bowman, S. L. (1993, March). *Career counseling for gay, lesbian, and bisexual people: Issues and theory.* Presentation at the annual convention of the American College Personnel Association, Kansas City, MO.

Gay, Lesbian, and Bisexual Identity Development

Boston Lesbian Psychologies Collective (Eds.). (1987). *Lesbian psychologies: Explorations and challenges.* Urbana and Chicago: University of Illinois Press.

Cass, V. C. (1979). Homosexuality identity formation: A theoretical model. *Journal of Homosexuality, 4*(3), 219–235.

Cass, V. C. (1984a). Homosexual identity: A concept in need of definition. *Journal of Homosexuality, 9*(2/3), 105–126.

Cass, V. C. (1984b). Homosexuality identity formation: Testing a theoretical model. *Journal of Sex Research, 20*(2), 143–167.

Coleman, E. (1985). Developmental stages of the coming out process. In J. C. Gonsiorek (Ed.), *A guide to psychotherapy with gay and lesbian clients* (pp. 31–43). New York: Harrington Park Press.

Dworkin, S. H., & Gutiérrez, F. (1989). Gay, lesbian, and bisexual issues in counseling [Special issue]. *Journal of Counseling and Development, 68*(1).

Fassinger, R. E. (1991). The hidden minority: Issues and challenges in working with lesbian women and gay men. *The Counseling Psychologist, 19*(2), 157–176.

Greene, B., & Herek, G. M. (1994). *Lesbian and gay psychology: Theory, research, and clinical applications.* Thousand Oaks, CA: Sage.

Klein, F. (1993). *The bisexual option.* New York: Harrington Park Press.

Levine, H., & Evans, N. J. (1991). The development of gay, lesbian, and bisexual identities. In N. J. Evans & V. A. Wall (Eds.), *Beyond tolerance: Gays, lesbians, and bisexuals on campus* (pp. 1–24). Alexandria, VA: American College Personnel Association.

Sophie, J. (1986). A critical examination of stage theories of lesbian identity development. *Journal of Homosexuality, 12*(2), 39–51.

Troiden, R. R. (1989). The formation of homosexual identities. *Journal of Homosexuality, 17*(1/2), 43–74.

Wall, V. A., & Evans, N. J. (1991). Using psychosocial development theories to understand and work with gay and lesbian persons. In N. J. Evans & V. A. Wall (Eds.), *Beyond tolerance: Gays, lesbians, and bisexuals on campus* (pp. 25–38). Alexandria, VA: American College Personnel Association.

General Career Counseling

Jepsen, D. A. (1990). Developmental career counseling. In W. B. Walsh & S. H. Osipow (Eds.), *Career counseling: Contemporary topics in vocational psychology* (pp. 117–157). Hillsdale, NJ: Erlbaum.

Kapes, J. T., Mastie, M. M., & Whitfield, E. A. (1994). *A counselor's guide to career assessment instruments* (3rd ed.). Alexandria, VA: National Career Development Association.

Leong, F. T. (1995). *Career development and vocational behavior of racial and ethnic minorities.* Mahwah, NJ: Erlbaum.

Rounds, J. B., & Tracey, T. J. (1990). From trait-and-factor to person-environment fit counseling: Theory and process. In W. B. Walsh & S. H. Osipow (Eds.), *Career counseling: Contemporary topics in vocational psychology* (pp. 1–44). Hillsdale, NJ: Erlbaum.

Walsh, W. B., & Osipow, S. H. (Eds.). (1993). *Career counseling for women.* Hillsdale, NJ: Erlbaum.

Career Center Materials for Lesbian, Gay, and Bisexual Career Clients

The Advocate (national gay and lesbian newsmagazine). 6922 Hollywood Blvd., 10th floor, Los Angeles, CA 90028.

Baker, D. B., Strub, S. O., & Henning, B. (1995). *Cracking the corporate closet.* New York: HarperCollins.

Blank, R., & Slipp, S. (1994). *Voices of diversity: Real people talk about problems and solutions in a workplace where everyone is not alike.* New York: Amacom (American Management Association).

Cohen, D. (Ed.). (1994). *The lesbian and gay pink pages.* Chicago: DAC Marketing (3023 North Clark St., No. 779, Chicago, IL 60657; tel: 312-472-4552; fax: 312-472-0576).

Coming Out (professional quality twofold brochure for clients). Available for purchase in any quantity from the Student Counseling Center at the University of Illinois at Urbana-Champaign, 212 Student Services Building, 610 East John St., Champaign, IL 61820.

Diamant, L. (1993). *Homosexual issues in the workplace.* Bristol, PA: Taylor & Francis.

Domestic Partners Project Research. Standing Committee for Lesbian, Gay, and Bisexual Awareness (SGLBA) Resource Clearinghouse, John Leppo, 907 Floyd Ave., VCU Box 842032, Richmond, VA 23284-2032 (tel: 804-828-6500; email: jleppo @ cabell.vcu.edu).

Evans, N. J., & Wall, V. A. (1991). *Beyond tolerance: Gays, lesbians, and bisexuals on campus.* Alexandria, VA: American College Personnel Association.

Federation of Parents and Friends of Lesbians and Gays. (1992). *Is homosexuality a sin?* Washington, DC: Author (PFLAG, P.O. Box 96519, Washington, DC 20090-6519).

Geller, T. (Ed.). (1990). *Bisexuality: A reader and sourcebook.* Novato, CA: Times Change Press.

Green, F. (1994). *GAYELLOW PAGES.* New York: Renaissance House (P. O. Box 533, New York, NY 10014-0533; tel: 212-674-0120).

Hunter, N. D., Michaelson, S. E., & Stoddard, T. B. (1992). *The rights of lesbians and gay men: The basic ACLU guide to a gay person's rights* (3rd ed.). Carbondale, IL: Southern Illinois University Press.

Hutchins, L., & Kaahumanu, L. (Eds.). (1991). *Bi any other name: Bisexual people speak out.* Boston: Alyson.

McNaught, B. (1993). *Gay issues in the workplace.* New York: St. Martin's Press.

Marcus, E. (1993). *Is it a choice? Answers to 300 of the most frequently asked questions about gays and lesbians.* San Francisco: HarperSanFrancisco.

National Association of Student Personnel Administrators (NASPA). *Network for Gay, Lesbian, and Bisexual Concerns Newsletter.* Available to members (1875 Connecticut Ave., NW, Suite 418, Washington, DC 20009; tel: 202-265-7500).

National Gay and Lesbian Switchboard. Tel: 202-371-9491.

National Gay and Lesbian Task Force. (1996). *Listing of corporations, organizations, and educational institutions offering domestic partner benefits* (Rev. ed.). Washington, DC: Author. Available from National Gay and Lesbian Task Force Policy Institute, Publications Dept., 2320 17th St., NW, Washington, DC 20009 (tel: 202-332-6483, ext 3327).

Out on Campus (newsletter). Available free to any member of the Standing Committee for Lesbian, Gay, and Bisexual Awareness (SCLGBA), American College Personnel Association.

Out! Resource Guide. (1994). Chicago: Lambda Publications (3059 North Southport, Chicago, IL 60657).

Progressive Resources Catalogue. Contains materials with a progressive-left perspective, such as books, posters, buttons, bumper stickers, pins, postcards, and T-shirts. Available from Donnely/Colt, Box 188, Hampton, CT 06247.

Organizations/Agencies

American Counseling Association, National Career Development Association, Gay/Lesbian/Bisexual Career Development Special Interest Group (SIG): ACA Customer Service tel: 800-347-6647.

American College Personnel Association (ACPA) Standing Committee for Lesbian, Gay, and Bisexual Awareness (SCLGBA). Publishes the newsletter *Out on Campus*; free to any ACPA member joining the SCLGBA.

American Psychological Association Committee on Lesbian and Gay Concerns, 750 First St., NE, Washington, DC 20002-4242 (tel: 202-336-5500).

American Psychological Association Division 44: The Society for Psychological Study of Lesbian and Gay Issues, 750 First St., NE, Washington, DC 20002-4242 (tel: 202-336-5500).

Association of Gay and Lesbian Psychiatrists, 209 North Fourth St., Suite D-5, Philadelphia, PA 19106 (tel: 215-925-5008; fax: 215-925-9309; email: aglpnat@aol.com).

Lambda Legal Defense and Education Fund (LLDEF), Inc., 666 Broadway, Suite 1200, New York, NY 10012-2317 (tel: 212-955-8585; email: lldefny@aol.com). Has two regional offices: Midwest Regional Office, 17 East Monroe, Suite 212, Chicago, IL 60603 (tel: 312-759-8110; email: lldefmro@aol.com); Western Regional Office, 6030 Wilshire Blvd., Suite 200, Los Angeles, CA 90036-3617 (tel: 213-957-2728; email: lldefla@aol.com).

Lesbian and Gay People in Medicine, c/o American Medical Students Association, 1910 Association Drive, Reston, VA 22091 (fax: 703-620-5873; email: amsatf@aol.com).

Lesbian and Gay Teachers Association, P. O. Box 021052, Brooklyn, NY 11202-0023 (tel: 714-596-1864). Publishes a newsletter.

National Gay and Lesbian Task Force, 2320 17th St. NW, Washington, DC 20009 (tel: 202-332-6483).

Parents, Families, and Friends of Lesbians and Gays (PFLAG), P.O. Box 96519, Washington, DC 20090-6519. National Office: 1101 14th St., NW, Suite 1030, Washington, DC 20005 (tel: 202-638-4200; fax: 202-638-0243; email: pflagnt1@aol.com).

Resource Lists

Available from National Gay and Lesbian Task Force Policy Institute. (1996). *Listing of Corporations, Organizations, Unions, and Educational Institutions Offering Domestic Partner Benefits* (Rev. ed.). Washington, DC: Author (Publications Dept., 2230 17th St., NW, Washington, DC 20009 (tel: 202-332-6483, ext 3327)..

In Dworkin, S. H., & Gutiérrez, F. J. (Eds.). (1992). *Counseling Gay Men and Lesbians: Journey to the End of the Rainbow.* Alexandria, VA: American Association for Counseling and Development. Professional Associations and Resources for Lesbians, Gays, and Bisexuals, pp. 341–348.

In Evans, N. J., & Wall, V. A. (Eds.). (1991). *Beyond Tolerance: Gays, Lesbians, and Bisexuals on Campus.* Alexandria, VA: American College Personnel Association. Resources listed (Brooks, pp. 213–232) include 75 organizations as well as information on gay, lesbian, and bisexual lifestyles; family issues; counseling issues; spirituality, religion and gay, lesbian, and bisexual issues; gay and lesbian literature; programming resources; movies/videos; journals and magazines; travel guides; gay and lesbian organizations.

Available from Standing Committee for Lesbian, Gay, and Bisexual Awareness (SCLGBA) Resource Clearinghouse, John Leppo, 907 Floyd Ave., VCU Box 842032, Richmond, VA 23284-2032 (tel: 804-828-6500; email: jleppo@cabell.vcu.edu.). Resource lists cover general resources, diversity-based organizations, gay and lesbian youth, gay and lesbian parents, advocacy and educational organizations, college-related organizations, switchboards and hotlines, media, religious-based organizations, and gay and lesbian bookstores.

Available from American Civil Liberties Union, Lesbian and Gay Rights Project, 132 West 43rd St., New York, NY 10036 (tel: 212-944-9800, ext 545).

Available from Human Rights Campaign, 1101 14th St., NW, Washington, DC 20005 (tel: 800-777-4723). This is the largest national lesbian and gay political organization with members throughout the country. It lobbies Congress, provides campaign support, and educates the public to secure equal rights for lesbian and gay Americans and ensure that they can live free from discrimination at home, at work, and in the community.

In American Psychological Association, Public Interest Directorate. (1993). *Graduate Faculty Interested in Lesbian and Gay Issues.* Washington, DC: Author (750 First St., NE, Washington, DC 20002-4242; tel: 202-336-5500).

Heterosexism and Homophobia

American Psychological Association. (1991). Avoiding heterosexual bias in language. *American Psychologist, 46*(9), 973–974.

Blumenfeld, W. J. (Ed.). (1992). *Homophobia: How we all pay the price.* Boston: Beacon Press.

Croteau, J. M., & Lark, J. S. (1995). A qualitative investigation of biased and exemplary student affairs practice concerning lesbian, gay, and bisexual issues. *Journal of College Student Development, 36*(5), 472–482.

Garnets, L., Hancock, K. A., Cochran, S. D., Goodchilds, J., & Peplau, L. A. (1991). Issues in psychotherapy with lesbians and gay men: A survey of psychologists. *American Psychologist, 46*(9), 964–972.

Pharr, S. (1988). *Homophobia: A weapon of sexism.* Inverness, CA: Chardon Press.

Professional Development as an Ally

Chojnacki, J. T., & Gelberg, S. (1995). The facilitation of a gay/lesbian/bisexual support-therapy group by heterosexual therapists. *Journal of Counseling and Development, 73*(3), 352–354.

Gelberg, S., & Chojnacki, J. T. (1995). Developmental transitions of gay/lesbian /bisexual-affirmative career counselors. *Career Development Quarterly, 43*(3), 267–273.

Holahan, W., & Gibson, S. A. (1994). Heterosexual therapists leading lesbian and gay therapy groups: Therapeutic and political realities. *Journal of Counseling and Development, 72*, 591–594.

Thompson, C. (1992). On being heterosexual in a homophobic world. In W. J. Blumenfeld (Ed.), *Homophobia: How we all pay the price* (pp. 235–248). Boston: Beacon Press.

Washington, J., & Evans, N. J. (1991). Becoming an ally. In N. J. Evans & V. A. Wall (Eds.), *Beyond tolerance: Gays, lesbians, and bisexuals on campus* (pp. 195–204). Alexandria, VA: American College Personnel Association.

Career Counseling With Racial and Ethnic Minorities

Greene, B. (1994). Ethnic-minority lesbians and gay men: Mental health and treatment issues. *Journal of Consulting and Clinical Psychology, 62*(2), 243–251.

Hoyt, K. B. (1989). The career status of women and minority persons: A 20-year retrospective. *Career Development Quarterly, 37*, 202–212.

Leong, F. T. (1995). *Career development and vocational behavior of racial and ethnic minorities.* Mahwah, NJ: Erlbaum.

Reynolds, A. L., & Pope, R. (1991). The complexity of diversity: Exploring multiple oppressions. *Journal of Counseling and Development, 70*, 174–180.

Salamone, P. R. (Ed.). (1991). Career development of racial and ethnic minorities [Special issue]. *Career Development Quarterly, 39*(3).

Section III: Diverse Populations. (1992). In S. H. Dworkin F. J. Gutiérrez (Eds.), *Counseling gay men and lesbians: Journey to the end of the rainbow.* Alexandria, VA: American Association of Counseling and Development.

Sue, D. W., Arredondo, P., & McDavis, R. J. (1992). Multicultural counseling competencies and standards: A call to the profession. *Journal of Multicultural Counseling and Development, 20,* 64–88.

Sample Letter Requesting Career Center Resources

We sent this letter (adapted from Hradsky & Comey, 1992) to gay/ lesbian/bisexual agencies (e.g., those listed in Organizations/Agencies) to request career center resources and received a number of free or inexpensive materials. These materials were placed in binders and shelved in our career center libraries.

Dear _____:

As we expand the materials for the Career Services Center at Illinois State University, we would like to include in our career resource files, information helpful to gay, lesbian, and bisexual students.

We would appreciate receiving any information from your organization that would assist students in career exploration or job search activities. Appropriate materials would include information about:

- lists of gay/lesbian/bisexual-friendly employers
- legal issues associated with the workplace
- employee benefits for workers and domestic partners
- military issues
- AIDS/HIV and employment
- career and lifestyle counseling
- job search concerns (e.g., resúmés, self-disclosure issues)
- homophobia and heterosexism in the workplace
- other related information.

Please send any relevant information to _____.

Thank you for any materials you could forward. We appreciate your assistance in helping our staff make the Career Services Center more responsive to gay, lesbian, and bisexual student needs.

Sincerely,

_____

Title

Reference

Hradsky, R. D., & Comey, D. M. (1992). *Creating a career center responsive to gay/lesbian/bisexual student needs.* Presentation at the annual conference of the American College Personnel Association, San Francisco.

APPENDIX 4:

Developmental Transitions and Mentoring of Gay, Lesbian, and Bisexual Allies

Allies are, and will continue to be, an important part of the movement toward equal rights and the end of oppression of g/l/b persons. As Washington and Evans (1991) wrote, ". . .although an oppressed person can certainly be a supporter and advocate for his or her own group, the impact and effect of such activity are different on the dominant group, and are often more powerful when the supporter is not a member of the oppressed population" (p. 195).

The development of heterosexuals who are seeking to develop professionally as g/l/b allies has recently begun to receive attention (e.g., Gelberg & Chojnacki, 1995; Gelberg, Chojnacki, Benn, Woodburn, & Chagnon, 1994; Gelberg, Chojnacki, & Chagnon, 1993; Gelberg, Chojnacki, Gibson, Benn, & Holahan, 1992; Geller, 1992; Thompson, 1992; Washington & Evans, 1991). Persons wishing to become allies can find the task difficult, however. Obstacles include both societal and internalized homophobia (Blumenfeld, 1992; Obear, 1991; Pharr, 1988) as well as *heterophobia*, which refers to negative reactions that g/l/b persons may have toward heterosexuals (Triplett & Busher, 1994). Because of heterosexism, homophobia, and heterophobia, allies' initial efforts to become active in the field of g/l/b issues can be hampered (Gelberg, Chojnacki, & Chagnon, 1993; Gelberg et al., 1992, 1994). Mentoring may be especially helpful as allies cope with the heterosexism, heterophobia, and homophobia associated with work in the field of g/l/b issues.

Although the use of mentoring to enhance the professional development of g/l/b allies has not been described, the topic of mentoring is receiving increased attention in the literature (e.g., Atkinson, Neville, & Casas, 1991; Blackwell, 1989; Burlew, 1991; Carden, 1990; Noe, 1988). In a review of theoretical and empirical literature on mentoring, Carden (1990) recommended that future studies focus on the use of mentoring with subjects from those populations less often included in research, that is, those who are under the influence of such isms as racism, sexism, and ageism. Most articles that address mentoring with special populations do not mention heterosexism as a specific ism, but mentoring is suggested as a way to help g/l/b individuals progress through the developmental stages of coming out as a g/l/b person (Hetherington, 1991). It seems logical to assume that mentoring might also be helpful to allies as they deal with internalized and externalized homophobia, heterosexism, and heterophobia (Gelberg et al., 1994).

We propose a six-stage framework for ally development that details the affective, cognitive, and behavioral components of each stage. In addition, we suggest mentoring activities for each of the developmental stages. We hope that these conceptualizations provide a useful cognitive framework to help allies set concrete professional objectives and to seek the type of professional support that is most beneficial given their own particular level of professional development as an ally.

Before describing our model, we define three terms important to understanding the model and examine the theoretical assumptions on which the model is based. The presentation of the model includes a graphic overview. The final part of this appendix is a handout we have developed for use in workshops on g/l/b ally professional development.

Definition of Terms

Mentoring

Definitions of mentoring vary with each conceptual or empirical study. We have adapted the definitions developed by Carden (1990) and Noe (1988). In our view, mentors are individuals who serve as role models, teachers, and coaches, and who provide career direction for less experienced individuals who are commonly termed *protégés*. Mentoring functions can be classified as having both psychosocial functions (e.g., the enhancement of the protégé's sense of competence and work-role effectiveness) and career functions (e.g., the provision of feedback regarding strategies for accomplishing work objectives) (Kram, 1983). Mentoring behaviors identified by Henderson (1985) include teaching, guiding, advising, counseling, sponsoring, role modeling, validating, motivating, protecting, communicating, being subtle, and not expecting credit.

Protégé

Protégés, also commonly termed *mentees* or *mentorees* (Carden, 1990), are the recipients of mentors' personal and professional assistance. Henderson (1985) identified a number of pertinent protégé behaviors: an upwardly mobile attitude, competence in one's role, dependability, interest in the mentor's work, discretion, and a sense of propriety.

Ally

We use the definition of ally provided by Washington and Evans (1991): "a person who is a member of the 'dominant' or 'majority' group who works to end oppression in his or her personal and professional life through support of, and as an advocate with and for, the oppressed population" (p. 195).

Theoretical Assumptions of Mentoring Model of Gay, Lesbian, and Bisexual Allies

1. Development as an ally is a lifelong process that involves a number of hierarchical stages, each of which is characterized by unique affective, cognitive, and behavioral components

We view development as a g/l/b ally as a lifelong process that involves cycling through six developmental stages as new professional developmental tasks are addressed over the life span (Gelberg et al., 1994). A developmental approach has also been taken by Washington and Evans (1991), who briefly described four levels of ally development: awareness, knowledge/education, skills, and action. Geller (1992) also outlined four levels of ally development: the recognition of the need to learn about g/l/b people, information gathering and self-education, increased networking and contact with g/l/b persons, and increased confidence as an ally. We have proposed six developmental stages for allies who work in the area of career counseling with g/l/b persons: awareness, ambivalence, empowerment, activism, pride, and integration (Gelberg & Chojnacki, 1995). These six stages are modified, refined, and expanded into more generalized uses in this appendix.

The ally developmental model we present is grounded in the developmental theories of counseling that view growth as resulting from the mastery of specific developmental tasks (Havighurst, 1980). Using a developmental perspective, we view growth as a continuous process that is irreversible and can be differentiated into patterns or stages. We view these stages as showing increased differentiation and integration of new parts, and as proceeding from dependence to independence and from egocentric to socially relevant behavior (Jepsen, 1990).

Thus in order to generate hypotheses about the nature of ally developmental tasks, we examined and adapted general principles of life-span developmental counseling (e.g., Erikson, 1968; Gilligan, 1982; Levinson, 1986; Levinson et al., 1978) and theories of g/l/b identity development (Cass, 1979, 1984a, 1984b; Coleman, 1985; D'Augelli, 1991; Fox, 1993; Levine & Evans, 1991; Miranda & Storms, 1989). In addition, we adapted the specific developmental tasks that characterized allies who worked as career counselors (Gelberg & Chojnacki, 1995) in order to describe more generalized work as allies. These approaches for generating ally developmental tasks were necessary because empirical research has not to date addressed the nature of the specific developmental tasks that characterize ally development.

In order to more fully understand the affective components of the developmental transitions, we have applied the notion of "developmental bridges" to ally development. According to Levinson (1986; Levinson et al., 1978), developmental bridges—or developmental transitions—occur between each developmental stage. Levinson viewed these developmental bridges as being characterized by disequilibrium, anxiety, confusion, a lack of cognitive clarity, and instability.

We have used other developmental principles in our proposed theory of ally development. In particular, we have drawn from Schmidt and Davison's (1983) work as we reflect about the level of challenge that mentors should provide for their protégés. Schmidt and Davison advocated the notion of the use of "plus-one staging," which recommended that challenges be presented that are only moderately discrepant from the individual's present developmental stage. Plus-one staging thus encourages cognitive development through avoiding the presentation of information that is too discrepant with the individual's present cognitive schemata. Blocher and Siegal (1981) similarly referred to the importance of supplying "optimally discrepant or novel information." Without this "optimal mismatch," allies may find it too difficult to relate to mentors who model behavioral, cognitive, or affective correlates reflecting developmental stages too discrepant with the ally's own present developmental stage.

2. Development as an ally involves affective, cognitive, and behavioral components that have some parallels with identity development for g/l/b persons

As detailed in chapter 4, g/l/b identity development involves progression through a number of stages. We propose that the stages of coming out as a g/l/b person have developmental parallels with the stages that characterize coming out as an ally. For example, although individuals may wish to become more affirmative to sexual orientation, they may not be aware of the affective, behavioral, or cognitive components that characterize the role of ally. Self-esteem as an ally may be initially low, and there may be a confusion about how to begin to develop professionally as an ally. Self-disclosure of the ally's interests in g/l/b issues may at first be low because of internalized homophobia and heterosexism. Allies may also experience societal homophobia as they begin to work in the area of g/l/b issues, and they may be viewed through stereotypes about the personal and professional attributes of allies.

Another parallel between ally development and g/l/b development is the fact that locus of control for allies may initially be external rather than internal. Thus allies may at first be more dependent on others as they begin to assume an active stance on g/l/b issues.

Allies may experience high levels of frustration, depression, anxiety, and anger as they respond to internal and societal homophobia and heterosexism (Gelberg & Chojnacki, 1995; Gelberg, Chojnacki, & Chagnon, 1993; Gelberg et al., 1992, 1994). The parallels between g/l/b persons and allies have been incorporated into the six stages of ally development in our proposed model.

Although there are strong parallels between the professional development of allies and g/l/b identity development, there are some differences worth noting. Being an ally is a choice, whereas it appears that sexual orientation is not. At the end of a day of advocacy, allies are still heterosexual and enjoy all of the benefits and advantages in society not available to g/l/b persons (i.e., heterosexual privilege). In addition, although allies can experience a good deal of psychological stress and anxiety in initially assuming affirmative roles, it is difficult to equate this stress with the experience of g/l/b persons living in a homophobic and heterosexist society. The parallels depicted in the developmental model are not intended to trivialize the experiences of g/l/b persons.

3. The ally's progression through the six developmental stages can be facilitated through the challenges and support provided by mentors

In order to facilitate the ally's progression through the six stages, mentors should provide a balance between support and challenge appropriate to the specific developmental stage of the ally. Mentors can thus help facilitate development through exposing the ally to information and experiences that are slightly discrepant with the ally's current understandings in order to encourage the development of new concepts. This makes use of Schmidt and Davison's (1983) assumption of plus-one staging as well as Blocher and Siegal's (1981) notion of the optimal mismatch. Because the mentoring of g/l/b allies has not been addressed in the literature, specific tasks for mentoring allies were generated through modifying the mentoring functions suggested by Atkinson et al. (1991), Carden (1990), Gram (1992), and Noe (1988).

The Mentoring Model With Stages of Development of G/l/b Allies: Affective, Cognitive, and Behavioral Correlates and Facilitative Roles of Mentors

The Model

Stage I—Awareness

The new ally becomes aware of a need to become more personally, professionally, or politically active on g/l/b issues. This need may spring from significant professional or personal relationships with g/l/b persons that create a heightened awareness of the problems of heterosexism and homophobia.

- **Affective correlates**. An ally at this stage senses an initial desire to become more active in addressing g/l/b issues. There is, however, a sense of confusion about how to best address the newly set objectives linked to becoming a g/l/b ally. Because the new ally may be in an environment that lacks allies to serve as role models, there may be a sense of social and professional isolation.

- **Cognitive correlates**. The new ally tends to have a limited knowledge about sexual orientation as well as cognitive biases regarding g/l/b issues. Thus the ally's understanding of g/l/b issues tends to be stereotypical and dualistic due to limited knowledge about g/l/b persons. There is also a lack of awareness of the roles and behaviors of allies as well as no awareness of heterosexual privilege, which refers to "the power and privileges that one receives, accepts, and experiences as a heterosexual person" (Washington & Evans, 1991, p. 196).

- **Behavioral correlates**. The new ally may have personal or professional associations with g/l/b persons but shows a lack of professional activity on g/l/b issues. Self-disclosures about interests and objectives associated with becoming a g/l/b ally are minimal, possibly due in part to homophobia, heterosexism, or heterophobia.

- **Facilitative role of mentor.** The mentor's role is initially an educative one. The mentor attempts to facilitate the new ally's gathering of information regarding g/l/b issues. At the beginning of this stage, the mentor should initially attempt to tolerate, rather than challenge, the current developmental level of the ally. As the relationship between the mentor and ally strengthens, mentors should begin to challenge their protégés in order to stimulate advancement to the second developmental level. In providing this challenge, the mentor should strive to provide an optimal balance between support and challenge in order to facilitate the ally's progression to the next developmental stage. Mentors should support protégé contacts with g/l/b persons and deepen their sensitivities and awareness as they experience these relationships.

Stage II—Ambivalence

Ambivalence is experienced as the new ally first desires to become more active professionally but then is held in check by homophobia and heterophobia.

- **Affective correlates.** The ally begins to have more personal or professional experiences that create feelings increasingly incongruent with professional inaction. Because the personal or professional skills to become active as an ally are still lacking, however, the ally may experience high levels of depression and anxiety due in part to the perceived incongruence between the objectives the ally has set for himself or herself and the lack of professional or personal actions in the role of ally. Thus the ally shows continued low self-efficacy as an ally and fails to value fully the role of ally. Additional ambivalence, anxiety, and depression are experienced with the ally's newly developed awareness of the extent of both internalized heterosexism and homophobia. The ally has continued difficulties in fully valuing ally-related goals and may experience personal feelings of guilt as he or she becomes more sensitized to the issue of heterosexual privileges.

- **Cognitive correlates.** As the ally becomes more informed about g/l/b issues, stereotypical thinking decreases and more enlightened thinking about g/l/b issues occurs.

- **Behavioral correlates.** The ally begins to have deepened professional and personal contacts with other allies and with g/l/b persons and shows an increased incidence of information gathering and other educational activities.

- **Facilitative role of mentor.** Mentors should continue to provide assistance in gathering written information about g/l/b issues. In addition, the mentor should normalize the ally's ambivalent feelings while also supporting the ally's continued questioning and exploration of g/l/b issues. Finally, the mentor should continue to support the new ally's networking with other allies and with g/l/b persons.

Stage III—Empowerment

The new ally experiences greater empowerment as a result of a perceived progression through stages I and II. The ally begins to demonstrate public signs of involvement in g/l/b issues.

- **Affective correlates.** Because of the ally's awareness of professional and personal growth as an ally, there is an embryonic self-valuing and self-efficacy in the role of ally. There is thus a greater motivation to address internalized homophobia and heterosexism, although the ally still experiences strong fear concerning homophobic and heterophobic responses to ally actions.

- **Cognitive correlates.** There is an increased intellectual commitment to, and knowledge of, g/l/b issues.

- **Behavioral correlates.** The ally begins demonstrating more g/l/b-affirmative behaviors, although there remains a continued dualism in self-presentation as an ally, depending in part on the ally's perception of the level of heterosexism, homophobia, or heterophobia of a particular environment. Thus there may still be limited self-disclosures about ally-related goals in some professional or personal environments.

- **Facilitative role of mentor.** At this stage the mentor should strive to provide empathetic listening and support of the ally's goals as the ally attempts to cope with self-esteem and self-efficacy issues. Mentors may also assist in the development of such interpersonal skills as (1) assertiveness training in dealing with heterosexism and homophobia experienced in response to work as an ally, (2) enhancement of stress management skills, and (3) assistance in values clarification linked to their protégés' new role of g/l/b ally. Finally, mentors may provide supportive confrontation about their protégés' dualistic self-presentation as an ally, and about any remaining internalized heterosexism and homophobia.

Stage IV—Activism

The new ally becomes more professionally, personally, socially, and politically active as the ally's locus of control moves from external to internal.

- **Affective correlates.** The ally experiences a stronger self-valuing of ally roles because of an enhanced ability to cope with perceived homophobia and heterosexism. Thus there is a greater sense of satisfaction, reduced anxiety, and lower levels of depression because of this increased activism and greater congruence between the ally's professional objectives and affirmative behaviors. At the same time, the ally may experience an increased alienation toward others who are perceived as homophobic or heterosexist.

- **Cognitive correlates.** The ally shows a more multiplistic view of g/l/b issues, although a dualistic view of the world as being either heterosexist/homophobic or g/l/b-affirmative begins to develop. The ally exhibits a greater self-awareness of remaining internalized homophobia and heterosexism.

- **Behavioral correlates.** There is an overall increase in professional activity in g/l/b issues. The ally also shows greater assertiveness in addressing perceived homophobia and heterosexism because of increased sophistication in his or her knowledge of g/l/b issues, enhanced interpersonal skills, and an internal locus of control. The ally also shows increased self-disclosure in the role of ally. These self-disclosures are also less dependent on the ally's perception of the level of homophobia or heterosexism in specific environments.

- **Facilitative role of mentor.** Mentors should provide assistance in helping their protégés develop long- and short-term action plans in order to help them implement the objectives they have set as an ally. Mentors should also reinforce the gains which their protégés have made as an ally.

Stage V—Pride

The ally experiences increased self-valuing because of greater congruence between the ally's professional objectives and affirmative behaviors.

- **Affective correlates.** Allies at this stage experience high levels of pride and self-valuing as an ally because of the increased activism and feelings of self-worth in the role of ally. Anger can begin to develop toward heterosexist individuals or cultures, and allies may show a decreased tolerance of professionals who are in earlier stages of ally development.

- **Cognitive correlates.** Although the ally shows a more sophisticated level of awareness of g/l/b issues, there continues to be a cognitive dualism regarding the ally's view of the world as being either primarily heterosexist/homophobic or g/l/b affirmative.

- **Behavioral correlates.** The ally shows high professional, personal, and social visibility in the role of ally. There is active confrontation of heterosexism and homophobia.

- **Facilitative role of mentor.** Mentors should continue to provide support for their protégés' professional activism. In addition, mentors need to help allies productively channel the anger they experience due to being part of a heterosexist society. Mentors need to stress the importance of meeting people where they are developmentally, invoking the developmental model so that their protégés do not become overly frustrated. Mentors should also help allies in the management of emotions (e.g., anger) in order to avoid immobilization due to intensity of emotions linked to the feelings of alienation toward heterosexist individuals or agencies.

Stage VI—Integration

The ally integrates professional and personal work as an ally into all areas of his or her life. The ally shows a tolerance of people who are in different stages of development, and there is an awareness of the lifelong processes involved in the role of developing as an ally.

- **Affective correlates.** At this stage, a balance exists between the ally's self-appreciation and an awareness of the ally's personal and professional growth areas. The ally views this new role as a lifelong developmental process, so there is potential recycling through the six developmental stages as the ally takes on new professional or personal tasks related to g/l/b issues. The ally also experiences a strong motivation linked to the role of ally, due to a now internal locus of control, to a more sophisticated awareness of the issues, to a more informed mindset, and, finally, to a stronger sense of connection with other g/l/b-affirmative individuals. As the ally gains a greater appreciation of the lifelong processes involved in the role of developing as an ally, the ally experiences a decrease in anger and an increase in the appreciation of others who are at various developmental stages of becoming g/l/b-affirmative.

- **Cognitive correlates.** Allies show more multiplistic views of g/l/b issues. In addition, the ally gains a greater appreciation for the strengths and limitations of work as a heterosexual in g/l/b issues. There is a greater recognition of the ally's previous tendencies to stereotype both heterosexuals and g/l/b persons.

- **Behavioral correlates.** The ally shows an enhanced effectiveness in ally-related activities due to a more multiplistic view of the issues, of self, and of society. There is also an increase in networking activities with both heterosexuals and g/l/b persons. All sexual orientations are now viewed by the ally as being equally attractive, despite the ally's own personal sexual orientation. There is the potential for recycling through the six developmental stages as the ally takes on new developmental tasks related to g/l/b issues.

- **Facilitative role of mentor.** Mentors now assume a more collaborative, consultative role with their protégés, as their protégés' autonomy increases. If the ally again progresses through the six stages in addressing future professional challenges, the earlier teaching and facilitative roles of the mentor should be temporarily reassumed in response to the new anxieties and dependence that the ally may experience as newer, more difficult professional objectives are established. Mentors should help allies understand the normalization of this recycling through stages, as tasks of increasing difficulty are taken on by the ally. At the same time, mentors should continue to offer constructive challenges in order to help allies maintain momentum and avoid complacency in the role of ally.

Using the Mentoring Model

As allies strive to become more affirmative in the g/l/b communities, a confusing array of feelings, including anxiety and depression, may surface. Viewing this experience from a developmental perspective can be helpful. Such feelings can potentially incapacitate professionals if these feelings are not understood as signs of an impending developmental transition, that is, as signs of a new need to grow professionally or personally. When viewed as positive signs of the need to address an impending developmental transition (Levinson, 1986; Levinson et al., 1978), anxiety and depression can serve to motivate (rather than incapacitate) professionals to master specific ally developmental tasks. Allies can thus expect to see a reduction in anxiety and isolation as new developmental tasks linked to being an ally are mastered. The expectation of the time-limited nature of anxiety and depression that is characteristic of a developmental transition can help allies more easily tolerate these strong emotions.

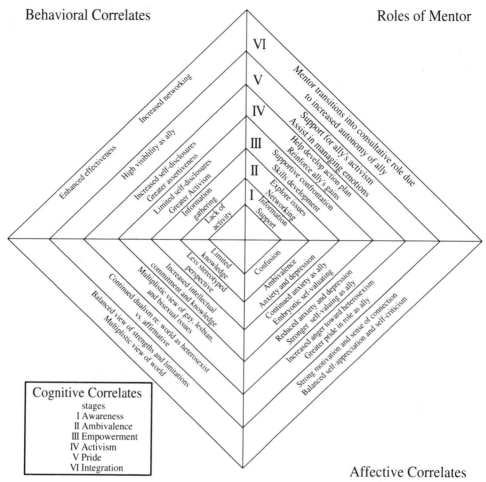

Figure 6. Overview of the stages of development of gay, lesbian, and bisexual allies: Affective, cognitive, and behavioral correlates and the role of mentoring

The adoption of a life-span developmental perspective thus helps new allies tolerate negative feelings that may accompany a heightened need to become more affirmative toward g/l/b issues, so that the ally is able to continue to strive to become more educated about g/l/b issues. The adoption of a life-span perspective also encourages allies to strive toward higher levels of professional development as earlier developmental tasks are mastered as well as avoid complacency as a particular task is mastered.

This model was developed with the assumption that mentors were heterosexual. Different sexual orientations may offer differing contributions in their role as mentors. Heterosexual mentors may be helpful to allies at certain stages of development, just as heterosexuals may have different impacts on g/l/b persons who are at certain stages of coming out as a g/l/b person (Chojnacki & Gelberg, 1995). Thus the contributions made in the role of a nonhomophobic heterosexual mentor may differ in some respects from the contributions made in the role of a g/l/b mentor. Although the impact of g/l/b mentors in comparison to the impact of heterosexual mentors on the professional development of allies has not been studied to date, Atkinson, Neville, and Casas (1991) found that European American professors successfully served as mentors to ethnic minority students and novice professionals. A better understanding of the impact of dissimilar sexual orientations on the mentor-protégé relationship will facilitate mentor-protégé assignment in formalized mentor programs.

The optimal situation for a mentor-protégé relationship seems to be one in which the mentor is more advanced professionally than the ally. There may be the potential for a mismatch, however. For example, the protégé could be at Stage V—Pride (in our proposed model) while the mentor is at Stage I—Awareness (in our proposed model). In this case, the mentor could be making stereotypic and dualistic statements based on limited knowledge of g/l/b issues while the protégé could be showing more sophisticated knowledge of g/l/b issues. Thus we should not automatically assume that a mentor is at a higher developmental stage than the protégé.

Because some environments have no self-identified allies, peer relationships may be a useful substitute for mentor-protégé relationships. Gram (1992), who studied peer relationships for human service professionals working in hospital settings, found that peer relationships were beneficial to professional collaboration. Comparative studies exploring the impact of the developmental level of the mentor and the protégé could facilitate mentor-protégé assignment in structured mentor programs focusing on g/l/b professional ally development.

Future inquiry and research in the development and mentoring of g/l/b allies is essential, as we believe that it is important to involve the majority culture in addressing the isms linked to sexual orientation. Just as European Americans can assist in addressing African American racism, as the young can help society address ageism, and as the able bodied address discrimination based on physical disabilities, so, too, can heterosexuals make a substantial contribution as allies in the field of g/l/b issues. Mentoring can be a useful tool to help professionals as they seek to develop professionally as g/l/b allies.

Handout
Gay/Lesbian/Bisexual Allies: Professional Development Guidelines

- **Developmental nature of ally growth.** Just as gay, lesbian, and bisexual persons go through developmental stages, allies also progress through a series of stages. The experiences that you have as an ally may show some similarities to gay, lesbian, and bisexual identity developmental stages. There will, however, also be some important differences in your experiences and development as experienced by gay, lesbian, and bisexual persons.

- **The highs and lows of ally development.** In your work as an ally, you should expect to experience some degree of anxiety, confusion, and isolation, along with the joys and satisfactions of working in the field. This is inevitable for two reasons. First, you will be exposed to heterosexism and homophobia from heterosexuals as they observe your actions. Second, you may experience some concerns from gay, lesbian, and bisexual persons about your qualifications and motivations for working in the field. In responding to these concerns, it is crucial to address your own homophobia and heterosexism, become knowledgeable about gay, lesbian, bisexual, and ally issues, and know your strengths and limitations in working in this field.

- **Role of support systems.** Professional and personal support systems are crucial to your development as an ally. For some issues, you will benefit more from the help of gay, lesbian, and bisexual persons, but other issues may be effectively addressed with the help of other allies. It is important to maintain a strong, diverse support system that will help you become more aware of your strengths and limitations as an ally.

- **The role of education: motivation is not enough.** Continued, lifelong education in gay, lesbian, and bisexual issues should occur through formal course work, independent reading, supervision, and positive relationships with gay, lesbian, and bisexual persons and with allies. Just as individuals working in other diversity areas must be aware of the impacts of racism, sexism, ableism, and ageism, allies must also become cognizant of the impact of heterosexism, homophobia, and heterophobia on personal development, individual career behaviors, personal and professional relationships, and organizational development.

- **Work environment factors.** Organizations have unique personalities that are more or less affirmative to gay, lesbian, and bisexual issues. In addition, organizations may pass through a series of developmental stages as they address homophobia and heterosexism. Some organizations are clearly both formally and informally heterosexist, although others may have differing degrees of overt and covert heterosexism. In addressing the heterosexism of your work organization, you will experience personal and professional dilemmas. Consultation and supervision will help you more effectively address these dilemmas.

■ **The scope of the "ally problem."** There is no centralized ally movement. There is the need for a strong, national support system for allies. Because this is a new field, there are unique and important opportunities for everyone. There is room in the field for individuals of all sexual orientations. We all make contributions in unique ways, and we all have limitations that may best be addressed by individuals whose sexual orientations differ from our own. In reflecting on sexual orientation as it relates to clinical competencies in working with g/l/b clients, Schwartz and Hartstein (1986) stated that sexual orientation per se neither qualifies one to lead a gay therapy group nor disqualifies a therapist from doing so. It is important for everyone, regardless of sexual orientation, to gain a greater awareness of homophobic attitudes, become knowledgeable about gay, lesbian, and bisexual issues, and achieve an appreciation and *valuing* of the positive role of diversity in sexual orientation. In that way, we can all play a part in the addressing of personal and societal heterosexism and homophobia.

Schwartz, R. D., & Hartstein, N. B. (1986). Group psychotherapy with gay men: Theoretical and clinical considerations. In T. S. Stein & C. J. Cohen (Eds.), *Contemporary perspectives on psychotherapy with lesbians and gay men* (pp. 157–177). New York: Plenum Press.
Handout adapted from Gelberg, S., Chojnacki, J. T., & Benn, M. (1995). *Gay, lesbian, and bisexual allies: Where are we today?* Round table held at the 1995 annual convention of the American College Personnel Association, Boston, MA.

REFERENCES

Adler, A. (1964). *The individual psychology of Alfred Adler* (H. L. Ansbacher & R. R. Ansbacher, Eds.). New York: Basic Books.

Agor, W. H. (1986, Winter). The logic of intuition: How top executives make important decisions. *Organizational Dynamics*, p. 5.

Agor, W. H. (Ed.). (1989). *Intuition in organizations.* Newbury Park, CA: Sage.

American Psychiatric Association. (1987). *Diagnostic and statistical manual of mental disorders* (3rd ed., rev.). Washington, DC: Author.

American Psychological Association, Public Interest Directorate. (1993). *Graduate faculty interested in lesbian and gay issues.* Washington, DC: Author.

American Psychological Association. (1991). Avoiding heterosexual bias in language. *American Psychologist, 46,* 973–974.

Anderson, M. Z., Tracey, T. J., & Rounds, J. (1995). *Examining the invariance of Holland's vocational interest model across gender.* Manuscript submitted for publication.

Anthony, B. D. (1985). Lesbian client–lesbian therapist: Opportunities and challenges in working together. In J. C. Gonsiorek (Ed.), *A guide to psychotherapy with gay and lesbian clients* (pp. 45–57). New York: Harrington Park Press.

Ariel, J., & Stearns, S. M. (1992). Challenges facing gay and lesbian families. In S. H. Dworkin & F. J. Gutiérrez (Eds.), *Counseling gay men and lesbians: Journey to the end of the rainbow* (pp. 95–112). Alexandria, VA: American Association for Counseling and Development.

Arnold, K. D. (1987). *Values and vocations: The career aspirations of academically gifted females in the first 5 years after high school.* Urbana-Champaign: University of Illinois, College of Education.

Arnold, K. D., & Denny, T. (1985). *The lives of academic achievers.* Urbana-Champaign: University of Illinois, College of Education.

Astin, H. S. (1984a). The meaning of work in women's lives: A sociopsychological model of career choice and work behavior. *The Counseling Psychologist, 12*(4), 117–126.

Astin, H. S. (1984b). A rejoinder: In appreciation of the richness of the commentaries. *The Counseling Psychologist 12*(4), 151–152.

Atkinson, D. R., Neville, H., & Casas, A. (1991). The mentorship of ethnic minorities in professional psychology. *Professional Psychology: Research and Practice, 22*(4), 336–338.

Baker, D. B., Strub, S. O., & Henning, B. (1995). *Cracking the corporate closet.* New York: HarperCollins.

Bandura, A. (1977). Self-efficacy: Toward a unifying theory of behavior change. *Psychological Review, 84*, 191–215.

Barnard, C. I. (1981). Cooperation. In O. Grusky & G. A. Miller (Eds.), *The sociology of organizations* (2nd ed., pp. 84–97). New York: Free Press.

Belz, J. R. (1993). Sexual orientation as a factor in career development. *Career Development Quarterly, 41*(3), 197–200.

Bennett, G. K., Seashore, H. G., & Wesman, A. G. (1990). *Differential aptitude tests* (5th ed.). San Antonio, TX: Psychological Corporation.

Benyamini, Y., & Gati, I. (1987). Perceptions of occupations: Aspects versus dimensions. *Journal of Vocational Behavior, 30*, 309–329.

Berger, R. (1982). The unseen minority: Older gays and lesbians. *Social Work, 27*, 236–241.

Bernard, C. B. (1984). Commentary on the meaning of work. *The Counseling Psychologist 12*(4), 139–140.

Betz, N. E. (1988). Advances in the assessment of career development and maturity. In W. B. Walsh & S. H. Osipow (Eds.), *Advances in vocational psychology: Vol. 2. Career decision making* (pp. 77–136). Hillsdale, NJ: Erlbaum.

Betz, N. E. (1989). Implications of the null environment hypothesis for women's career development and for counseling psychology. *The Counseling Psychologist, 17*, 136–144.

Betz, N. E. (1992). Career assessment: A review of critical issues. In S. D. Brown & R. W. Lent (Eds.), *Handbook of counseling psychology* (2nd ed., pp. 453–484). New York: Wiley.

Betz, N. E., & Fitzgerald, L. F. (1987). *The career psychology of women.* Orlando, FL: Academic Press.

Betz, N. E., & Hackett, G. (1981). The relationship of career-related self-efficacy expectations to perceived career options in college women and men. *Journal of Counseling Psychology, 28*, 399–410.

Betz, N. E., & Hackett, G. (1986). Applications of self-efficacy theory to understanding career choice behavior. *Journal of Social and Clinical Psychology, 4*, 279–289.

Blackwell, J. E. (1989). Mentoring: An action strategy for increasing minority faculty. *Academe, 75*(5), 8–14.

Blank, R., & Slipp, S. (1994). *Voices of diversity: Real people talk about problems and solutions in a workplace where everyone is not alike.* New York: Amacom (American Management Association).

Blocher, D. H., & Siegal, R. (1981). Toward a cognitive developmental theory of leisure and work. *The Counseling Psychologist, 9,* 33–44.

Blumenfeld, W. J. (Ed.). (1992). *Homophobia: How we all pay the price.* Boston: Beacon Press.

Blumenfeld, W. J., & Raymond, D. (1988). *Looking at gay and lesbian life.* Boston: Beacon Press.

Boden, R. (1992). Psychotherapy with physically disabled lesbians. In S. H. Dworkin & F. J. Gutiérrez (Eds.), *Counseling gay men and lesbians: Journey to the end of the rainbow* (pp. 157–174). Alexandria, VA: American Association for Counseling and Development.

Bolles, R. (1990). *The new quick job hunting map.* Berkeley, CA: Ten-Speed Press.

Bolles, R. (1995). *What color is your parachute?* Berkeley, CA: Ten-Speed Press.

Bolman, L. G., & Deal, T. E. (1991). *Reframing organizations: Artistry, choice, and leadership.* San Francisco: Jossey-Bass.

Boston Lesbian Psychologies Collective (Eds.). (1987). *Lesbian psychologies: Explorations and challenges.* Urbana and Chicago: University of Illinois Press.

Botkin, M., & Daly, J. (1987, March). *Occupational development of lesbians and gays.* Paper presented at the annual meeting of the American College Personnel Association, Chicago.

Boyd, M., & Wilson, N. L. (Eds.). (1991). *Amazing grace: Stories of lesbian and gay faith.* Freedom, CA: The Crossing Press.

Bozarth, J. D., & Fisher, R. (1990). Person-centered career counseling. In W. B. Walsh & S. H. Osipow (Eds.), *Career counseling: Contemporary topics in vocational psychology* (pp. 45–78). Hillsdale, NJ: Erlbaum.

Bradford, J., Ryan, C., & Rothblum, E. D. (1994). National lesbian health care survey: Implications for mental health care. *Journal of Consulting and Clinical Psychology, 62*(2), 228–242.

Brady, S., & Busse, W. J. (1994). The gay identity questionnaire: A brief measure of homosexual identity information. *Journal of Homosexuality, 26*(4), 1–22.

Bridges, W. (1994). *JobShift: How to prosper in a workplace without jobs.* Reading, MA: Addison-Wesley.

Brooke, S. L. (1993). The morality of homosexuality. *Journal of Homosexuality, 25*(4), 77–99.

Brooks, S. (1991). Resources. In N. J. Evans & V. A. Wall (Eds.), *Beyond tolerance: Gays, lesbians, and bisexuals on campus* (pp. 213–232). Alexandria, VA: American College Personnel Association.

Brown, S. D., & Lent, R. W. (Eds.). (1992). *Handbook of counseling psychology* (2nd ed.). New York: Wiley.

Browning, C. (1987). Therapeutic issues and intervention strategies with young adult lesbian clients: A developmental approach. *Journal of Homosexuality, 14*(1/2), 45–52.

Buhrke, R. A. (1989). Incorporating lesbian and gay issues into counselor training: A resource guide. *Journal of Counseling and Development, 68*(1), 77–80.

Buhrke, R. A., & Douce, L. A. (1991). Training issues for counseling psychologists in working with lesbian women and gay men. *The Counseling Psychologist, 19*(2), 216–234.

Burlew, L. D. (1991). Multiple mentor model: A conceptual framework. *Journal of Career Development, 17*(3), 213–221.

Caballo-Diéguez, A. (1989). Hispanic culture, gay male culture, and AIDS: Counseling implications. *Journal of Counseling and Development, 68*(1), 26–30.

Cammermeyer, M. (1994). *Serving in silence.* New York: Viking Press.

Campbell, D. (1994). *Campbell Interest and Skills Survey (CISS).* Minneapolis, MN: National Computer Systems.

Campbell, R. E., & Cellini, J. V. (1981). A diagnostic taxonomy of adult career problems. *Journal of Vocational Behavior, 19,* 175–190.

Carden, A. D. (1990). Mentoring and adult career development: The evolution of a theory. *The Counseling Psychologist, 18*(2), 275–299.

Carl, D. (1990). *Counseling same-sex couples.* New York: Norton.

Carlson, J. (Ed.). (1995). Counseling homosexuals and bisexuals [Special issue]. *Individual Psychology: The Journal of Adlerian Theory, Research, and Practice, 51*(2).

Carney, C. G., Wells, C. F. (1987). *Career planning: Skills to build your future.* Monterey, CA: Brooks/Cole.

Cass, V. C. (1979). Homosexuality identity formation: A theoretical model. *Journal of Homosexuality, 4*(3), 219–235.

Cass, V. C. (1984a). Homosexuality identity: A concept in need of definition. *Journal of Homosexuality, 9*(2/3), 105–126.

Cass, V. C. (1984b). Homosexual identity formation: Testing a theoretical model. *Journal of Sex Research, 20*(2), 143–167.

Chan, C. S. (1989). Issues of identity development among Asian American lesbians and gay men. *Journal of Counseling and Development, 68*(1), 16–20.

Chan, C. S. (1992). Cultural considerations in counseling Asian American lesbians and gay men. In S. H. Dworkin & F. J. Gutiérrez (Eds.), *Counseling gay men and lesbians: Journey to the end of the rainbow* (pp. 115–124). Alexandria, VA: American Association for Counseling and Development.

Chapman, B. E., & Brannock, J. C. (1987). Proposed model of lesbian identity development: An empirical examination. *Journal of Homosexuality, 14*(3/4), 69–80.

Chickering, A. W. (1969). *Education and identity.* San Francisco: Jossey-Bass.

Chickering, A. W., & Reisser, L. (1993). *Education and identity* (2nd ed.). San Francisco: Jossey-Bass.

Chojnacki, J. T., & Gelberg, S. (1994). Toward a conceptualization of career counseling for gay, lesbian, and bisexual persons. *Journal of Career Development, 21*(1), 3–10.

Chojnacki, J. T., & Gelberg, S. (1995). The facilitation of a gay, lesbian, and bisexual support-therapy group by heterosexual therapists. *Journal of Counseling and Development, 73*(3), 352–354.

Chronicle Guidance Publications. (1989). *Chronicle Occupational Briefs* (Rev. ed.). Moravia, NY: Author.

Chung, Y. B. (1994, January). Career choice and decision making of lesbian, gay, and bisexual individuals. Paper presented at the annual conference of the National Career Development Association, Albuquerque, NM.

Chung, Y. B., & Harmon, L. W. (1994). The career interests and aspirations of gay men: How sex-role orientation is related. *Journal of Vocational Behavior, 45*, 223–239.

Cohen, D. (Ed.). (1994). *The lesbian and gay pink pages.* Chicago: DAC Marketing.

Coleman, E. (1985). Developmental stages of the coming out process. In J. C. Gonsiorek (Ed.), *A guide to psychotherapy with gay and lesbian clients* (pp. 31–43). New York: Harrington Park Press.

Crites, J. O. (1965). Measurement of vocational maturity in adolescence: I. Attitude Test of the Vocational Development Inventory. *Psychological Monographs, 79*(2), No. 595.

Crites, J. O. (1974). Career counseling: A review of major approaches. *The Counseling Psychologist, 4*, 3–23.

Crites, J. O. (1978). *Theory and research handbook for the Career Maturity Inventory* (2nd ed.). Monterey, CA: CTB/McGraw-Hill.

Croteau, J. M., & Destinon, M. V. (1994). A national survey of job search experiences of lesbian, gay, and bisexual student affairs professionals. *Journal of College Student Development, 35*, 40–45.

Croteau, J. M., & Hedstrom, S. M. (1993). Integrating commonality and difference: The key to career counseling with lesbian women and gay men. *Career Development Quarterly, 41*(3), 201–209.

Croteau, J. M., & Lark, J. S. (1995). A qualitative investigation of biased and exemplary student affairs practice concerning lesbian, gay, and bisexual issues. *Journal of College Student Development, 36*(5), 472–482.

Croteau, J. M., & Morgan, S. (1989). Combating homophobia in AIDS education. *Journal of Counseling and Development, 68*(1), 86–91.

Curnow, T. J. (1989). Vocational development of persons with disability. *Career Development Quarterly, 37*(3), 269–278.

D'Augelli, A. R. (1991). Gay men in college: Identity processes and adaptations. *Journal of College Student Development, 32*, 140–146.

D'Augelli, A. R. (1994). Lesbian and gay male development: Steps toward an analysis of lesbians' and gay men's lives. In B. Greene & G. M. Herek (Eds.), *Lesbian and gay psychology: Theory, research, and clinical applications* (pp. 118–132). Thousand Oaks, CA: Sage.

Dawis, R. V., & Lofquist, L. H. (1984). *A psychological theory of work adjustment.* Minneapolis: University of Minnesota Press.

Dawis, R. V., Lofquist, L. H., & Weiss, D. J. (1968). *A theory of work adjustment (a revision). Minnesota studies in vocational rehabilitation* (Vol. 23). Minneapolis: University of Minnesota, Department of Psychology, Work Adjustment Project.

De Monteflores, C. (1986). Notes on the management of difference. In T. S. Stein & C. J. Cohen (Eds.), *Contemporary perspectives on psychotherapy with lesbians and gay men* (pp. 73–101). New York: Plenum Press.

Dent, H. S. (1995). *Job shock: Four new principles transforming our work and business.* New York: St. Martin's Press.

Dern, D. P. (1994). *The Internet guide for new users.* New York: McGraw-Hill.

Diamant, L. (1993). *Homosexual issues in the workplace.* Bristol, PA: Taylor & Francis.

Dorn, F. J. (1990). Career counseling: A social psychological perspective. In W. B. Walsh & S. H. Osipow (Eds.), *Career counseling: Contemporary topics in vocational psychology* (pp. 193–223). Hillsdale, NJ: Erlbaum.

Dunker, B. (1987). Aging lesbians: Observations and speculations. In Boston Lesbian Psychologies Collective (Eds.), *Lesbian psychologies: Explorations and challenges* (pp. 72–82). Urbana and Chicago: University of Illinois Press.

Dworkin, S. H. (1992). Some ethical considerations when counseling gay, lesbian, and bisexual clients. In S. H. Dworkin & F. J. Gutiérrez (Eds.), *Counseling gay men and lesbians: Journey to the end of the rainbow* (pp. 325–334). Alexandria, VA: American Association for Counseling and Development.

Dworkin, S. H., & Gutiérrez, F. (Eds.). (1989). Gay, lesbian, and bisexual issues in counseling [Special issue]. *Journal of Counseling and Development, 68*(1).

Dworkin, S. H., & Gutiérrez, F. J. (Eds.). (1992). *Counseling gay men and lesbians: Journey to the end of the rainbow.* Alexandria, VA: American Association for Counseling and Development.

Eldridge, N. S., & Barnett, D. C. (1991). Counseling gay and lesbian students. In N. J. Evans & V. A. Wall (Eds.), *Beyond tolerance: Gays, lesbians, and bisexuals on campus* (pp. 147–178). Alexandria, VA: American College Personnel Association.

Elliott, J. E. (1990, August). *Career development with lesbian and gay clients.* Paper presented at the 98th annual convention of the American Psychological Association, Boston.

Elliott, J. E. (1993). Career development with lesbian and gay clients. *Career Development Quarterly, 41*(3), 210–226.

Elmer-Dewitt, P. (1995, July 3). On a screen near you: Cyberporn. *Time, 146*(1), 38–45.

Epstein, C. F. (1970a). Encountering the male establishment: Sex-status limits on women's careers in the professions. *American Journal of Sociology, 75,* 965–982.

Epstein, C. F. (1970b). *Woman's place.* Berkeley: University of California Press.

Erikson, E. H. (1950). *Childhood and society.* New York: Norton.

Erikson, E. H. (1968). *Identity: Youth and crisis.* New York: Norton.

Espín, O. M. (1987). Issues of identity in the psychology of Latina lesbians. In Boston Lesbian Psychologies Collective (Eds.), *Lesbian psychologies: Exploration and challenges* (pp. 35–55). Urbana and Chicago: University of Illinois Press.

Etringer, B. D., Hillerbrand, E., & Hetherington, C. (1990). The influence of sexual orientation on career decision making: A research note. *Journal of Homosexuality, 19*(4), 103–111.

Evans, N. J., & Wall, V. A. (Eds.). (1991). *Beyond tolerance: Gays, lesbians, and bisexuals on campus.* Alexandria, VA: American College Personnel Association.

Faderman, L. (1984). The "new gay" lesbians. *Journal of Homosexuality, 10*(3/4), 85–95.

Farmer, H. S. (1984). A shiny fresh minted penny. *The Counseling Psychologist, 12*(4), 141–144.

Farmer, H. S. (1985). Model of career and achievement motivations for women and men. *Journal of Counseling Psychology, 32*, 363–390.

Fassinger, R. E. (1985). A causal model of career choice in college women. *Journal of Vocational Behavior, 27*, 123–153.

Fassinger, R. E. (1991). The hidden minority: Issues and challenges in working with lesbian women and gay men. *The Counseling Psychologist, 19*(2), 157–176.

Fassinger, R. E. (1994, January). *Identity and work: Issues in the vocational psychology of lesbians.* Paper presented at the annual conference of the National Career Development Association, Albuquerque, NM.

Fassinger, R. E., & Schlossberg, N. K. (1992). Understanding the adult years: Perspectives and implications. In S. D. Brown & R. W. Lent (Eds.), *Handbook of counseling psychology* (2nd ed., pp. 217–249). New York: Wiley.

Figler, H. (1988). *The complete job-search handbook.* New York: Holt, Rinehart, & Winston.

Fitzgerald, L. F., & Betz, N. E. (1984). Astin's model in theory and practice: A technical and philosophical critique. *The Counseling Psychologist, 12*(4), 135–138.

Foster, W. (1986). *Paradigms and promises: New approaches to educational administration.* Buffalo, NY: Prometheus.

Fox, A. (1991). Development of a bisexual identity: Understanding the process. In L. Hutchins & L. Kaahumanu (Eds.), *Bi any other name: Bisexual people speak out* (pp. 29–36). Boston: Alyson.

Fox, R. C. (1993, August). *Coming out bisexual: Identity, behavior, and sexual orientation self-disclosure.* Paper presented at the annual convention of the American Psychological Association, Toronto, Canada.

Freeman, J. (1975). How to discriminate against women without really trying. In J. Freeman (Ed.), *Women: A feminist perspective* (pp. 194–208). Palo Alto, CA: Mayfield.

Freiberg, P. (1995, June). Psychologists examine attacks on homosexuals. *APA Monitor*, pp. 30–31.

Friedrich, J. R. (1987). Perceived control and decision making in a job hunting context. *Basic and Applied Social Psychology, 8*, 163–176.

Fry, R. (1995a). *Your first interview* (3rd ed.). Hawthorne, NJ: Career Press.

Fry, R. (1995b). *Your first resúmé* (4th ed.). Hawthorne, NJ: Career Press.

Furnham, A., & Gunter, B. (1993). *Corporate assessment: Auditing a company's personality.* New York: Routledge.

Garcia, N., Kennedy, C., Pearlman, S. F., & Perez, J. (1987). The impact of race and culture differences: Challenges to intimacy in lesbian relationships. In Boston Lesbian Psychologies Collective (Eds.), *Lesbian psychologies: Explorations and challenges* (pp. 142–160). Urbana and Chicago: University of Illinois Press.

Garnets, L., Hancock, K. A., Cochran, S. D., Goodchilds, J., & Peplau, L. A. (1991). Issues in psychotherapy with lesbians and gay men: A survey of psychologists. *American Psychologist, 46*(9), 964–972.

Gati, I. (1979). A hierarchical model for the structure of vocational interests. *Journal of Vocational Behavior, 15*, 90–106.

Gati, I. (1986). Making career decisions: A sequential elimination approach. *Journal of Counseling Psychology, 33*(4), 408–417.

Gati, I., Fassa, N., & Houminer, D. (1995). Applying decision theory to career counseling practice: The sequential elimination approach. *Career Development Quarterly, 43*(3), 211–220.

Gati, I., & Tikotzki, Y. (1989). Strategies for collection and process of occupational information in making career decisions. *Journal of Counseling Psychology, 36*(3), 430–439.

Gelatt, H. B. (1989). Positive uncertainty: A new decision-making framework for counseling. *Journal of Counseling Psychology, 36*(2), 252–256.

Gelberg, S. (1988). *Computer anxiety and personality type.* Unpublished master's thesis equivalency, University of Illinois at Urbana-Champaign.

Gelberg, S. (1990). Relationships among vocational interests, gender, previous experience with computers, computer self-efficacy, and math anxiety in predicting computer anxiety (Doctoral dissertation, University of Illinois at Urbana-Champaign, 1990). *ProQuest—Dissertation Abstracts,* No. AAC 9021683.

Gelberg, S., & Chojnacki, J. T. (1995). Developmental transitions of gay/lesbian/bisexual-affirmative, heterosexual career counselors. *Career Development Quarterly, 43*(3), 267–273.

Gelberg, S., Chojnacki, J. T., Benn, M., Woodburn, J., & Chagnon, J. (1994, March). *Mentoring gay, lesbian, and bisexual allies: A developmental theory* (Sponsored by Standing Committee for Lesbian, Gay, and Bisexual Awareness). Presentation at the annual convention of the American College Personnel Association, Indianapolis, IN.

Gelberg, S., Chojnacki, J. T., & Chagnon, J. (1993). *Becoming gay/lesbian/bisexual-affirmative: A dialogue between counselors.* Presentation at the Third Annual Midwestern Conference on Diversity, University of Illinois, Urbana.

Gelberg, S., Chojnacki, J. T., Gibson, S., Benn, M., & Holahan, W. (1992). *Coming out as gay affirmative: Developmental transitions of heterosexual therapists.* Presentation at the annual convention of the American College Personnel Association, San Francisco.

Gelberg, S., Foldesi, N., Prieto, S., Rademacher, B., & Spearman, P. (1993). *Diversity in career counseling: Addressing the isms.* Presentation at the annual convention of the American College Personnel Association, Kansas City, MO.

Gelberg, S., & Harnisch, D. L. (1988, August). *Vocational interests as related to attitudes toward computers and computer skills.* Paper presented at the 96th annual convention of the American Psychological Association, Atlanta, GA.

Geller, B. (1992, August). Thoughts on being an ally. *NASPA Network on Gay, Lesbian, and Bisexual Concerns Newsletter*, pp. 1, 4.

Geller, T. (Ed.). (1990). *Bisexuality: A reader and sourcebook.* Novato, CA: Times Change Press.

Gerstein, L. H., & Shullman, S. L. (1992). Counseling psychology and the workplace: The emergence of organizational counseling psychology. In S. D. Brown & R. W. Lent (Eds.), *Handbook of counseling psychology* (2nd ed., pp. 581–625). New York: Wiley.

Gilbert, L. A. (1984). Comments on the meaning of work in women's lives. *The Counseling Psychologist 12*(4), 129–130.

Gilligan, C. (1982). *In a different voice.* Cambridge, MA: Harvard University Press.

Golden, C. (1987). Diversity and variability in women's sexual identities. In Boston Lesbian Psychologies Collective (Eds.), *Lesbian psychologies: Explorations and challenges* (pp. 19–34). Urbana and Chicago: University of Illinois Press.

Gonsiorek, J. C. (Ed.). (1985). *A guide to psychotherapy with gay and lesbian clients.* New York: Harrington Park Press.

Gonyea, J. C. (1995). *The on-line job search companion.* New York: McGraw-Hill.

Gottfredson, L. S. (1981). Circumscription and compromise: A developmental theory of occupational aspirations. *Journal of Counseling Psychology Monograph, 28,* 545–579.

Gottfredson, G. D., & Holland, J. L. (1989). *The Dictionary of Holland Occupational Codes* (DHOC) (2nd ed., rev.). Odessa, FL: Psychological Assessment Resources.

Gram, A. M. (1992). Peer relationships among clinicians as an alternative to mentor-protégé relationships in hospital settings. *Professional Psychology: Research and Practice 23*(5), 416–417.

Gray, J. D. (1979). *Role conflicts and coping strategies in married professional women.* Unpublished doctoral dissertation, University of Pennsylvania.

Gray, J. D. (1980). Role conflicts and coping strategies in married professional women. *Dissertation Abstracts International, 40,* 3781–A.

Green, F. (1994). *GAYELLOW PAGES.* New York: Renaissance House.

Greene, B. (1994). Ethnic-minority lesbians and gay men: Mental health and treatment issues. *Journal of Consulting and Clinical Psychology, 62*(2), 243–251.

Greene, B., & Herek, G. M. (1994). *Lesbian and gay psychology: Theory, research, and clinical applications.* Thousand Oaks, CA: Sage.

Greenfield, T. B. (1980). The man who comes back through the door in the wall: Discovering truth, discovering self, discovering organizations. *Educational Administration Quarterly, 16*(3), 26–59.

Gutiérrez, F. J., & Dworkin, S. H. (1992). Gay, lesbian, and African American: Managing the integration of identities. In S. H. Dworkin & F. J. Gutiérrez (Eds.), *Counseling gay men and lesbians: Journey to the end of the rainbow* (pp. 141–156). Alexandria, VA: American Association for Counseling and Development.

Hackett, G., & Betz, N. E. (1981). A self-efficacy approach to the career development of women. *Journal of Vocational Behavior, 18*, 326–339.

Hackett, G., & Lent, R. W. (1992). Theoretical advances and current inquiry in career psychology. In S. D. Brown & R. W. Lent (Eds.), *Handbook of counseling psychology* (2nd ed., pp. 419–451). New York: Wiley.

Hahn, H., & Stout, R. (1995). *The Internet yellow pages* (2nd ed.). Berkeley, CA: Osborne McGraw-Hill.

Hakim, C. (1993). *When you lose your job: Laid off, fired, early retired, relocated, demoted, unchallenged.* San Francisco: Berrett-Koehler.

Hall, D. T. (1972a). A model of coping with role conflict: The role behavior of college educated women. *Administrative Science Quarterly, 17*, 471–489.

Hall, D. T. (1972b). Role and identity processes in the lives of married women. Unpublished paper, quoted in N. E. Betz & L. F. Fitzgerald (1987), *The career psychology of women.* Orlando, FL: Academic Press.

Hammer, A. L., Borgen, F. H., Hansen, J. C., & Harmon, L. W. (1994). *Strong Interest Inventory.* Palo Alto, CA: Consulting Psychologists Press.

Hansen, J. C. (1984). Response to the meaning of work in women's lives. *The Counseling Psychologist 12*(4), 147–149.

Hansen, J. C., & Campbell, D. P. (1985). *Manual for the Strong Interest Inventory* (4th ed.). Stanford, CA: Stanford University Press.

Harmon, L. W. (1984). What's new? A response to Astin. *The Counseling Psychologist 12*(4), 127–128.

Harmon, L., Hansen, J. C., Borgen, F. H., & Hammer, A. L. (1994). *Strong Interest Inventory: Applications and technical guide.* Palo Alto, CA: Consulting Psychologists Press.

Harren, V. A. (1979). A model of career decision making for college students. *Journal of Vocational Behavior, 14*, 119–133.

Harren, V. A. (1980). *Assessment of Career Decision Making (ACDM) preliminary manual.* Carbondale, IL: Author.

Harren, V. A. (1985). *Assessment of Career Decision Making.* Los Angeles: Western Psychological Services.

Harrington, T. F., & O'Shea, A. J. (Eds.). (1984). *Guide for occupational exploration* (2nd ed.). Indianapolis, IN: JIST Works.

Harris, M. B., & Turner, P. H. (1986). Gay and lesbian parents. *Journal of Homosexuality, 12*(2), 101–113.

Harris-Bowlsbey, J., Spivack, J. D., & Lisansky, R. S. (1991). *Take hold of your future.* Iowa City, IA: American College Testing Program.

Havighurst, R. J. (1980). Social and developmental psychology: Trends in influencing the future of counseling. *Personnel and Guidance Journal, 58,* 328–333.

Hawkins, R. L. (1992). Therapy with the male couple. In S. H. Dworkin & F. J. Gutiérrez (Eds.), *Counseling gay men and lesbians: Journey to the end of the rainbow* (pp. 81–94). Alexandria, VA: American Association for Counseling and Development.

Hawks, B. K., & Muha, D. (1991). Facilitating the career development of minorities: Doing it differently this time. [Special issue: Career development of racial and ethnic minorities]. *Career Development Quarterly, 39*(3), 251–260.

Henderson, A. (1984). Homosexuality in the college years: Developmental differences between men and women. *Journal of American College Health, 32,* 216–219.

Henderson, D. W. (1985). Enlightened mentoring: A characteristic of public management professionalism. *Public Administration Review, 45*(6), 857–863.

Herek, G. M. (1984). Beyond "homophobia": A social psychological perspective on attitudes toward lesbians and gay men. *Journal of Homosexuality, 10*(1/2), 1–21.

Herek, G. M. (1989). Hate crimes against lesbians and gay men: Issues for research and policy. *American Psychologist, 44*(6), 948–955.

Herek, G. M. (1993). Documenting prejudice against lesbians and gay men on campus: The Yale Sexual Orientation Survey. *Journal of Homosexuality, 25*(4), 15–30.

Hetherington, C. (1991). Life planning and career counseling with gay and lesbian students. In N. J. Evans & V. A. Wall (Eds.), *Beyond tolerance: Gays, lesbians, and bisexuals on campus* (pp. 131–145). Alexandria, VA: American College Personnel Association.

Hetherington, C., Hillerbrand, E., & Etringer, B. D. (1989). Career counseling with gay men: Issues and recommendations for research. *Journal of Counseling and Development, 67,* 452–454.

Hetherington, C., & Orzek, A. (1989). Career counseling and life planning with lesbian women. *Journal of Counseling and Development, 68*(1), 52–57.

Hetrick, E. S., & Martin, A. D. (1987). Developmental issues and their resolution for gay and lesbian adolescents. *Journal of Homosexuality, 14*(1/2), 25–43.

Hillerbrand, E., Hetherington, C., & Etringer, B. D. (1986, March). Career counseling with gay and lesbian students. Paper presented at the annual meeting of the American College Personnel Association, New Orleans, LA.

Hoffman, M. A. (1991). Counseling the HIV-infected client: A psychosocial model for assessment and intervention. *The Counseling Psychologist, 19*(4), 467–542.

Holahan, W., & Gibson, S. A. (1994). Heterosexual therapists leading lesbian and gay therapy groups: Therapeutic and political realities. *Journal of Counseling and Development, 72,* 591–594.

Holland, J. L. (1973). *Making vocational choices: A theory of careers.* Englewood Cliffs, NJ: Prentice-Hall.

Holland, J. L. (1985a). *Making vocational choices: A theory of vocational personalities and work environments* (2nd ed.). Englewood Cliffs, NJ: Prentice-Hall.

Holland, J. L. (1985b). *The Self-Directed Search: A guide to educational and vocational planning* (Rev. ed.). Odessa, FL: Psychological Assessment Resources.

Holland, J. L. (1985c). *Vocational Preference Inventory (VPI)* (Rev. ed.). Odessa, FL: Psychological Assessment Resources.

Holland, J. L. (1992). *Making vocational choices: A theory of vocational personalities and work environments* (2nd ed.). Lutz, FL: Psychological Assessment Resources.

Holland, J. L., Daiger, D. C., & Power, P. G. (1980). *My Vocational Situation.* Palo Alto, CA: Consulting Psychologists Press.

Hopson, B., & Hough, P. (1973). *Exercises in personal and career development.* New York: APS.

House, R. M. (1991). Counseling gay and lesbian clients. In D. Capuzzi & D. R. Gross (Eds.), *Introduction to counseling: Perspectives for the 1990s* (pp. 323–394). Boston: Allyn & Bacon.

House, R. M., & Holloway, E. L. (1992). Empowering the counseling professional to work with gay and lesbian issues. In S. H. Dworkin & F. J. Gutiérrez (Eds.), *Counseling gay men and lesbians: Journey to the end of the rainbow* (pp. 307–323). Alexandria, VA: American Association for Counseling and Development.

House, R. M., & Tyler, V. (1992). Group counseling with gays and lesbians. In D. Capuzzi & D. R. Gross (Eds.), *Introduction to group counseling* (pp. 183–204). Denver, CO: Love.

Hoyt, K. B. (1989). The career status of women and minority persons: A 20-year retrospective. *Career Development Quarterly, 37,* 202–212.

Hradsky, R. D., & Comey, D. M. (1992). *Creating a career center responsive to gay/lesbian/bisexual student needs.* Presentation at the annual convention of the American College Personnel Association, San Francisco.

Hradsky, R. D., Waldrep, L. W., Hill, C. K., & Paul, N. A. (1995, March). *Transforming the career center with technology: Assessment, intervention, and evaluation.* Presentation at the annual convention of the American College Personnel Association, Boston.

Humphreys, L. (1972). *Out of the closets: The sociology of homosexual liberation.* Englewood Cliffs, NJ: Prentice-Hall.

Hunter, N. D., Michaelson, S. E., & Stoddard, T. B. (1992). *The rights of lesbians and gay men: The basic ACLU guide to a gay person's rights* (3rd ed.). Carbondale: Southern Illinois University Press.

Hutchins, L., & Kaahumanu, L. (Eds.). (1991). *Bi any other name: Bisexual people speak out.* Boston: Alyson.

Iasenza, S. (1989). Some challenges of integrating sexual orientations into counselor training and research. *Journal of Counseling and Development, 68,* 73–76.

Jackson, D. N. (1984). *Multidimension aptitude battery*. Port Huron, MI: Research Psychologists Press.

Jepsen, D. A. (1984). The developmental perspective on vocational behavior: A review of theory and research. In S. D. Brown & R. W. Lent (Eds.), *Handbook of counseling psychology* (pp. 178–215). New York: Wiley.

Jepsen, D. A. (1990). Developmental career counseling. In W. B. Walsh & S. H. Osipow (Eds.), *Career counseling: Contemporary topics in vocational psychology* (pp. 117–157). Hillsdale, NJ: Erlbaum.

Jordan, J. V., Kaplan, A. G., Miller, J. B., Stiver, I. P., & Surrey, J. L. (1991). *Women's growth in connection: Writings from the Stone Center*. New York: Guilford Press.

Jung, P. B., & Smith, R. F. (1993). *Heterosexism: An ethical challenge*. Albany: State University of New York Press.

Kahn, S. E. (1984). Astin's model of career development: The working lives of women and men. *The Counseling Psychologist 12*(4), 145–146.

Kanfer, R., & Hulin, C. L. (1985). Individual differences in successful job searches following lay-off. *Personnel Psychology, 38*, 835–847.

Kapes, J. T., Mastie, M. M., & Whitfield, E. A. (1994). *A counselor's guide to career assessment instruments* (3rd ed.). Alexandria, VA: National Career Development Association.

Kaschak, E. (1992). *Engendered lives: A new psychology of women's experience*. New York: Basic Books.

Kehoe, M. (1986a). Lesbians over 65: A triply invisible minority. *Journal of Homosexuality, 12*(3/4), 139–152.

Kehoe, M. (1986b). A portrait of the older lesbian. *Journal of Homosexuality, 12*(3/4), 157–161.

Keita, G. P., & Hurrell, J. J. (Eds.). (1994). *Job stress in a changing workforce: Investigating gender, diversity, and family issues*. Washington, DC: American Psychological Association.

Kennedy, J. L. (1995). *Hook up, get hired!* New York: Wiley.

Kennedy, J. L., & Morrow, T. J. (1994). *Electronic job search revolution*. New York: Wiley.

Kimmel, D. C. (1978). Adult development and aging: A gay perspective. *Journal of Social Issues, 34*, 113–130.

Kinsey, A. C., Pomeroy, W. B., & Martin, C. E. (1948). *Sexual behavior in the human male*. Philadelphia: Saunders.

Kinsey, A. C., Pomeroy, W. B., Martin, C. E., & Gebhard, P. H. (1953). *Sexual behavior in the human female*. Philadelphia: Saunders.

Klein, F. (1993). *The bisexual option*. New York: Harrington Park Press.

Klein, F., Sepekoff, B., & Wolf, T. J. (1985). Sexual orientation: A multivariable dynamic process. *Journal of Homosexuality, 11*(1/2), 35–49.

Kohlberg, L. (1981). *The philosophy of moral development*. San Francisco: Harper & Row.

Kram, K. E. (1983). Phases of the mentoring relationship. *Academy of Management Journal, 26*(4), 608-625.

Krumboltz, J. D. (1988). *Career Beliefs Inventory.* Palo Alto, CA: Consulting Psychologists Press.

Krumboltz, J. D., & Hamel, D. A. (1977). *Guide to career decision making skills.* New York: College Entrance Examination Board.

Krumboltz, J. D., & Nichols, C. W. (1990). Integrating the social learning theory of career decision making. In W. B. Walsh & S. H. Osipow (Eds.), *Career counseling: Contemporary topics in vocational psychology* (pp. 159–192). Hillsdale, NJ: Erlbaum.

LaFevre, J. L. (1992). *How you really get hired* (3rd ed.). New York: Prentice Hall.

Lamb, R. R., & Prediger, D. J. (1981). *Technical report for the unisex edition of the ACT Interest Inventory (UNIACT).* Iowa City, IA: American College Testing Program.

Lapierre, E. D. (1990). Homophobia and its consequences for gay and lesbian clients. In R. J. Kus (Ed.), *Keys to caring: Assisting your gay and lesbian clients* (pp. 90–104). Boston: Alyson.

Lent, R. W., & Hackett, G. (1987). Career self-efficacy: Empirical status and future directions [Monograph]. *Journal of Vocational Behavior, 30*, 347–382.

Lent, R. W., Larkin, K. C., & Brown, S. D. (1989). Relation of self-efficacy to inventoried vocational interests. *Journal of Vocational Behavior, 34*, 279–288.

Leong, F. T. (1995). *Career development and vocational behavior of racial and ethnic minorities.* Mahwah, NJ: Erlbaum.

Levine, H., & Evans, N. J. (1991). The development of gay, lesbian, and bisexual identities. In N. J. Evans & V. A. Wall (Eds.), *Beyond tolerance: Gays, lesbians, and bisexuals on campus* (pp. 1–24). Alexandria, VA: American College Personnel Association.

Levinson, D. J. (1986). A conception of adult development. *American Psychologist, 41*(1), 3–13.

Levinson, D. J., Darrow, C. N., Klein, E. B., Levinson, M. H., & McLee, B. (1978). *The seasons of a man's life.* New York: Knopf.

Lock, R. D. (1988). *Taking charge of your career direction.* Pacific Grove, CA: Brooks/Cole.

Loiacano, D. K. (1989). Gay identity issues among Black Americans: Racism, homophobia, and the need for validation. *Journal of Counseling and Development, 68*(1), 21–25.

Mancini, M. (1994). *Time management.* New York: Business One Irwin/Mirror Press.

Marcus, E. (1993). *Is it a choice? Answers to 300 of the most frequently asked questions about gays and lesbians.* San Francisco: HarperSanFrancisco.

Martin, J. L. (1988). Psychological consequences of AIDS-related bereavement among gay men. *Journal of Consulting and Clinical Psychology, 56*(6), 856–862.

Maslow, A. (1970). *Motivation and personality* (2nd ed.). New York: Harper & Row.

Matteson, M. T., & Ivancevich, J. M. (Eds.). (1987). *Controlling work stress: Effective human resource and management strategies.* San Francisco: Jossey-Bass.

McCandlish, B. M. (1985). Therapeutic issues with lesbian couples. In J. Gonsiorek (Ed.), *A guide to psychotherapy with gay and lesbian clients* (pp. 71–78). New York: Harrington Park Press.

McDermott, D., Tyndall, L., & Lichtenberg, J. W. (1989). Factors related to counselor preference among gays and lesbians. *Journal of Counseling and Development, 68*(1), 31–35.

McDonald, G. J. (1982). Individual differences in the coming out process for gay men: Implications for theoretical models. *Journal of Homosexuality, 8*(1), 47–60.

McKay, M., Davis, M., & Eshelman, B. (1995). *Relaxation and stress reduction workbook.* Oakland, CA: New Harbinger.

McKay, M., Davis, M., & Fanning, P. (1983). *Messages: The communication book.* Oakland, CA: New Harbinger.

McNaught, B. (1993). *Gay issues in the workplace.* New York: St. Martin's Press.

McWhirter, D. P., & Mattison, A. M. (1985). Psychotherapy for gay male couples. In Gonsiorek, J. C. (Ed.), *A guide to psychotherapy with gay and lesbian clients* (pp. 79–91). New York: Harrington Park Press.

Meyer, J. W., & Rowan, B. (1977). Institutionalized organizations: Formal structure as myth and ceremony. *American Journal of Sociology, 83*(2), 349–363.

Michael, R. T., Gagnon, J. H., Laumann, E. O., & Kolata, G. (1994). *Sex in America: A definitive survey.* Boston: Little, Brown.

Mickens, E. (1994). *The 100 best companies for gay men and lesbians.* New York: Pocket Books.

Miles, R. E. (1965). Human relations or human resources? *HBR, 7,* 148–163.

Minton, H. L., & McDonald, G. J. (1984). Homosexual identity formation as a developmental process. *Journal of Homosexuality, 9*(2/3), 91–104.

Miranda, J., & Storms, M. (1989). Psychological adjustments of lesbians and gay men. *Journal of Counseling and Development, 68*(1), 41–45.

Moos, R. (1986). *Work Environment Scale manual* (2nd ed.). Palo Alto, CA: Consulting Psychologists Press.

Moos, R. H. (1987). Person-environment congruence in work, school, and health care settings. *Journal of Vocational Behavior, 31,* 231–247.

Morales, E. S. (1992). Counseling Latino gays and Latina lesbians. In S. H. Dworkin & F. J. Gutiérrez (Eds.), *Counseling gay men and lesbians: Journey to the end of the rainbow* (pp. 125–139). Alexandria, VA: American Association for Counseling and Development.

Murphy, B. C. (1992). Counseling lesbian couples: Sexism, heterosexism, and homophobia. In S. H. Dworkin & F. J. Gutiérrez (Eds.), *Counseling gay men and lesbians: Journey to the end of the rainbow* (pp. 63–79). Alexandria, VA: American Association for Counseling and Development.

Murray, H. A. (1938). *Explorations in personality.* New York: Oxford University Press.

Murray, S. O. (1991). "Homosexual occupations" in Mesoamerica? *Journal of Homosexuality, 21*(4), 57–65.

Myers, P. B., & Myers, K. D. (1992). *MBTI career report*. Palo Alto, CA: Consulting Psychologists Press.

Myers, L. J., Speight, S. L., Highlen, P. S., Cox, C. I., Reynolds, A. L., Adams, E. M., & Hanley, C. P. (1991). Identity development and worldview: Toward an optimal conceptualization. *Journal of Counseling and Development, 70*, 54–63.

National Gay and Lesbian Task Force. (1994). *Fortune 1000 survey: Domestic partner benefits*. Washington, DC: Author.

Nelson, J. B. (1985). Religious and moral issues in working with homosexual clients. In J. C. Gonsiorek (Ed.), *A guide to psychotherapy with gay and lesbian clients* (pp. 163–175). New York: Harrington Park Press.

Nevill, D. D. (1984). The meaning of work in women's lives: Role conflict, preparation, and change. *The Counseling Psychologist 12*(4), 131–133.

Noe, R. A. (1988). An investigation of the determinants of successful assigned mentoring relationships. *Personnel Psychology, 41*(3), 457–479.

Obear, K. (1991). Homophobia. In N. J. Evans & V. A. Wall (Eds.), *Beyond tolerance: Gays, lesbians, and bisexuals on campus* (pp. 39–66). Alexandria, VA: American College Personnel Association.

Okiishi, R. W. (1987). The genogram as a tool in career counseling. *Journal of Counseling and Development, 66*, 139–143.

Orzek, A. M. (1992). Career counseling for the gay and lesbian community. In S. H. Dworkin & F. J. Gutiérrez (Eds.), *Counseling gay men and lesbians: Journey to the end of the rainbow* (pp. 23–33). Alexandria, VA: American Association for Counseling and Development.

Osipow, S. H. (1983). *Theories of career development* (3rd ed.). Englewood Cliffs, NJ: Prentice Hall.

Osipow, S. H. (1987a). Applying person-environment theory to vocational behavior. *Journal of Vocational Behavior, 31*, 333–336.

Osipow, S. H. (1987b). *Manual for the Career Decision Scale*. Odessa, FL: Psychological Assessment Resources.

Osipow, S. H., Carney, C. G., Winer, J. L., Yanico, B., & Koschier, M. J. (1980). *The Career Decision Scale* (3rd ed., rev.). Columbus, OH: Marathon Consulting Press.

Out! Resource guide. (1994). Chicago: Lambda Publications.

Parker, Y. (1988). *The resúmé catalog*. Berkeley, CA: Ten-Speed Press.

Parsons, F. (1909). *Choosing a vocation*. Boston: Houghton-Mifflin.

Peplau, L. A. (1982). Research on homosexual couples: An overview. *Journal of Homosexuality, 8*(2), 3–8.

Perry, W. G., Jr. (1970). *Forms of intellectual and ethical development in the college*. New York: Holt, Rinehart, and Winston.

Pfeffer, J. (1981). Who governs? In O. Grusky & G. A. Miller (Eds.), *The sociology of organizations* (2nd ed., pp. 228–247). New York: Free Press.

Pharr, S. (1988). *Homophobia: A weapon of sexism.* Inverness, CA: Chardon Press.

Phillips, S. D. (1992). Career counseling: Choice and implementation. In S. D. Brown & R. W. Lent (Eds.), *Handbook of counseling psychology* (2nd ed., pp. 513–547). New York: Wiley.

Phillips, S. D., & Pazienza, N. J. (1988). History and theory of the assessment of career development and decision making. In W. B. Walsh & S. H. Osipow (Eds.), *Career decision making* (pp. 1–32). Hillsdale, NJ: Erlbaum.

Plummer, K. (1975). *Sexual stigma: An interactionist account.* London: Routledge & Kegan Paul.

Pope, M. (1992). Bias in the interpretation of psychological tests. In S. H. Dworkin & F. J. Gutiérrez (Eds.), *Counseling gay men and lesbians: Journey to the end of the rainbow* (pp. 279–291). Alexandria, VA: American Association for Counseling and Development.

Pope, M. (1995). The "salad bowl" is big enough for us all: An argument for the inclusion of lesbians and gay men in any definition of multiculturalism. *Journal of Counseling and Development, 73*(3), 301–304.

Pope, R. L., & Reynolds, A. L. (1991). Including bisexuality: It's more than just a label. In N. J. Evans & V. A. Wall (Eds.), *Beyond tolerance: Gays, lesbians, and bisexuals on campus* (pp. 205–212). Alexandria, VA: American College Personnel Association.

Prediger, D. P. (1976). A world-of-work map for career exploration. *Vocational Guidance Quarterly, 24*(3), 198–208.

Prediger, D. P. (1981). Mapping occupations and interests: A graphic aid for vocational guidance and research. *Vocational Guidance Quarterly, 30*, 21–36.

Prince, J. P. (1994, January). Career development of gay men: Implications for research. Paper presented at the annual conference of the National Career Development Association, Albuquerque, NM.

Raphael, S. M. (1974). "Coming out": The emergence of the movement lesbian. *Dissertation Abstracts International, 35*, 5536A. (University Microfilms No. 75-5084)

Rayman, J. R. (1990). Computers and career counseling. In W. B. Walsh & S. H. Osipow (Eds.), *Career counseling: Contemporary topics in vocational psychology* (pp. 225–262). Hillsdale, NJ: Erlbaum.

Rayman, J. R., Bryson, D. L., & Bowlsbey, J. H. (1978). The field trial of DISCOVER: A new computerized interactive guidance system. *Vocational Guidance Quarterly, 26*, 349–360.

Reynolds, A. L., & Pope, R. (1991). The complexity of diversity: Exploring multiple oppressions. *Journal of Counseling and Development, 70*, 174–180.

Ritter, K. Y., & O'Neill, C. W. (1989). Moving through loss: The spiritual journey of gay men and lesbian women. *Journal of Counseling and Development, 68*(1), 9–15.

Robbins, S. P. (1993). *Organizational behavior: Concepts, controversies, and applications* (6th ed.). Englewood Cliffs, NJ: Prentice-Hall.

Rochlin, M. (1985). Sexual orientation of the therapist and therapeutic effectiveness with gay clients. In J. C. Gonsiorek (Ed.), *A guide to psychotherapy with gay and lesbian clients* (pp. 21–29). New York: Harrington Park Press.

Rogers, C. R. (1959). A theory of therapy, personality, and interpersonal relationships, as developed in the client-centered framework. In S. Koch (Ed.), *A study of a science. Study 1: Conceptual and systematic. Vol. 3. Formulations of the person and the social context* (pp. 184–256). New York: McGraw Hill.

Rotter, J. B. (1966). Generalized expectancies for internal versus external control of reinforcement. *Psychological Monographs, 80*(1), No. 609, 1–28.

Rounds, J. B., Jr., Henley, G. A., Dawis, R. V., Lofquist, L. H., & Weiss, D. J. (1981). *Manual for the Minnesota Importance Questionnaire.* Minneapolis: Vocational Psychology Research, University of Minnesota.

Rounds, J. B., & Tracey, T. J. (1990). From trait-and-factor to person-environment fit counseling: Theory and process. In W. B. Walsh & S. H. Osipow (Eds.), *Career counseling: Contemporary topics in vocational psychology* (pp. 1–44). Hillsdale, NJ: Erlbaum.

Rudolph, J. (1988). Counselors' attitudes toward homosexuality: A selective review of the literature. *Journal of Counseling and Development, 67,* 165–168.

Rudolph, J. (1989). Effects of a workshop on mental health practitioners' attitudes toward homosexuality and counseling effectiveness. *Journal of Counseling and Development, 68,* 81–85.

Salomone, P. R. (Ed.). (1991). Career development of racial and ethnic minorities [Special issue]. *Career Development Quarterly, 39*(3).

Sang, B. E. (1989). New directions in lesbian research, theory, and education. *Journal of Counseling and Development, 68*(1), 92–96.

Savickas, M. L. (1984). Career maturity: The construct and its measurement. *Vocational Guidance Quarterly, 32,* 222–231.

Savin-Williams, R. C. (1994). Verbal and physical abuse as stressors in the lives of lesbian, gay male, and bisexual youths: Associations with school problems, running away, substance abuse, prostitution, and suicide. *Journal of Consulting and Clinical Psychology, 62*(2), 261–269.

Schmidt, J. A., & Davison, M. L. (1983). Helping students think. *Personnel and Guidance Journal, 61,* 563–569.

Schmitz, T. J. (1988). Career counseling implications with the gay and lesbian population. *Journal of Employment Counseling, 25,* 51–56.

Schwanberg, S. L. (1990). Attitudes towards homosexuality in American health care literature: 1983–1987. *Journal of Homosexuality, 19*(3), 117–136.

Schwartz, R. D., & Hartstein, N. B. (1986). Group psychotherapy with gay men: Theoretical and clinical considerations. In T. Stein & C. J. Cohen (Eds.), *Perspectives on psychotherapy with lesbians and gay men* (pp. 157–177). New York: Plenum Press.

Schwartzberg, S. S. (1992). AIDS-related bereavement among gay men: The inadequacy of current theories of grief. *Psychotherapy, 29*(3), 422–429.

Sergiovanni, T. J., & Corbally, J. E. (1986). *Leadership and organizational culture: New perspectives on administrative theory and practice.* Urbana: University of Illinois Press.

Shawver, L. (1995). *And the flag was still there: Straight people, gay people, and sexuality in the U. S. military.* New York: Haworth Press.

Sher, B. (1994). *I could do anything if I only knew what it was: How to discover what you really want and how to get it.* New York: Delacorte Press.

Sher, B., & Gottlieb, A. (1986). *Wishcraft: How to get what you really want.* New York: Ballantine.

Shuster, R. (1987). Sexuality as a continuum: The bisexual identity. In Boston Lesbian Psychologies Collective (Eds.), *Lesbian psychologies: Explorations and challenges* (pp. 56–71). Urbana and Chicago: University of Illinois Press.

Sobocinski, M. R. (1990). Ethical principles in the counseling of gay and lesbian adolescents: Issues of autonomy, competence, and confidentiality. *Professional Psychology: Research and Practice, 21*(4), 240–247.

Sophie, J. (1986). A critical examination of stage theories of lesbian identity development. *Journal of Homosexuality, 12*(2), 39–51.

Spokane, A. R. (Ed.). (1987). Conceptual and methodological issues in person-environment fit research [Special issue]. *Journal of Vocational Behavior, 31,* 217–221.

Starzecpyzel, E. (1987). The Persephone complex: Incest dynamics and the lesbian preference. In Boston Lesbian Psychologies Collective (Eds.), *Lesbian psychologies: Explorations and challenges* (pp. 261–282). Urbana and Chicago: University of Illinois Press.

Strader, S. C., & Bowman, S. L. (1993, March). *Career counseling for gay, lesbian, and bisexual people: Issues and theory.* Presentation at the annual convention of the American College Personnel Association, Kansas City, MO.

Stumpf, S. A., Brief, A. P., & Hartman, K. (1987). Self-efficacy expectations and coping with career-related events. *Journal of Vocational Behavior, 31,* 91–108.

Sue, D. W., Arredondo, P., & McDavis, R. J. (1992). Multicultural counseling competencies and standards: A call to the profession. *Journal of Multicultural Counseling and Development, 20,* 64–88.

Super, D. E. (1957). *The psychology of careers.* New York: Harper & Row.

Super, D. E. (1963). Toward making self-concept theory operational. In D. E. Super, R. Starishevsky, N. Matlin, & J. P. Jordaan (Eds.), *Career development: Self-concept theory* (pp. 17–32). New York: College Entrance Examination Board.

Super, D. E. (1973). The Work Values Inventory. In D. G. Zytowski (Ed.), *Contemporary approaches to interest measurement.* Minneapolis: University of Minnesota Press.

Super, D. E. (1980). A life-span, life-space approach to career development. *Journal of Vocational Behavior, 16*, 282–298.

Super, D. E. (1983). Assessment in career guidance: Toward truly developmental counseling. *Personnel and Guidance Journal, 61*, 555–562.

Super, D. E. (1992, April). *Integrating career theories: Problems and prospects—Developmental theory.* Presentation at the Conference of Convergence in Theories of Career Choice and Development, Michigan State University, East Lansing.

Super, D. E., & Nevill, D. D. (1986). *The Values Scale.* Palo Alto, CA: Consulting Psychologists Press.

Super, D. E., Thompson, A. S., Lindeman, R. H., Jordaan, J. P., & Myers, R. A. (1981). *The Career Development Inventory.* Palo Alto, CA: Consulting Psychologists Press.

Super, D. E., Thompson, A. S., Lindeman, R. H., Myers, R. A., & Jordaan, J. P. (1985). *Adult Career Concerns Inventory.* Palo Alto, CA: Consulting Psychologists Press.

Tannen, D. (1994). *Talking from 9 to 5: How women's and men's conversational styles affect who gets heard, who gets credit, and what gets done at work.* New York: Morrow.

Task Force on the Status of Lesbian and Gay Male Psychologists. (1977, November). Removing the stigma. *APA Monitor 8*(11), pp. 16, 28.

Thomas, R., & Chickering, A. W. (1984). Education and identity revisited. *Journal of College Student Personnel, 25*, 392–399.

Thompson, C. (1992). On being heterosexual in a homophobic world. In W. J. Blumenfeld (Ed.), *Homophobia: How we all pay the price* (pp. 235–248). Boston: Beacon Press.

Tiedeman, D. V. (1961). Decisions and vocational development: A paradigm and its implications. *Personnel and Guidance Journal, 40*, 15–20.

Tiedeman, D. V., & O'Hara, R. P. (1963). *Career development: Choice and adjustment.* New York: College Entrance Examination Board.

Tinsley, D. J., & Schwendener-Holt, M. J. (1992). Retirement and leisure. In S. D. Brown & R. W. Lent (Eds.), *Handbook of counseling psychology* (2nd ed., pp. 627–662). New York: Wiley.

Triplett, M., & Busher, E. (1994, March). *The masculinity gap: Homophobia and heterophobia in relationships between men.* Presentation at the annual convention of the American College Personnel Association, Indianapolis, IN.

Troiden, R. R. (1989). The formation of homosexual identities. *Journal of Homosexuality, 17*(1/2), 43–74.

U. S. Department of Labor. (1991). *Dictionary of occupational titles* (4th ed., rev.). Indianapolis, IN: JIST Works.

U. S. Department of Labor. (1994). *Occupational outlook handbook, 1994–1995.* Indianapolis, IN: JIST Works.

Vargo, S. (1987). The effects of women's socialization on lesbian couples. In Boston Lesbian Psychologies Collective (Eds.), *Lesbian psychologies: Explorations and challenges* (pp. 161–173). Urbana and Chicago: University of Illinois Press.

Vondracek, F. W., Lerner, R. M., & Schulenberg, J. E. (1986). *Career development: A life-span developmental approach.* Hillsdale, NJ: Erlbaum.

Vroom, V. (1964). *Work and motivation.* New York: Wiley.

Waldrep, L. (1994, Summer). The future is closer than you think: The electronic job search. *Career Development,* pp. 1, 6.

Wall, V. A., & Evans, N. J. (1991). Using psychosocial development theories to understand and work with gay and lesbian persons. In N. J. Evans & V. A. Wall (Eds.), *Beyond tolerance: Gays, lesbians, and bisexuals on campus* (pp. 25–38). Alexandria, VA: American College Personnel Association.

Wall, V. A., & Washington, J. (1991). Understanding gay and lesbian students of color. In N. J. Evans & V. A. Wall (Eds.), *Beyond tolerance: Gays, lesbians, and bisexuals on campus* (pp. 67–78). Alexandria, VA: American College Personnel Association.

Walsh, W. B. (1987). Person-environment congruence: A response to the Moos perspective. *Journal of Vocational Behavior, 31,* 347–352.

Walsh, W. B., & Betz, N. E. (1990). *Tests and assessment* (2nd ed.). Englewood Cliffs, NJ: Prentice-Hall.

Walsh, W. B., & Osipow, S. H. (Eds.). (1990). *Career counseling: Contemporary topics in vocational psychology.* Hillsdale, NJ: Erlbaum.

Walsh, W. B., & Osipow, S. H. (Eds.). (1993). *Career counseling for women.* Hillsdale, NJ: Erlbaum.

Washington, J., & Evans, N. J. (1991). Becoming an ally. In N. J. Evans & V. A. Wall (Eds.), *Beyond tolerance: Gays, lesbians, and bisexuals on campus* (pp. 195–204). Alexandria, VA: American College Personnel Association.

Watkins, C. E., & Savickas, M. L. (1990). Psychodynamic career counseling. In W. B. Walsh & S. H. Osipow (Eds.), *Career counseling: Contemporary topics in vocational psychology* (pp. 79–116). Hillsdale, NJ: Erlbaum.

Weick, K. E. (1976). Educational organizations as loosely coupled systems. *Administrative Science Quarterly, 21*(1), 1–19.

Westbrook, B. W. (1983). Career maturity: The concept, the instrument, and the research. In W. B. Walsh & S. H. Osipow (Eds.), *Handbook of vocational psychology: Vol. 1. Foundation* (pp. 263–304). Hillsdale, NJ: Erlbaum.

Wittstock, M. (1990). The best of both worlds and still nothing: Bisexuals come out to talk. In T. Geller (Ed.), *Bisexuality: A reader and sourcebook* (pp. 26–33). Novato, CA: Times Change Press.

Woodrick, C. (1979). *The development and validation of an attitude scale to measure career myths held by college students.* Unpublished doctoral dissertation, Texas A&M University, College Station, TX.

Woods, J. D. (1994). *The corporate closet.* New York: Free Press.

Yates, M. (1994). *Power on the job: The legal rights of working people.* Boston: South End Press.

Youngblood, J. H., Nichols, L., & Wilson, B. (1995, March). *Transforming career centers: Where organizational and developmental approaches collide.* Presentation at the annual convention of the American College Personnel Association, Boston.

Zinik, G. (1985). Identity conflict or adaptive flexibility? Bisexuality reconsidered. *Journal of Homosexuality, 11*(1/2), 7–19.

Index

academic aptitude tests, 31
Adler, A., 14
adult career development models, 51–52
adult development models, general, 45–51
African Americans, workplace
    discrimination and, 64
Age Discrimination in Employment Act,
    4
aggressive communications, 102–3
allies, 5, 155, 157–67
Amazing Grace (Boyd and Wilson), 53
America On-Line, Gay and Lesbian
    Community Forum on, 96
American College Personnel Association
    Standing Committee for
Lesbian, Gay, and Bisexual Awareness
    (SCLGBA), 67–68, 96
American College Testing (ACT)
    Assessment, 31
American College Testing (ACT)
    Program, 16, 32
    ACT Interest Inventory, 35
    ACT Job Families, 34
American Psychiatric Association, 17
American Psychological Association
    Committee on Lesbian and Gay
    Concerns (CLGC), 14
    guidelines for heterosexual bias in
    language, 23
    Public Interest Directorate, 68
Americans With Disabilities Act, 4, 66
Anderson, M. Z., 30
androgyny, 30

Apple Computer, antidiscrimination
    policy, 65
Arnold, K. D., 18
assertiveness, 102–3
assessing the work environment, 63–64
    assessment of employment factors, 60
    g/l/b professional organizations, 67–68
    heterosexism in the workplace, 44, 63,
    64–65, 85, 86, 94
    homophobia in the workplace, 1, 44,
    63, 64, 85, 86, 100–101,
    103
    legal and geographical considerations,
    73–74
    networking and informational
    interviewing, 68–73
    person-environment interactions,
    112–16
    recent publications, 66–67
    resources for, 65–73
    women and gender issues in the
    workplace, 50
    workplace personal safety, 62
    world of work resources, 33–35
    See also job search
Assessment of Career Decision Making
    (ACDM) inventory, 33, 83
assessment of interests, values,
    experiences, and skills, 27–28
    assessing career interests, 28–30
    assessing experiences, 31
    assessing skills/abilities, 31
    assessing values/needs, 30–31
    assessment instruments, 28–33

Note. For brevity, the acronym g/l/b refers to gay, lesbian, and bisexual persons.

191